'A powerful and inspiriting book. Its authors understand that the growth of global markets privil...   ...f learning and some ways of descri[b]...  ...hallenge people working with adult... ...l perspectives rooted in local exp[e]...   ...to be read.'

CW01066864

...KETT, *Director,*
...*ning (NIACE)*

'A very current and   ...dult education to its political and economic environment. In it the reader will find discussion of continuing and recently emerging issues that break new conceptual and empirical ground as well as promise crucial lessons for other developing regions. Contains a wealth of information for popular educators seeking to improve their understanding and practice.'

PROFESSOR NELLY STROMQUIST, *University of Southern California*

'The global market forces of the late twentieth century have created a completely new terrain on which socially committed adult education and training will have to operate in the twenty-first century. This stimulating new book brings together a variety of perspectives (from an appropriately international set of authors) that can help adult educators the world over to analyse the new conjuncture and formulate strategies that will support struggles against domination by the market. It is warmly commended as one of the few books in the field that challenge the prevailing neo-liberal orthodoxy and offer an alternative approach.'

PROFESSOR FRANK YOUNGMAN, *author of*
A Socialist Pedagogy of Adult Education

'This book, highlighting the impact of globalization on the education sector, is both appropriate and timely, and will be a valuable contribution to the existing body of literature on adult education.'

LALITA RAMDAS, *President, International Council for*
Adult Education (ICAE)

'Essential reading for adult educators worldwide who are concerned about recent global trends and aware of the challenges that they pose to adult education and adult educators.'

PAT ELLIS, *Pat Ellis Associates, the Caribbean*

Global Perspectives on Adult Education and Training

Series editors: Budd Hall with Carol Medel-Anonuevo and Griff Foley

Series advisors: Peggy Antrobus, Phyllis Cunningham, Chris Duke, Patricia Ellis, Matthias Finger, Heribert Hinzen, Agneta Lind, Peter Mayo, Derek Mulenga, Jorge Osorio, Lalita Ramdas, Te Rippowe, Nelly P. Stromquist, and Rajesh Tandon

This new Series is designed to provide for the first time a genuinely global basis to the theory and practice of adult education and learning worldwide. A key goal is to introduce readers to issues, debates and understandings related to centrally important areas in adult education and training, particularly but not exclusively in the majority (or 'Third') world, and to provide a forum where practitioners from the South, women, and other social groups historically under-represented in AET, can find a voice. To this end, the new Series will contribute to redressing an imbalance in the literature whereby our understanding and debates in adult education and training in the English-speaking world have been unduly dominated by bodies of knowledge and theoretical perspectives drawn from experience in the USA and Britain and relatively unrepresentative of class, race and gender.

Among the issues of immediate and vital interest to adult educators throughout the world which new titles in this Series will address are: popular education, adult learning and civil society, post-colonial perspectives, women's perspectives, informal learning in peoples' struggles, worker education, environmental adult education, participatory research, the political economy of adult education, indigenous knowledge and adult learning, and the impact on them of globalization and other social trends.

Shirley Walters, ed., *Globalization, Adult Education and Training: Impacts and Issues*

Derek C. Mulenga, ed., *Knowledge, Empowerment and Social Transformation: Participatory Research in Africa*

In preparation:

Matthias Finger: *Adult Education at the Crossroads*

Peter Mayo: *Gramsci, Freire and Adult Education: Possibilities for Transformative Action*

Moacir Gadotti et al., eds, *Paulo Freire: A BioBibliography* (in 2 volumes)

Moacir Gadotti and Carlos A. Torres, eds, *Popular Education in Latin America: A Reader*

Globalization, Adult Education and Training

Impacts and Issues

Edited by Shirley Walters

ZED BOOKS
London & New York

IIZ–DVV
Bonn

UIE/UNESCO
Hamburg

ICAE
Toronto

CACE Publications
Cape Town

NIACE
Leicester

Globalization, Adult Education and Training was first published in 1997 by
Zed Books Ltd, 7 Cynthia Street, London N1 9JF, UK, and
Room 400, 175 Fifth Avenue, New York, NY 10010, USA

in association with
the Institute for International Cooperation of the German Adult Education
Association (IIZ–DVV), Obere Wilhelmstrasse 32, D-53225 Bonn, Germany,
and the International Council on Adult Education (ICAE), 720 Bathurst Street,
Suite 500, Toronto, Ontario, Canada M5S 2R4,
and Unesco Institute for Education (UIE), Feldbrunnenstrasse 58,
D-20148 Germany

Published in Southern Africa by CACE Publications,
Centre for Adult and Continuing Education, University of the Western Cape,
Private Bag X17, Bellville, 7535, South Africa

Published in paperback in the United Kingdom by NIACE, the National
Organization for Adult Learning, 21 De Montfort Street, Leicester LE1 7GE, UK

Cover designed by Lee Robinson/AdLib Designs
Typeset in Monotype Garamond by Illuminati, Grosmont
Printed and bound in Great Britain
by Biddles Ltd, *www.biddles.co.uk*

A catalogue record for this book is available from the British Library

Library of Congress Cataloging-in-Publication Data
Globalization, adult education and training : impacts and issues /
edited by Shirley Walters.
p. cm.
Based on an international conference held in Cape Town in Nov.
1995, hosted by the Centre for Adult and Continuing Education
from the University of the Western Cape, South Africa, and the
Centre for Adult Education from the University of Linkoping,
Sweden.
Includes bibliographical references.
ISBN 1–85649–511–6. ISBN 1–85649–512–4 (pbk.)
1. Adult education—Congresses. 2. International education—
Congresses. 3. Continuing education—Congresses. 4. Occupational
training—Congresses. 5. Education—International cooperation—
Congresses. I. Walters, Shirley.
LC5209.G56 1997
374—dc21   97-9161 CIP

ISBN 1 85649 511 6 Cased
ISBN 1 85649 512 4 Limp

In the United Kingdom
ISBN 1 86201 026 9 Limp

Contents

PART IV Life-long Learning Reconsidered

Acknowledgements

This book is based on issues raised at an international conference on *Adult Education and Training in Reconstruction and Development: Lessons from the South and the North*, held in Cape Town in November 1995. The conference was hosted by the Centre for Adult and Continuing Education (CACE) from the University of the Western Cape, South Africa, and the Centre for Adult Education (CAE) from the University of Linköping, Sweden and attended by 150 leading academics, professional practitioners and education activists from over 25 countries.

We would like to thank Professor Sibusiso Bengu and Mr Carl Tham, Ministers of Education in the South African and Swedish governments, for participating in the conference. In addition we wish to thank Anette Svensson of CAE and Joe Samuels from CACE, together with the organizing team of Minnie Venter-Hildebrand and the CACE staff, for constructing a very stimulating learning event which inspired this publication.

An editorial committee, formed at the conference, met twice during 1996 to formulate the framework for this book. The editorial committee consists of Maurice Amutabi of the Moi University, Kenya; Keith Jackson of Fircroft College, UK; Ove Korsgaard of the Royal Danish School of Educational Studies, Denmark; Pauline Murphy of the University of Ulster, Northern Ireland; Teresa Quiroz Martin of the University of Arts and Social Science, Chile; and Shirley Walters of the University of the Western Cape, South Africa. The committee's commitment to this publication and their creativity as experienced academics, researchers and adult educators have made the production of this book a pleasure. Their individual and collective contributions are gratefully acknowledged.

All the contributors who have written for the book have shown enthusiasm and good humour in response to our many reminders and requests. They are part of a community of adult educators and trainers, located in different sites of practice in twelve different countries, who share a common concern for democratic, socially relevant adult education and training.

Special acknowledgement goes to Minnie Venter-Hildebrand, whose role was to provide editorial support and co-ordination. She did this with dedication and in a spirit of solidarity. Julie-Anne Justus's style editing was invaluable.

The financial support of the Swedish International Development Agency (SIDA) contributed both to the conference and the book's production. This support is appreciated and gratefully acknowledged. Finally we would like to thank Robert Molteno of Zed Books for his support in publishing this book.

The book is published to coincide with Unesco's Fifth International Conference on Adult Education in July 1997 in Hamburg, Germany.

1
Introduction

Background

This was not just another adult education and training conference. It was a magical moment which gave hope, inspiration and opportunities to begin to rethink adult education and training globally.

Eighteen months before, South Africa had emerged from a long struggle against apartheid. In this struggle South Africans were assisted by people from all over the world through diverse acts of solidarity. For several international participants who had for many years been involved in the anti-apartheid solidarity movements, it was a moment of hope and renewed energy as they engaged in dialogue, participated in songs, popular theatre and visits with the local educators who were working for a participatory, democratic future.

The conference was more than an opportunity to 'feel good'. It provided the space for a radical rethinking of adult education and training. South Africa was in a situation of rapid transition, in which policies and practices were being redeveloped. The issues raised resonated with other situations around the world, but were having to be resolved in a very short, concentrated period. The conference had not only participants from different countries but also a combination of grassroots practitioners, academics and professionals. The richness of these diverse experiences and locations is reflected in this book.

This book is concerned with the role of adult education and training within a context of globalization. It is concerned to look at how adult education and training for the majority of people is being shaped by the radical restructuring of the economic, political, cultural and social life around the globe, and how practitioners are responding to the new and often contradictory pressures. The world is currently in transition from one paradigm to another. The dominant paradigm has been that of

modernization, and we would suggest that we are shifting to a new paradigm of globalization. This has major implications for our understanding
of 'progress' and for notions of civil society, the state, the market and
their relationships to one another. Some of the questions include: what
are the implications for understanding democracy? What does this shift
mean for the majority of people who are poor, live in rural areas or
urban slums, and are marginal to decision-making processes in their
societies? What does it mean for adult education and training concerned
with the interests of this majority? What are the contradictory pressures
under which practitioners are engaging? How is adult education and training being redefined in this current period?

This book attempts to address some of these questions in tentative
ways from the perspectives of both practitioners and academics. It opens
up debates and discussions in order to engage reflective practitioners in
them. It claims neither to grasp all the implications nor to give final
answers. It reflects the strengths and weaknesses of its origin, a conference within a particular time and place.

The collection

This book consists of twenty-five chapters, by thirty-one authors (eighteen of whom are women) from twelve countries. The editorial committee
selected most of the papers from conference submissions that related to
the theme of the book. While some of the chapters reflect the submissions
in their original form, others have been substantially reworked and four
new chapters were commissioned. Most of the authors come from an
adult-education rather than a vocational-training background.

The fact that seven of the chapters centre on South Africa reflects the
fact that the conference was held in that country. South Africa's process
of democratization throws up in stark relief many of the issues confronting adult education and training globally. For adult educators and trainers
concerned with democracy, social justice and equity, the South African
case is not of parochial interest only: it provides space to examine the
political and social contexts within which learning occurs, and asks searching questions about the social purposes and the provision of adult education and training globally. We can do this while acknowledging that
global similarities are rooted and shaped in national and historical uniqueness.

The chapters have been grouped under four headings. The first is 'The
Impact of Globalization on Adult Education and Training'. The chapters
in this section focus on the changing nature of the state, market and civil
society and their impact on adult education and training practices. The
second theme is 'Adult Education and Training Strategies', where a range
of different responses to the diverse contexts are described. The third is

'Participation: Problems and Possibilities'. This section presents descriptions and analyses of local, engaged practices of adult educators and trainers as they work with the majority of people who are poor, working class, women and children, living in urban and rural areas. The chapters are illustrative of issues and concerns that manifest in different sites of practice, including primary health care, local and national politics, indigenous education and civil society organizations. The fourth theme is 'Life-long Learning Reconsidered'. These chapters redefine and reconceptualize the meaning of adult education and training to challenge the dominant human-capital school.

Reconstruction and development in South Africa

A key question for many adult educators and trainers is what they should be doing in order to enhance the possibilities for a more people-centred social and economic programme of transformation to succeed in South Africa, at a political moment when global economies dictate neo-liberal market-based policies as the only acceptable solutions.

The new South African government has adopted a policy framework, the Reconstruction and Development Programme (RDP), which contains the long-standing demands of the democratic movement for a more radical social and economic programme of transformation. Fundamental transformation is urgent: South Africa, among comparable middle-income developing countries, has one of the worst records in terms of social indicators (health, education, safe water, fertility) and of income inequality. Poverty in South Africa has a strong racial dimension, as nearly 95 per cent of the poor are black. To turn around the poverty-stricken reality of 70 per cent of the population will not only take a long time but also require political will and a great deal of resources.

The RDP is an ambitious framework that aims to meet basic needs, develop human resources, build the economy and democratize the state and civil society. Underpinning the RDP is a strong concern with redress, equity and economic development. As adult education and training is integral to social, economic, political and cultural development, it is centrally involved in the RDP and therefore implicated in its success or failure.

The impact of globalization and the neo-liberal policies on the restructuring of South African political, economic, social and cultural realities is no doubt very powerful. The critical question that the South African government is confronting is how to combine formal democracy, an open, growing economy and people-centred development. South Africa is having to 'build a nation' at a time when the nation-state has become less important in the world. The globalizing forces minimize differences and national borders at a time when South Africa is needing to build

unity and recognize differences amongst its diverse population of 40
million people who speak eleven languages, who have been sytematically
organized along racial lines, and who vary widely across divisions of
culture, gender, social class and region. There is a sense among educators
that the tide is so powerful that there is no alternative but to go with it.
But there are those who recognize that they must join forces with others
in a process of 'globalization from below' in which solidarity discourses
are reasserted. A example of this is in parts of the trade-union movement, described by Marshall in Chapter 6. A key challenge is to build
solidarity in a context of competition.

The South African case throws up the starkness of developments
around the world and the widening gap between the rich and the poor.
It provides the space to rethink the social purposes of and strategies for
adult education and training.

Some key issues

Globalization

Globalization reflects social relations that are not only linked at the
economic level. As Korsgaard elaborates in Chapter 2, they are also
present in the political, social, cultural and environmental spheres. The
shift towards a global perspective means that the well-known adage, 'think
global, act local' takes on new significance. The slogan is now beginning
to be reformulated as 'think, feel and act both globally and locally'.

Experiences at the local level need to be rethought, taking into account
the forces that are moving the world towards the destruction of the
natural resources of the planet and constructing more competitive relations among people, groups, nations and regions. Adult education and
training are directly implicated in these processes on many levels, including the development of environmental awareness and alternative environmentally sustainable energy strategies.

The processes of globalization are breaking down dichotomies and
distinctions. The concept of the division of the world into North, South,
East and West is being increasingly challenged. The hegemonic neo-liberal
capitalist system is encouraging the minimizing of different identities and
the homogenization of cultures. Globalization leads to the aggregation of
states, so that economies of scale and ease of technological transfer can
be achieved. The economic importance of the nation-state is in rapid
decline, while its importance on the political level is being reasserted, for
instance in South Africa. It is no longer nation-states that are the keys
to economic growth but economic blocs and multinational corporations.
Capital accumulation knows no boundaries. The discourse of global competitiveness prevails, while the discourse of solidarity is reemerging in

new forms, as the chapters by Marshall (6), Manicom and Walters (7) and Murphy (10) illustrate.

The traditional dichotomies and distinctions between home-life and work-life are also being reshaped in some cases. Employment and un-employment, paid work and unpaid work come together in people's lives in new ways, sometimes because it suits capital, sometimes because people choose it that way. The flexibilization of work, which enables people to create a 'virtual office' at home with the use of new technology, is an illustration of how work-life and home-life can become totally intertwined. Some social theorists who are projecting the future of work within a context of jobless growth stress the importance of civil society as the sector in which most jobs will need to be created. The distinction be-tween civil society and the economy is becoming more blurred. For many people in the South, and particularly for women who work in the infor-mal economy, the clear distinction between work-life and home-life has never existed. Also, in many situations trade unions have taken up issues that exist both on the factory floor and in the community. For example, struggles have been waged at the workplace for improved transport, housing and education for workers' families. Trade unionists also often offer leadership in civic associations. In daily life economic and commu-nity activities have been closely linked.

The relations between the state, economy and civil society are being restructured in a variety of ways within the processes of globalization. In Chapters 3 and 5, by Welton and Jackson, the restructuring of Canada and Britain respectively are analysed. Each describes how global market forces have reduced the capacity of individual nation-states to create social policies in the interests of their people, and the way the nation-states have constrained democratic participation in civil society to facili-tate neo-liberal policies. In both Britain and Canada state support for organizations of civil society has fallen off dramatically, and many of these organizations, which were concerned mainly with issues of social justice, have closed down. Many of the social services that were provided by the state now have to be provided by civil society, for example, certain health and welfare services. In Chapter 4, Quiroz Martin, presenting the situation in Chile, describes how it is primarily women who carry the burden of the economic and political restructuring.

In Chapter 8, Heng makes the link between the individual, local and global contexts. She highlights the psychological oppression that links to local and regional cultural forms that are used directly in the economy. Women are silent and silenced by this oppression and it is this condition that is traded by capital and by, in this instance, the Malaysian state. The women on the global assembly lines of the world have very poor working conditions that barely allow them and their families to survive.

In considering democracy within the context of globalization a wide range of issues are raised. Democracy is seen here not just as formal voting and constitutions but as a process involving decision-making in the family, the community, the workplace and the state. Some of these issues are touched on in Chapter 2, by Korsgaard.

In general terms the trend is for decision-making power to move away from the local and the national to the international levels. The challenge for adult education then is how to ensure that people at the local level achieve power to determine economic, political, social and cultural relations in new ways which reflect local and global factors. In the chapters by Marshall (6), Manicom and Walters (7) and Murphy (10), the strategy of developing global relations 'from below' in the contexts of the trade union and women's movements is put forward as a means to reassert power and influence at both the local and global levels. They argue that the prospects for democracy are poor if the values of capital continue to drive globalization. Democracy will increase only if the values and interests of the majority of women and men are able to assert themselves out of activities which are embedded in many local situations. This perspective informs the book's general approach to adult education and training, which might increase the participation of the majority in all aspects of society.

Integrating adult education and training

The use of the term 'adult education and training' signals a move in some parts of the world away from adult education and vocational training as discrete entities. The former has been concerned mainly with community, political and cultural issues, whilst the latter has focused on work-related skills training. They have coexisted as two separate tracks barely communicating with one another. This move to integration has also been signposted particularly in Europe with the use of the term 'adult learning'.

Much of the literature on adult education and development emphasizes the need for adult education to be an integral part of people's survival strategies, otherwise it will seldom be prioritized by potential learners. There is a recognition amongst some adult educators that they must engage in economic development. This is seen to cover all aspects of the economy, including both the formal and informal employment sectors. There is acknowledgement amongst some trainers that general education is an important component of people's development in the workplace. There are also increasing numbers of trainers working in the informal sectors. The majority of contributors to the book come from the adult education tradition.

The dominant paradigm in adult education and training literature has a human-capital, free-market perspective. It emphasizes the economic value of adult education and training (AET) within narrow terms of reference. It is most concerned with AET for people located within the industrialized urban centres, that is, 'skyscraper economies'. The majority of women and men in the world do not inhabit the industrial heartlands of nations or regions. Many of them subsist in 'shanty-town economies' in the shadows of the cities. We recognize that each nation, each region, and the world in general consists of skyscrapers and shanty-towns, existing side by side. They are not separate and exclusive ways of life, but integrally bound up with one another, different manifestations of an integral reality – a global skyscraper and shanty-town economy.

In Chapter 24, on life-long learning, Gustavsson points out that there are historically two different and important theoretical and ideological strands which argue for life-long education and training. The dominant trend in the Western world is the human-capital school, mostly supported by neo-liberal ideology. The theory of human capital expresses a view concerning the economic reasons for education and training, but has nothing to say about the learning process. The other trend is the humanistic school, which is concerned with a democratic and holistic approach to people's education and training.

In South Africa adult education has traditionally been concerned more with social, political, personal and cultural development than with economic development. It has been very closely tied in the last fifty years to the political struggle against apartheid. As Gumede argues (Chapter 23), this is a major limitation as for many adults the primary concern is economic survival. About 50 per cent of South Africans are unemployed and, not surprisingly, in a recent survey the need for jobs was rated the top priority. For the rural poor, piped water was almost as high a priority.

A key initiative in the movement towards a new adult education and training system in South Africa came from the formal economic sector and more particularly from the trade-union movement. The unions realized that even radical improvement of the existing industrial training system would still leave their members in a second-class position. They needed to improve their own skills and knowledge to get better jobs. They needed to improve educational and development opportunities in their communities to obtain a better life for their families and neighbours. They also needed to contribute to a more productive and world competitive economy to pay for these policies.

The trade unions recognized the necessary connection between economic, social and political development. This view was rooted possibly in the political, community and economic struggles they had waged as part of the liberation movement through the 1980s. They entered discussions and debates with representatives from the business and state sectors, and made concrete policy proposals in 1994. These had integration as the cornerstone of national policy development, insisting on equivalence of adult basic education, vocational training and schooling.

One of the proposals was for a national qualifications grid, the National Qualifications Framework (NQF), which would secure integration, equivalency and access across a new national education and training system. A broad 'competency model' was adopted to define and assess learning outcomes at all levels of the NQF. In Chapter 13 Lugg presents some of the issues and debates related to the possibilities for the NQF to contribute to economic development and simultaneously to the achievement of redress for those people excluded from the education and training system by apartheid.

The question of integration of adult education and training is an important one which has opened up spaces to engage different traditions and potentially to challenge the human-capital notion. As Lugg points out, in the structures of the NQF, in the designing of outcomes-based curricula, in the teaching methodologies, in all aspects of the teaching and learning processes, there need to be struggles to ensure that the human-capital and technicist views do not become predominant. Many of the concepts can be interpreted in conservative or progressive ways, for example, recognition of prior learning (RPL) has transformative and conservative possibilities as Michelson elaborates in Chapter 14. At present, as Gamble and Walters argue in Chapter 12, the power of the concept of integration lies in the fact that opportunities are being created for practitioners 'to live in the gaps' between sectors and traditions of education and training. It is, for example, forcing community adult educators to take the needs of economic development seriously, and workplace trainers to remember the needs of a democratic civil society. At a time of rapid change in South Africa and the world more generally it is important to rethink adult education and training theories and practices in a radical way. Living in the gaps between the adult education and vocational training traditions can help us to do this.

In South Africa, as in many other parts of the world, the human-capital paradigm seems to be dominant. There is concern among adult educators that the integration debate is being driven by interests in the formal economic sector, by both organized labour and employers. But it is in the informal sector, or the 'shanty-town economy', that most people work and live. If policies are developed with only the formal sector in mind, the majority of people will in all likelihood not benefit. Even in the formal sector, Breier shows that education and training can work against workers' interests (Chapter 20). She challenges the human capital theory with its narrow utilitarian purposes. But the concern for a more holistic perspective is not to deny the critical importance of adult education and training for highly skilled, high-level people. Similar concerns echo in a number of the chapters which describe the realities in either Kenya (Amutabi), Australia (Holt, Christie and Fry), Canada (Welton), Chile (Quiroz Martin) or Northern Ireland (Murphy).

An additional concern is expressed by Jackson, who argues in Chapter 5 that there is a real danger that if the dominant values driving adult education and training are those of human resource development, it is possible to see an economism pervading and eventually colonizing society. He argues that for the majority to benefit, the drive must come from an approach to economic and social development which recognizes the inter-relatedness of society and the economy where human values – not human capital – predominate. This is a strong theme that runs throughout the book.

Everyday learning and education

The relation between everyday learning and education (organized learning) is one of the most fundamental questions in educational discourse. In Chapter 25 Larsson discusses this relationship in the context of life-long learning. He states that adult education must be understood as something that can change the results or the character of everyday learning.

Everyday learning is also discussed by Michelson who argues in Chapter 14 that the recognition of prior learning as a strategy to bring historically marginalized people into educational institutions needs to challenge what knowledge is accredited by whom. She points out that there are Euro-centric, sexist biases built into assessment practices internationally. The question of what knowledge is affirmed through education is also tackled from an Australian Aboriginal viewpoint by Holt, Christie and Fry in Chapter 18. They make a plea for the value of indigenous knowledge – not only for Aboriginal people but for all Australians – as it affirms human and environmentally sustainable values. The resurgence of the arguments for the valorization of indigenous knowledge from indigenous people around the world, which has strong echoes in the women's move-ments, is an important critique of the human-capital paradigm. There is an argument that humanity must work towards a renewed consciousness about future human existence rather than being dominated by narrow economic imperatives.

Important insights into the relationship between everyday learning and education are made by Breier in Chapter 20. Drawing on her research on the social uses of literacy in South Africa, she describes how schooling does not necessarily lead to social, political or economic empowerment. She gives examples of unschooled taxi drivers who learn to drive and survive through imitation, apprenticeships and social networks. In another example of workers on a farm she shows how education is gendered, with unschooled men being rewarded with better jobs than the more highly educated women.

The link between everyday learning and education and Habermas's concepts of the system-world and the life-world is highlighted by both

Welton (Chapter 3) and Gustavsson (Chapter 24).The system-world, put simply, consists of the market and the state – the world of money and power. This sphere uses expert knowledge as its base. The rationality used is instrumental. The system is driven by strategic action rather than the search for rightness and truth. The life-world is a sphere where individuals create their own identities, values and meanings and search for truth, justice and beauty. The argument is made that the world of money and power tends to colonize the life-world. This process leads to diminishing possibilities for people to understand their everyday lives and act as free human beings – a precondition for a free and democratic society.

The educational institutions which are set up to facilitate learning are colonized by rules and curricula, traditions and behaviour, that often diminish possibilities for learning. They are part of the system-world. This raises the question as to whether authentic learning can be realized within the formal system. Murphy (Chapter 10) and Shefer, Samuels and Sardien (Chapter 16) begin to answer this with examples of educational practices which take seriously the personal, political and professional concerns of the learners, in this case women and black people, within the curricula.

Gustavsson, Jackson and Welton all point to the essential role that social movements play in the contribution to the production of knowledge and learning processes. Many people have, as their starting-point, the learning processes from studies and experiences in social movements. Social movements are considered the carriers of historical projects of importance to all people, which address universal questions such as the relations between men and women highlighted through the women's movements, between nature and people through the environmental movements, between master and slave through the liberation and civil rights movements. In their search for knowledge through their actions, people produce culture and new knowledge. A social movement can therefore be characterized by its cognitive praxis.

Globally, the majority of people manifestly engage with learning for their own purposes and interest when it is to meet a social, economic, political or technical need. Through the liberation movement in South Africa, the most innovative, creative learning took place. The political and organizing processes were educational. As part of the movement for democracy, thousands of non-governmental organizations (NGOs) and community-based organizations (CBOs) participated in educational and organizational activities that cut across, for example, health, work, media, culture, childcare, human rights and adult literacy. The chapters by Matiwana (21), Venter-Hildebrand and Houston (22) and Shefer, Samuels and Sardien (16) describe educational practices located within this tradition.

The significant role of NGOs as expressions of the relationship between local action and globally significant social movements on the one hand, and between the locality and the state on the other, is illustrated in several of the chapters. For example, Matiwana describes the training of community health committees which oversee primary health care in an informal housing settlement. They connect to a national NGO in delivery of health services. Marshall and Moshenberg both argue for solidarity amongst workers around the world in order to connect the very local struggles to global struggles against domination by the market. Both the chapter by Manicom and Walters and that by Quiroz Martin describe feminist popular education as a critical response by NGOs at a very local level to the processes of globalization. In the current climate, it is through NGOs and social movements that the majority of marginalized women and men have some hope of being able to survive and improve their everyday realities. These arguments build on the long tradition of social movement adult education, but, as Korsgaard argues in Chapter 2, adult educators and trainers have to go further to construct a global civil society to counterbalance globalizing economic forces.

A very significant development in the discussion of the relationship between everyday learning and education is the emphasis being placed on learning. The concept of learning throughout life has emerged as one of the keys to the next century. It has helped to put the learner, rather than the educator or practitioner, at the centre of policy and implementation. It also draws attention to all the ways in which adults learn at different points in their lives outside recognized educational institutions. The ways in which life-long learning is conceptualized and operationalized will inevitably be very different in the South and the North.

The role of the adult educators and trainers is foregrounded particularly in the chapters by Gamble and Walters (12), Shefer, Samuels and Sardien (16) and Lugg (13). They argue that practitioners are critical to the achievement of new integrated, holistic and non-oppressive ways of practising adult education and training. With the concept of learning, however, the mediators of learning can often become the technological software and hardware rather than the practitioners. The designers of the software then become key.

Breier raises the issue of the mediators of learning differently. As already mentioned, the subjects of her research were the taxi drivers who work long hours in a cut-throat business environment, who find it impossible to attend adult education and training classes. Much of their acquisition of new knowledge or skills is mediated by a range of people around them, through imitation and informal apprenticeships. The study came to the conclusion that it is the mediators of social processes who should form a focus of training attention. For example, most people in urban areas use banks. The bank tellers are in a position to assist clients, for example, to learn how to use a credit card. This approach refocuses the problem, away from the masses of poorly schooled people, to the mediators. It is up to the mediators to learn to serve people across differences of class, language and culture so that learning can occur more effectively through everyday life experiences. This may help in situations like that in Kenya, as described by Amutabi, where structural adjustment programmes (SAPs) demand erosion of social services. Though Breier's argument does not diminish the need for improved adult education and training provision for learners, it does shift the focus of the problem to an additional area of need.

As discussion of these key issues shows, in rethinking adult education and training in the context of globalization we are entering uncharted waters swirling with contradictory currents. We have by no means grasped all the implications. Our hope is that the chapters in this book, in raising questions, reflecting on the different perspectives and possibilities and sharing strategies, will offer more understanding of the range of factors involved. To other adult educators and trainers who are concerned with enhancing prospects for people-centred social and economic programmes, the book offers strength to persist in searching for alternatives.

Limitations

This book in no way attempts to be comprehensive and we recognize a number of glaring omissions. Some examples of these are the lack of debate about information technology and educational delivery strategies as they are being shaped by the rapidly changing global context, and voter education as a massive thrust in adult education.

Words about words

A number of the terms used are contentious. We have not tried to standardize their use across chapters but have left authors to speak from their own contexts. For the sake of clarity we have avoided using inverted commas around certain terms. In some contexts it is the convention to refer to 'race' in this way to signal that the term is understood as not natural but a socially constructed category. While we share this understanding, we have not used the convention. We also use the terms North, South, West and Third World with some reservation, because of the way they often homogenize those regions and implicate all the inhabitants in the politics of imperialism, obscuring class, racial or ethnic differentiation. We understand these terms as designating constructs referring to degrees of relative poverty or affluence, rather than to geographic regions.

Editorial Committee: Maurice Amutabi, Keith Jackson, Ove Korsgaard, Pauline Murphy, Teresa Quiroz Martin and Shirley Walters

Part I
The Impact of Globalization on Adult Education and Training

Globalization reflects a process in which social relations are not only linked at the economic level but also permeate the political, social, cultural and environmental spheres, to impact on everyday life. At this moment the well-known adage 'think globally – act locally' takes on new significance and new meanings. The slogan is now beginning to be reformulated as 'think, feel and act both globally and locally'. The first chapter, by Korsgaard, analyses the meaning of globalization, and his broad brush-strokes form a useful background to the later chapters.

The chapters in this section focus on the changing nature of the state, market and civil society, and their impact on adult eduation and training practices. Welton, Quiroz Martin and Jackson then present country-specific descriptions of Canada, Chile and Britain respectively. They elaborate the fundamental implications in their countries of the hegemonic neo-liberal economic agenda for the majority of women and men, and for adult education and training. In her chapter Marshall presents the imperatives for the trade unions to 'globalize from below' in response to the processes of globalization. In turn, Manicom and Walters review how feminist popular education is being challenged and provoked by global reconfigurations. Heng focuses on the oppressive conditions for women on the global assembly lines, which have proved basic building-blocks in the movement of capital around the world. In particular she tells of the lived experiences of emotional subordination of Malaysian women workers. She argues for the importance of addressing these experiences and reconstructing subjectivities in and as educational work with women workers.

In all the chapters the importance of rethinking experiences at the local level is acknowledged, taking into account the world-wide forces towards the destruction of the natural resources of the planet, and for the construction of competitive relations among peoples, classes, groups, nations and regions. The building of a 'global civil society' is stressed as a way of reshaping and challenging the dominant economic and political relations in which human capital is placed before human values. They all, in different ways, problematize and grapple with the relationships between the local lived realities of the majority of people and global rule by the elites. They offer varying insights into how to begin to forge this new relationship, which would be in the interests of the majority, who are poor and are women.

2

The Impact of Globalization
on Adult Education

Ove Korsgaard

'Globalization' became a keyword at a conference in Cape Town, South Africa.[1] This surprised many participants. Was it because globalization is a fashionable term or was it because adult education is being confronted in new ways within a globalizing context? This chapter explores the notion of globalization and points to implications for adult education and training.

There is a distinction between increased internationalization of economic intercourse and the emergence of a qualitatively new global economy. The world-wide international economy is one in which the principal entities are nation-states and it involves the growing interconnection between national economies. Interactions are of the 'billiard ball' type where international events do not directly penetrate or permeate the domestic economy but are refracted through national policies and processes.

Economic globalization, on the other hand, involves qualitative change towards a system in which distinct national economies are subsumed and rearticulated into the system through international processes and transactions. The international system becomes homogenized, as markets and production become global. Intensified economic interdependence involves the increase of economic intercourse between national economies; true economic globalization invokes a qualitative shift toward a global economic system no longer based on autonomous national economies but on a consolidated global marketplace for production, distribution and consumption. Here the global economy dominates the national economies existing within it.[2]

The market

At the conference in Cape Town, Ben Turok described a number of the problems arising from the fact that South Africa is increasingly integrated into the global economy.[3]

South Africa has what he calls a skyscraper economy – economic domination by a few big enterprises – surrounded by shanty towns. 'The skyscraper economy, in recent times, has been benefiting a small elite and government budgets were designed to protect the interests of that small elite.' To a large extent then the skyscraper economy was only serving the interest of a small minority. 'Now our job is to change that, and it is very difficult. Also because of the World Trade Organization, which forces us to conform to international requirements. Of course, the speed at which we conform is controversial, but we have to conform to some extent.'

As South Africa has to be competitive in the global market, Turok urges an understanding of competitiveness in two ways:

> South Africa has to be competitive with imports from abroad. China has the cheapest labour in the world and Chinese imports are beginning to enter South Africa on the basis of labour which is much cheaper than South African labour. The same is true of many other countries such as India and others. [Second,] South Africa has to compete internationally in world markets and this is a healthy thing because it forces modernization and improved local products. So, the government has a major transformation task ahead in relation to the issue of competitiveness.

A key in the world of competitiveness is skilled people. According to Turok, South Africa is very low in the world scale of skilled people, 'so I think we need training institutions in every township to harness the skills we have.' But the state is not able to improve the skills of the people without help from the people. 'That is how I see the whole business of adult education and training – as a bottom-up process facilitated by government.'

According to Professor Dr Talvi Mårja from Tallinn Pedagogical University, the situation in the Baltic states is more or less the same.[4] The end of the Cold War was followed by the establishment of new nation-states with market economies. But these new states have been aspiring to political independence and democracy at the same time as Europe has been moving towards economic and political integration.

According to Mårja, adult education institutions have to play two different roles: one to safeguard the cultural heritage and identity of their people, and the other to train the people to be able to compete in the global market. She states:

> There is no doubt that without knowledge, skills and experiences, i.e. without well educated and competent people who are highly motivated and could orient adequately in the society, the process of democratization of the society and the transition to a market economy is not possible.

Today, transition to the market economy is part of a global economy. The global flow of capital sharpens international competition and undermines the possibility of the nation-state carrying out an economic policy based on national premisses. Increasingly, national governments are unable to control international capital, which crosses the borders with great speed. To compensate for this loss of political capability, new international institutions have been created in order to regulate and co-ordinate economic policy – for example, the World Trade Organization, the International Monetary Fund, the World Bank, Organization of Petroleum Exporting Countries and the European Union.

The dramatic consequences of globalization on the economic level have been analysed in a number of studies. According to Robert B. Reich,[5] the very idea of national economies is becoming meaningless, as are the notions of national corporation, national capital, national products and national technology.

This shift in economic relations is connected to a shift in the content of work. Reich makes the central point that physical work is being replaced by intellectual work, particularly in the North. The American standard of living in the future will not depend on well-known key industries such as the automobile industry. The standard of living will increasingly depend on the global demand for American skills and know-how.

Globalization is not really global. At least it is an uneven process in which there is a cleavage between skyscraper economies and shanty towns. It is essentially the symbol analysts who participate directly in the global economy and the global labour market. For Reich this growing number of people are about to 'blow up' the USA as a nation because highly educated and privileged people seem to have, regardless of nationality, more in common with each other than with their poor compatriots. Often they live and work in enclaves and have little contact with the local society in their direct environment. Their children go to private schools and private security guards see to their safety. Reich fears this development, but sees no possibility of stopping the process of globalization which is, according to him, weakening the nation-state and national democracy. The future standard of living in any country will depend on the ability of the population to sell its labour power in a global labour market.

Today, education and training are the gateway into the global market which demands that adults continue a process of further learning throughout their life. Life-long learning is the key concept for this way of life.

Education and training play a growing role for each individual, enterprise and nation because:

- education will give the individual better employment possibilities throughout life;
- it is a key variable for the competitiveness of the individual enterprise on the global labour market where symbol-work plays an increasing role;

- it is of overwhelming importance for the individual nation to per-
severe in the climate of international competition that has intensified
as a result of the different free-trade agreements.

The state

Today, nations are players in a highly competitive global game. When
capital moves freely and internationally, competition is intensified. It will
be a decisive political priority to create optimal conditions for the accumulation of capital and the establishment of new jobs within the framework
of the nation-state.

In this regard, education has become decisive. Practically the whole
educational world has apprehended the goals of labour-market policies,
and this has consequences for the education for individuals, enterprises
and nations. This accentuation of educational expectations within the
labour market has, however, meant that other goals for educational policies
have receded into the background.

The Norwegian educational researcher Alfred Telhaug[6] has analysed
the educational systems in different countries and identified a common
tendency which prevailed during the 1980s. Although Japan, China,
Germany, Great Britain, the USA, Russia and the Scandinavian countries
are extremely different regarding history, culture and political systems,
there is, according to Telhaug, a common tendency to shift from 'child-
centred' to 'economy-centred' motivation. When new school planning is
formulated, ideals about social justice and personal development are
exchanged for concepts from management discourse such as competition, quality and productivity.

In most countries during the last 15 years there has been a marked
change from language and objectives relating to the quality of life and of
the community, to the language of the marketplace. According to Keith
Jackson,[7] the new market language is widely used and has penetrated into
the heart of adult education and training in the UK.

This change has also been seen within adult education, where Unesco
and the OECD represent two different attitudes: one humanistic and the
other economic. The concept of life-long learning was introduced by
Unesco in the late 1960s and was related to a humanistic tradition where
education is connected with democracy and the development of the individual. Around 1980, however, the position of Unesco was clearly
weakened and the OECD had an increasing influence on educational
policies. The OECD stressed the importance of adult education for economic development. The philosophy is based on a neo-liberal way of
thinking, regarding education as an investment in 'human capital' and
'human resource development'.

At the same time that education became increasingly important for competition in the global labour market, ministries of labour and finance in many countries became more involved in fields which traditionally belonged to the ministries of education.

Robert Reich, the American Minister of Labour, became chief advocate for developing a national system for training and retraining workers. In a global economy, Reich says, there is little practical distinction between domestic and foreign firms. The only way to gain comparative advantages is to create a superior labour force that will attract global capital.[8] Until now, government-sponsored training programmes in the USA have been devoted to training the poor and disadvantaged and, to a lesser degree, retraining the unemployed. Reich would have the government take responsibility for continual training and upgrading of the entire labour force – including the 90 per cent who are employed.

All nations are faced with the fact that education and training are a decisive factor in international economic competition. In Japan, the situation has been accepted that a high level of education is a decisive competition parameter. Here it is an accepted truth that the very strong economic position of Japan is founded on intense educational competition, with schooling being the most important concern for Japanese parents and children. In no other country does education mean so much for a person's future as in Japan. This situation has created what Professor Yoshio Katageri[9] calls an 'education-record society' where the 'war of the entrance exam' to higher education institutions is indelibly stamped on all life situations.

While a number of states re-arm within science and education, other countries at the same time cut social programmes. The globalization of economies has restricted all states – including large and economically powerful ones – from carrying out social policy which is governed by national interests. The globalization of economies makes it more difficult to sustain regulation models based on the welfare-state and Keynesian policies which have underpinned economic policies since World War II, especially in Western Europe. Keynesianism was premised on the idea that national economies were real. The acceleration in globalization since the mid-1970s has nevertheless caused a loss of effectiveness of national policies in the sphere of welfare.

Several have argued that the present nation-states are too small to cope with the big problems of today's societal life and too large for the small problems. But it is not realistic to anticipate an early death of the nation-state. On the one hand, it is far from disappearing, and on the other it is in a process of transition. There are indications that the 'democratic safety state' is about to be replaced by the 'liberal competition state'.[10] This replacement seems to be a common phenomenon and is also carried out in countries with social democratic policies. Of course there are great differences as to what extent it has removed the base for the Keynesian regulation model: for example, in Chile it has meant radical social cuts while in Denmark the same has not happened.[11]

The shift from a social democratic safety state to a liberal competition state creates fundamental questions about the relation between the nation-state, democracy and national solidarity. In the UN research report entitled *State in Disarray, The Social Effects of Globalization*,[12] it is stressed that the modern state is established on two principles, namely, the concept of the sovereignty of the people and the concept of national solidarity. Democracy was built on the assumption that the worst off are an integral part of society and therefore have a right to necessary, minimum public expenditures. The report concludes, however, that national solidarity is internationally on the decline.

In the 1960s, the pressure for the expansion of educational opportunities had both economic and social roots. Greater equity in educational opportunity was seen as a major levelling force in society. However, since the 1980s the strong dominance of the economic imperative has been evident.

Civil society

In the liberal tradition of adult education and the Nordic tradition for *folkeoplysning* (popular and national education) concepts such as national community, democracy and the civil society have played an exceptionally large ideological role. One fundamental idea has been that democracy in the last instance was built on adult and popular education.[13]

The process of globalization is a tremendous challenge to democracy itself and to the notion of adult and popular education as fundamental for a democratic society. The fact that adult education and training are increasingly governed by the goals of labour market policies makes it necessary to consider the traditional links between adult education, national community, democracy and civil society. Historically, it is within the framework of the nation-state that the fight for freedom and equality, democracy and human rights has been won. The national struggles for freedom in the twentieth century were fought in the belief that democracy, human rights and social justice are central elements in the establishment of a sovereign state.

From recent experiences in Canada, Welton[14] claims that the Canadian state, the liberal democracy and the liberal tradition for adult education are in deep crisis and that Canada is in the midst of convulsive changes and agonizing societal learning processes. 'Many people do not think that Quebec will, in fact, separate, but the current controversies about Quebec's place in Canada speak of deeper problems about the very nature of the Canadian nation-state as we move into the 21st century.' Welton says 'the two crises – of liberal democracy and of adult education – are inextricably linked' because Canadian adult education has always been concerned with

issues of social action and public responsibility. Canadian adult education, for much of the twentieth century, has contained 'moral alternatives
to the market'. Welton claims that this tradition has weakened.

The answer as to why liberal democracy is in crisis is no doubt complex. It will, however, become clearer if one examines the changing configuration of the relationship between the three elements of society, namely
the market, the state and civil society.

Market, state and civil society

While the concept of a civil society as a separate area in relation to the
market and the state is as old as modern society, the understanding of
what is meant by civil society has changed. A backwards look to the
nineteenth century and the first wave of democracy shows different
positions on the relationship between state, market and civil society.[15] In
Europe, the fundamental meaning of the concept came from the commoners' fight against nobility and absolute monarchy. The civil society
became a category of liberty characterizing the public space where the
citizens acted politically.

It can be said that civil society was 'discovered' in the so-called Scottish
enlightenment. The main characters were Adam Ferguson and his pupil
Adam Smith. *An Essay on the History of Civil Society* was published in 1767
and in 1776 Adam Smith issued his *Wealth of Nations*. They 'discovered'
society as something independent, following its own mechanisms, which
cannot directly be derived from or subordinated to governmental actions.
While Smith emphasized the division between state and market, Ferguson
stressed the difference between the state and civil society. He argued the
legality of defending oneself against the state and emphasized the right
to assemble in voluntary societies.

It was the liberal Thomas Paine who, in his controversy with the
conservative Edmund Burke, took the radical step of confronting civil
society with the state. According to Paine, state power should be limited
in favour of civil society, which is founded on the principle that all
individuals have fundamental human rights. This revolutionary way of
thinking is also found in the American Declaration of Independence,
which states that the people have the right to oppose a government that
abuses fundamental human rights.

Within German cultural circles another perspective developed regarding
the relation between state and the individual. In this instance, the liberal
understanding of civil society did not get the same backing as in the
Anglo-American world. Civil society was conquered by the concept of
'folk' and 'nation', which Herder was the first to explain theoretically. For
him it was language, culture and mentality that defined the people, not
their legal status within the state. While Ferguson and Paine highlighted

the individual and his or her rights, Herder stressed the collective identity and 'the common best'.

It was not possible for the European working class to accept the liberal model, which was built on an alliance between the market and civil society against the absolute power of the state. Contrary to this perspective, the working class regarded the market as a destructive force: it was not the state but the market which should be tamed. Within socialism this perspective led to two different points of view.

The first point of view was expressed through the understanding that civil society was a bourgeois phenomenon that should be discarded. There were two sectors in society, namely the market and the state. For the labour movement, therefore, the struggle was to obtain the power of the state in order to fight against the power of capital. According to this model, socialism and the state are two sides of the same coin, namely state socialism.

The second point of view was that civil society is important for socialism. It is Antonio Gramsci who pointed out the importance of keeping civil society as an independent category in socialist thinking. But the liberal bourgeois model had to be changed because it is not civil society and the market which are in alliance against the state, but civil society and the state which are in alliance against the market.

This three-pole model experienced great difficulty within socialism, in contrast to the two-pole model where the state and the market stand face-to-face. It was not only in state communist ideology and practice that civil society slipped away, but also in social-democratic welfare states where it was difficult to attach an ideological and practical meaning to civil society. For many years, therefore, civil society was out of the theoretical limelight.

The concept was revived in the 1980s with agitation from critical intellectuals in Eastern Europe. This centred on the all-encompassing state that the dissidents attempted to create with free space where they could live as citizens outside of the shadow of totalitarianism. Similarly, the African National Congress (ANC) in South Africa contributed towards giving the concept 'civil society' a positive connotation for a self-definition in opposition to the totalitarian state.[16]

In the West, civil society was first dealt with by the American communitarians, who developed critiques directed against both the market and the state (and to some extent also the welfare state). For the communitarians civil society became the place where the individual and society mutually commit themselves in a morally obligated community. Neither the state nor the market can do this.

Christopher Lasch,[17] a leading American communitarian, says that we are in need of a third wave to relate to moral obligations – where obligation is placed neither with the state nor with the market but in ordinary common sense, common feelings and daily life. He supports the republican tradition that democratic society can only 'rest on publicly-practised citizens' virtues'. The prerequisite for both the market and state is 'non-economic ties of confidence and solidarity', which are moral virtues. To build a democratic society is an art which does not originate from the state or from the market but from the citizenship of civil society. If the key institutions of society do not support this art, it will be destroyed.

According to Welton and Jackson in this volume (Chapters 3 and 5), adult education in Canada and Great Britain no longer fulfils that function.

A global civil society

There is an important difference between the concepts 'international' and 'global'. Historically and conceptually the word 'international' is derived from the word 'national' and is based on the assumption that the decisive actors on the international scene are stable nation-states. For example, both the United Nations and Unesco are founded on the belief that it is nation-states that are the legitimate foundation of these institutions. On the other hand, the words 'global' and 'local' are mutually and deeply connected – as expressed in the slogans 'Think global – act local' and 'Act global – think local'.

Increasing globalization is a two-edged sword. On the one hand it is quite obvious that it removes competence from the national context and that it thus undermines the institutions which civil society and the democratic public hitherto have used for communication. On the other hand globalization opens up new possibilities for a democratic influence on essential common issues which by their nature are about the notion of the nation-state. Attempts to democratize are, therefore, forced to work for the establishment of global democratic structures, including international organs for civil society.

The question is whether democracy can develop outside the shell in which it was born, namely the nation-state. This is one of the current and fundamental political questions. According to the pessimists, the relationship between democracy and the nation-state is so close that the democratization of international institutions and structures is bound to fail. One thing is certain, however, and that is if democracy is to transcend the notion of the nation-state, a global civil society has to develop with concomitant international civil structures and corresponding public facilities. Such structures are not present in current international political processes. It is essentially on the technological and economic level that global integration takes place. It cannot be in the interest of civil society to leave the regulation of this integration to market forces alone or to naked competition between states. Instead, the fight should concern itself with the establishment of comprehensive global structures.

It seems that such processes are under way, although the networking of a global civil society has so far rested on weak and insecure foundations. One scholar has claimed that a global civil society 'is being constructed before our eyes'[18] with more and more non-governmental organizations working from a global perspective when they deal with issues such as human rights, women's equality, ecology and social relief endeavours.

Today, 'globalization from below'[19] is proceeding faster then one would have thought a few years ago. Many of the same ideas about the local and the global erupt all over the world. Local citizens' movements and alternative institutions are springing up to meet basic economic needs, to preserve local traditions, to establish ecological chains and to struggle for human rights and dignity. More and more people are crafting their own strategies for survival and development, and in the process are spinning their own transnational webs to embrace and connect people across the world.

The development of a global civil society opens up possibilities to dissolve the historical connection slowly between nation-state and 'civil citizen'. Such a development would nourish the concept that it is not only national solidarity that counts, but also the global entirety.[20]

Adult and popular education became a lever for national and democratic development in Europe about two hundred years ago. Because of what is called globalization, a new concept is needed in adult education. While no final definition was given, it became clear in South Africa that a number of attempts were being made to clarify this new idea with their 'rainbow nation'[21] concept.

A new concept must build upon the reality that today the global and the local are interconnected and interdependent in ways that humanity has not experienced before. Today, the many different local communities around the world share a common destiny and humanity is a geo-ecological entirety within the same biosphere. This way of understanding the world is completely new and unique.

This understanding will, in time, place the globe in a new form of togetherness. It will not extinguish the conflict between rich and poor but it will define it in a new way, based on global limits as a common denominator.

Notes

Translated by Erik Hogsbro Holm.

1. International Conference on Adult Education and Training: Its Role in Reconstruction and Development, 7–10 November 1995, Cape Town.

2. Holm and Sorensen 1995.
3. Turok 1995.
4. Mårja 1995.
5. Reich 1993.
6. Telhaug 1992.
7. Jackson 1997.
8. Reich 1993.
9. Kategiri 1991.
10. Hirsch 1995.
11. Quiroz Martin, Chapter 4 in this book.
12. United Nations 1995.
13. Korsgaard 1996.
14. Welton, Chapter 3 in this book.
15. Korsgaard 1996.
16. Walters 1989.
17. Lasch 1993.
18. Falk 1993.
19. Falk 1993.
20. Hirsch 1995.
21. The 'rainbow nation' is a concept that developed after South Africa's elections in 1994, encompassing all her people in a quest for reconciliation and nation-building.

References

Falk, R. (1993) 'The Infancy of Global Society' in Lundestad, G. and Westad, O.A. (eds), *Beyond the Cold War: New Dimensions in International Relations*, Scandinavian University Press, Oslo.

Hirsch, J. (1995) 'Fra fordistisk sikkerhedsstat til national konkurrencestat', *Grus,* 45–1996, Denmark.

Holm, H.H. and Sorensen, G. (1995) 'What has Changed?' in Holm, H.H. and Sorenson, G. (eds), *Whose World Order? Uneven Globalization and the End of the Cold War*, Westview Press, Boulder, CO.

Jackson, K. (1997) 'Adult Education and Globalization' in Walters, S. (ed.), *Adult Education and Training in the Age of Globalization*, Zed Books, London.

Kategiri, Y. (1991) 'Japanese Education in the Development of Economics', *The Bulletin of Aichi University of Education*, Vol. XXXVV, Kariya, Japan.

Korsgaard, O. (1996) *Kampen om lyset: Dansk voksenoplysning gennem 500 år*, Gyldendal, Denmark and Norway.

Lasch, C. (1993) *The Revolt of the Elites and the Betrayal af Democracy*, W.W. Norton, New York.

Mårja, T. (1995) 'The Role of Education in Restoring the Democratic Society: A Baltic Case', paper presented at the International Conference on Adult Education and Training: Its Role in Reconstruction and Development, 7–10 November, Cape Town.

Reich, R.B. (1993) *The Work of Nations*, Simon & Schuster, Hemel Hempstead.

Telhaug, A.F. (1992) *Norsk og internasional skoleutvikling*, Gyldendal, Denmark and Norway.

Turok, B. (1995) 'A Reflection on the Reconstruction and Development Program (RDP) after 18 Months', paper presented at the International Conference on

Adult Education and Training: Its Role in Reconstruction and Development, 7–10 November, Cape Town.

United Nations (1995) *State in Disarray, The Social Effect of Globalization*, UN research report, UNRISD, New York.

Walters, S. (1989) *Education for Democratic Participation*, University of the Western Cape, Bellville.

3

In Defence of Civil Society: Canadian Adult Education in Neo-conservative Times

Michael Welton

In 1983, the Catholic Bishops of Canada precipitated a major debate with their statement 'Ethical Reflections on the Economic Crisis'. The statement termed unemployment a 'moral disaster' and called for alternative, people-oriented and social policies. In particular, it urged government not to fight inflation at the cost of high unemployment. In 1993, the Canadian Conference of Bishops issued another pastoral letter, 'Widespread Unemployment: A Call to Mobilise the Social Forces of the Nation'. In this document they declared that unemployment was worse than it had been ten years previously. Estimating the unemployed and underemployed at one quarter of the labour force, the Bishops observed that 'widespread and sustained unemployment' generated a 'continuing social crisis', with increases in social pathologies like spousal and child abuse.

Through this period, which coincides with the neo-conservative regime of Brian Mulroney (1984–93), the Canadian welfare state began to shake and tremble as the neo-conservatives laid siege to what Canadians had fought so hard to achieve through the struggle years of the 1920s, 1930s and 1940s. But it was not only our economy and welfare state that were trembling. The very existence of the Canadian nation-state seemed more fragile than ever in this improbable bi-national country.

The October 1995 referendum on Quebec separation was bitterly contested and the outcome indecisive. The increasingly angry showdown between Quebec separatists and the rest of Canada has deepened the uneasiness and uncertainty felt by many Canadians, inside and outside Quebec. We do not know if our country will be fractured irrevocably, with a new Quebec wedged between the historically impoverished and economically underdeveloped Atlantic region to the east and wealthier Ontario to the west, with First Nations peoples carving out an ambiguous relationship with English Canada and the new Quebec. Canadian liberal democracy is in serious crisis. The continued existence of our nation-state is intimately tied to the existence of our welfare state.

But this epoch has had the salutary effect of shaking us out of our complacency, opening up possibilities for a radical rethinking of the purpose of socially responsible adult education and the meaning of democracy in our post-1989 world. One might argue that 'democratic theory' had reached an impasse by the early 1970s, with the utopian potential of the welfare state gradually exhausting itself. Social democracy in Canada has run out of steam – it has generated nothing of intellectual interest or excitement in the past two decades. In power it has acted like a neo-conservative government; out of power, a pall of silence has fallen over its national leader, Alexa McDonough. In the last election, the New Democratic Party lost its official party status, garnering about 6 per cent of the popular vote and winning only nine seats.

Our national political scene has been radically reconfigured with the separatist Bloc Quebec in opposition; the pseudo-populist Reform Party is just two seats behind. The right now appears to speak for the common people, addressing their fears that communities are unravelling, families falling apart and meaning eroding in the jungle of mass consumerism. They have convinced the ordinary Canadian, or at least quite a few of them, that the welfare state bred clientelism and dependency, and that curbing the deficit will invigorate a sluggish economy and revitalize morale.

The vitality of our democratic life in Canada has been sustained for the last three decades by a host of associations and movements within civil society, such as women's and indigenous people's networks, ecology groups, and so on. In my view, the revitalization of democratic theory requires the elaboration of a 'civil societarian' perspective on societal organization and transformation. This perspective requires that we develop an understanding of how our complex, late-modern societies actually work. The revolutionary fantasies of the 1960s must give way to a more chastened and modest utopianism: chastened because we have learned that political projects which totally remake 'society' have been disastrous, modestly utopian because one of the big lessons of the twentieth century appears to be that it is utterly catastrophic to human well-being for social learning processes to be constrained within civil society. I would like to argue that the core value structure of socially responsible adult education – the affirmation that the life-world is the foundation of meaning, solidarity and stable personality; our commitment to the enlightened, autonomous and reflective learner; the centrality of social learning processes to the formation of the active citizen; and the fostering of discussion, debate and dialogue amongst citizens – is compatible with 'discursive' or 'deliberative' approaches to democracy. And 'civil society' – the realm of communicative action and self-organization – is the key to understanding the meaning of deliberative democracy.

Surviving together: the Canadian public tradition

For one who has grown up in Canada's golden age of left-of-centre social democratic public culture, it has been shocking to experience the fraying and unravelling of the welfare state over the last decade and a half. It is shocking because the story of Canada can be told as a narrative of a collective struggle to forge a nation in the face of great geographical and political obstacles. We have always privileged the collective over the individual, and accentuated the organic community (think of Catholicism in Quebec and Anglicanism in early Ontario) over the individual's self-development. We have fundamentally valued the pursuit of life, liberty and happiness not for the isolated individual; rather, that peace, order and good government would prevail in the land. Our pre-eminent learning challenge as a nation-state has been survival. To survive, be it the harshness of the prairie winter or the pull from the south, Canadians have had to forge deep bonds with one another. We imagine not a frontier sliding towards the promised land of fortune and individual happiness, but a fortress, where we gather together against a mysterious and dangerous wilderness for comfort and hope.

Our greatest economic historian, Harold Innis, taught us that the very nature of our staples economy (fish, fur, wheat, oil) has required a collectively oriented state. Our state had to intervene to create the infrastructure to facilitate staple production and distribution, largely to the metropole. Canadian Prime Minister Sir John MacDonald fashioned our 'national policy' in the late nineteenth century through high tariffs and the building of a railway linking east and west. Canadians are at ease with an activist state. Deep within our collective psyches lies the belief that the state must act to foster human solidarity and ensure that the least among us is cared for. Both our real conservatives and our socialists share this belief.

Canadian collectivist culture survived the dislocation of acute suffering of the depression and war years. Catalysed by thousands of grassroots adult educators who led endless study and action groups, Canadians came to believe unquestioningly that the state should play a central role in social policy. This was largely a new role for the Canadian state. It is not surprising, in the light of our public traditions, that Canadians would adopt a version of Keynesian economic theory which was committed to economic activism in support of stabilization and full employment. The collective provision of social benefits and collective management of the economy became central features of Canadian life to an extent that clearly differentiated us from the United States. An Ontario Ministry of Intergovernmental Affairs document captures the essence of Canadian citizenship.

> Over time, the idea of a Canadian citizenship has evolved and broadened. Today, a national system of health care, an array of income support programmes,

free public and secondary education and affordable post-secondary education
are claims that all Canadians make on their governments. Taken together, these
programmes represent and symbolize Canadians' sense of themselves as members of a community where solidarity and mutual responsibility are fundamental
social norms.[1]

Times change quickly, however; only five years after the publication of
this statement, the neo-conservative government of Mike Harris has
engendered serious social upheaval and conflict in Ontario.

Throughout its history, Canadian adult education has been concerned
with issues of social action and public responsibility. When the Canadian
adult education community achieved communal identity in the depression
and war years, the welfare state had not yet emerged. Identifying the
'central problem' of their time as economic and political powerlessness,
and animated by a vision of participatory democracy, Canadian adult
educators in the 1930s and 1940s sought to mobilize people at the grassroots level to reflect collectively on their life situation and devise solutions to their problems.[2]

The leaders of the Antigonish Movement of Nova Scotia knew that
real adult education sprang from the heart and pains of the people.
Through participation in various co-operative ventures, men and women
acquired a set of critical competencies to engage their previously quite
baffling situation. Men and women did not become 'masters of their own
destiny' – none of us has yet – but they did achieve something like
'critical enablement' as they moved from defeatist pathos to taking some
control over their personal, economic and social destinies.[3] The Church
provided a meaningful, if contested, orientation to life (people were not
nihilistic and bereft of hope), forms of solidarity in communities were
strong, and people still had qualities of self-reliance. In more theoretical
terms, the strength of the traditional civil society was the cultural precondition enabling the Antigonish Movement to motivate its followers to
create co-operative forms of work and consumption. From this position
of strength, they confronted a piratical economy and laissez-faire state.

But these conditions required human leaders to activate the people, so
to speak. And these leaders came predominantly from the clergy, who
had a ready-made communications network in place. If Eastern Nova
Scotia had been less ethnically and religiously oriented, and the leadership confused or bewildered, it really is hard to imagine the movement
getting off the ground.[4] This orientation to collective social action, one
might argue, constitutes an original identity. Canadian adult education
particularly supported people to play a role in public debate, be it as
workers, citizens or social activists. Adult education acted as an agency,
mediating between the macro and micro levels of our existence.

'Amateurs out to change the world' – Alexander Laidlaw's memorable
phrase – captures the spiritual dynamism of many of our popular educa-

tors throughout the twentieth century in Canada. These amateurs fought fiercely for a learning process that would build and sustain community while simultaneously empowering men and women as collective actors to struggle for justice. I believe that many of our forefather and foremother educators of adults in farm, women's, worker and co-operative movements would be shocked and dismayed at the extent to which the modern practice of adult education has capitulated to a technocratic ideology, market-driven logic and rampant individualism. They understood adult education as part of the resistance movement to capital's maniacal drive to break into bits and create 'possessive individualists' out of us all. They knew, to use the language of adult education in the Canadian farm movement, that 'combined intelligence' enabled us to command our life-situations. Left to our individual resources, we would not be strong enough to counter those forces fracturing us – each against the other, class against class, men against women, group against group, region against region.[5]

Neo-conservatism comes to Canada

Our social nation-state is now under assault; our social legacy, forged in the bitter fires of the depression and war years and hammered into shape in the 1950s and 1960s, is in danger of being undermined. Canadian economists Errol Black and Robert Chernomas believe the neo-conservatives are trying to transform Canadian society from a 'form of social or communitarian capitalism to a miniature replica of the U.S. form of individualistic capitalism'.[6] In response to economic stagnation, escalating inflation and a restive labour movement in the 1970s, the federal liberals introduced disastrous monetary policies in 1981. Interest rates skyrocketed to 18 per cent, fuelling growth in public-sector debt, exacerbating the emerging fiscal crisis, accelerating unemployment and causing untold misery for many ordinary people.[7] In 1984, Brian Mulroney swept the moribund liberals out of office, offering us a platform of job creation and preservation of social programmes. But it did not take him very long to reveal his true colours.

By the mid-1970s the Western world had entered a period of profound change, both economically and ideologically. Global ruling elites, with the transnational corporations as their power base, began a complex process of dismantling social forms of capitalism in order to liberate market constraints or regulations. By now we are all familiar with the brutal consequences of global elite 'development' policies: World Bank and International Monetary Fund structural adjustment programmes have pushed Southern (and Northern) economies into the dirt, wreaking havoc with welfare policies. Capital had been wrestling itself free of tutelage from either the state or civil society. In fact, it was now going to teach civil society a thing or two. Taking his cues from his idols Reagan and

Thatcher, Mulroney fashioned his 'Agenda for Change'. Restraint was the keyword: he would reduce the deficit to deal with the fiscal crisis, and would rely on a 'free' market to foster economic growth. Deregulate transportation, communication, finance; privatize crown corporations to the common people; reduce spending on social welfare programmes: this was the neo-conservative agenda. This agenda, McBride and Shields observe,[8] was not a 'natural' response to the irresistible demands of globalization. To forgo tax revenues from corporations and to keep interest rates high were choices selected from a range of possibilities. Neo-conservatism is 'heavily imbued with ideology'.[9]

It is important to understand that neo-conservatism is not simply a tough-minded way of doing business efficiently. It is not just about economics, or the new relationship of the state to the economy. It is an illegitimate and very dangerous attempt to further 'colonize the life-world'.[10] By attacking the notion of universal social welfare provision, the neo-conservatives undermine forms of solidarity that were previously protected by the activist state.

The regressivity of the tax system, changes to unemployment insurance and the introduction of workfare divide the collectivity, setting up an insidious dichotomy between haves and have-nots. Indeed one notices that, increasingly, the rich and well-off live within a 'culture of contentment' (Galbraith's pointed phrase). Those within this culture have withdrawn compassion from the less fortunate, who are now held accountable for being out of work or simply out of their minds. The common wealth is rent apart by neo-conservative policies, making one wonder what they are conserving and leading one to despise what they think is new. There is a neo-fascist odour to the mean policies of Ontario's Mike Harris (drastic cuts to poor mums, abolition of anti-scab labour legislation, reduction in day-care facilities, etc.). We should take note, too, of the anti-union policies of the Harris government. Neo-conservatism does not seem to tolerate oppositional learning sites; here we simply observe that the federal neo-conservatives (in the guise of liberals) have, in the past two or three years, withdrawn the funding from numerous popular groups including the Canadian Association for Adult Education and about one hundred international education centres across the country, and radically reduced funding for labour education.

A 'truly civil society'[11] requires that associations of civil society such as trade unions be allowed to pursue freely their own learning processes and agendas. The American sociologist Robert Putnam speaks of 'social capital', which he defines as the 'processes between people which establish networks, norms and social trust and facilitate co-ordination and co-operation for mutual benefit'.[12] It is precisely within the domain of what we are now calling civil society (the social space which includes intimate relationships, social movements, public spheres) that social capital is produced. Relationships of mutuality, reciprocity and trust, when they occur, are carefully nurtured over time. Social capital is analogous to the growth of an oak tree. It starts out precariously as an acorn, then a small shoot, facing wind and cold. Over a hundred years ago or so, it reaches its full sturdiness. In a matter of minutes, modern technology can burst in on this tree and destroy it. Social capital is a little like that: it takes years of care and nurturing to foster meaningful relationships of respect and tolerance. The heedless action of the state can destroy accumulated social capital, and social capital is not so easy to replace. Eva Cox comments:

> Social capital should be the pre-eminent and most valued form of capital as it provides the basis on which we build a truly civil society. Without our social bases we cannot be fully human. We become vulnerable to social bankruptcy when our social connections fail. If most of our experiences enhance our senses of trust and mutuality, allowing us to feel valued and value others, then social capital increases.[13]

Adult education and the rebellious politics of civil society

The crisis of the welfare state and the weakening of civil society have thrown Canadian adult education into disarray and conflict. History teaches us that in times of major historical transition and power shifts adult education, interpreted here in the possible broadest sense to include the shaping of our outlook on the world and our modes of acting within it, will not simply be left to the professional adult educator. We are in the midst of a struggle for the heart and soul of adult education. But why am I surprised? Adult education has always been torn between serving two masters: the system or the life-world. As the market – discourse and logic – has become ascendant over the last decade or so, 'adult education' has coupled its caboose to the corporate training and development model. This model largely instrumentalizes adult education for the purpose of corporate development and growth. For neo-conservative federal government bureaucrats in charge of our training policy initiatives, life-long learning is a signifier for life-long adaptation to the 'needs' of the 'new' global economy. I have heard federal bureaucrats tell a group of educators that we should no longer use the phrase 'adult education' because, apparently, educators might raise questions about purposes, goals, meanings. No doubt about it, there has been a major shift in discourse in Western countries from education to learning. But the concept of 'learning' floats free from designated and concrete meaning. Unless civil societarian adult educators claim 'learning' for themselves, giving it a socially anchored, contextual meaning, the neo-conservatives will run away with it. And for them it will most assuredly mean the adaptation of isolated, individual learners to the corporate-determined status quo.

Professionalized Canadian adult education may well have jumped aboard the 'learning of earning' bandwagon. But rebellious forms of oppositional learning persist in all parts of Canada. In the late 1980s, Prime Minister Mulroney tried to constrain and muzzle open-learning processes within civil society regarding the North American Free Trade Agreement. He failed to do this, and numerous groups (but particularly Labour and the Action-Canada Network) exploded in civil space to make their arguments and identify problems with the agreement. For months, public learning processes were vibrant as hundreds of thousands of Canadians were drawn into the discussion. Although the agreement was passed (and we are suffering the consequences of this in massive job loss), forms of solidarity were fostered. A similar learning process occurred during the contentious debates about the 1992 Charlottetown Accord (a neo-conservative attempt to finesse Quebec into the federation). Widely denounced by ordinary people as an elite ('men in suits') attempt to manipulate Canadians into an agreement with Quebec that they had no say in, the Accord was soundly defeated. One of the by-products of the public learning process regarding the future of our nation-state were the 'Citizens' Forums', initiated ironically by the Tories, that sprang up everywhere. While many Canadians might not have understood that the very idea of a citizens' forum had originated with adult educators in the 1940s, these gatherings were deeply rooted in our public traditions of creating communicative spaces for reflection and action. That they were despised by neo-conservative journalists and politicians should not shock us either.

More recently, the two major centres of neo-conservative 'slash and burn' activity, Alberta and Ontario, have had their smooth ride ruptured. In November 1995, a small group of 120 laundry workers acted as a kind of lightning rod for anti-government protest by walking off their job to protest the contracting-out of their work. The strike quickly spread to other workers and hospitals in Calgary and threatened to affect hospitals in Edmonton. In the face of this growing unrest, the Klein government abandoned plans for further cuts to health care and contracting-out was put on hold.[14] Since December 1995 the Ontario labour movement has been mobilizing thousands of workers in numerous demonstrations. Throughout spring 1996 the newspapers were full of strike scenes, including the 100,000 assembled in steel city Hamilton, the heart of industrial Ontario. Black and Chernomas's judgement that the 'strategy in Ontario is based on a recognition that both capital and the state are collaborating in a campaign to weaken labour and reduce the standard of living of working people, and that the only way to derail this agenda is through solidarity and direct action that disrupts production and creates instability'[15] is accurate.

Labour, as one of the still important associational oppositional learning sites within civil society, will however have to undergo a difficult critical learning process if it is to play something more than a defensive role in our current upheavals. Defending jobs is worthwhile, but this in itself leaves the more fundamental questions we are currently facing unasked. As we move towards the twenty-first century, one of greatest societal learning challenges will not be 'deficit education'. It will be spreading joblessness and the decomposition of the relationship between wage, identity and work. I believe that the current political discourse of the federal government is based on the false promise of massive job creation following in the wake of information and communication's technological revolutions. Our challenge as critically oriented adult educators is therefore to figure out, imaginatively and creatively, how we can transform the meaning of 'job' into 'worthwhile activity', that is, producing goods and services for others that sustain life and foster solidarity. But here we must be realistic and not get too carried away. These latter goals are core values of civil society, of the life-world, and there will have to be a very profound mobilization within civil society in order to find receptors in the productive sphere for its democratic reordering. Canadians have always struggled to create communicative space – vital publics – within civil society.

Let me give three examples from current socially responsible adult education practice. First, the left-of-centre think-tank, the Ottawa-based Canadian Centre for Policy Alternatives and Choices, a Manitoba coalition for social justice, decided to create the alternative federal budget to precipitate critical social learning processes. Based on consultation with grassroots groups across Canada, the alternative budget challenges the neo-conservative ideology that the government can do nothing but cut spending. The alternative budget is used by locally based grassroots groups as an educational and mobilizing tool.

Second, in June 1995 in Halifax, Nova Scotia local justice groups responded to the presence of the G-7 leaders in their city by organizing a week-long series of workshops, rallies, forums, speeches, 'speak-outs', demonstrations, seminars and street theatre at a local community college. Never before had the unions, feminist groups, environmentalists, anti-racist workers, First Nations and Black activists, development educators and sustainable future devotees come together quite like this. The organizers of the People's Summit (P-7 as it came to be popularly called) did not, however, endeavour to create a coherent oppositional movement. Rather, they wanted to create a space for the expression of different viewpoints in order to communicate their alternative vision to the general public. P-7 organizers knew well that the mass media – 2,000 journalists were in the area – would attempt to occupy public space with the personality-oriented, media sound-bite approaches. (In retrospect, P-7 participants were pleasantly surprised at the attention they did get from mainstream press.) Some critics wanted the P-7 to take a stronger stand: to produce a 'manifesto' that would present a unified front to the world. Andrew Parkin, a scholarly observer of the events of the P-7, has argued that the P-7 was 'intended to be a democratic, participatory and inclusive public forum which would stand in stark contrast to plutocratic, elitist and exclusive political institutions such as the G-7.[16] He thinks that the P-7 is best understood within a civil societarian framework.

The grassroots groups, garnered from local and faraway places, ought to be understood as a family of social movements – 'new' social movements because of their self-limiting goals. These movements, he contends, fulfil four functions. First, they strengthen civil society by forming new independent associations and organizations within civil society. These associations produce social solidarity ('social capital' as we recall Putnam) and renew the spiritual and organizational resources needed for efficacious collective action. Second, by cracking open blocked public space, the new social movements ensure that reflective learning processes occur outside the control of government and private corporate interest. More public participation is demanded and new channels of communication are opened up beyond the grasp of the state and direct control of private capital.[17] Third, and particularly pertinent to the G-7 meeting, the new social movements converging in Halifax (I can still hear the Nicaraguan and Cameroonian female delegates to a forum on the destructive policies of the IMF speaking out of great agony but with great resolve and dignity) signal the importance of creating a global civil society to counterpoint the globalization of capital. Finally, the new social movements practise a politics of inclusion by incorporating marginalized perspectives into their public deliberations. 'Each of these four dimensions,' Parkin says, 'of new social movement practice – the strengthening, defending, and the expanding of the scope and inclusiveness of civil society – help to tilt the balance of power away from government, bureaucracies and privately owned corporations, in favour of individuals and independent public associations active within civil society'.[18]

My third and final example of rebelliousness within Canadian civil society flowed in the wake of the P-7. In February 1995, a group of socially responsible adult educators formed the Atlantic Popular Educators' Network. Many of its key members had assumed leading roles in the P-7 activities. In the fall of 1995, this modest network held a series of small workshops to bring together movement activists to share our experiences and to speak openly and honestly with one another in order to move towards a deeper common understanding. These meetings culminated in a January 1996 meeting facilitated by Budd Hall of the Ontario Institute for Studies in Education. The organizers invited people to explore several key questions: (1) How did we get to the present stage of economic and social crisis, and what has been the impact on our organization? (2) What is it that we want to accomplish in the near future and in the long run? Could we put our fears and wants on the table? (3) How can we begin a process of building a movement for social justice?

Sixty-seven people from a wide variety of civil society associations (Voice of Women, Nova Scotia Organic Growers, Amnesty International, Congress of Black Women, Metro Food Bank Society, Nova Scotia Youth Voices, and others) met for a full day of reflection. Out of this meeting came a deep sense – perhaps the deepest – that global restructuring and undermining of the welfare state had isolated us and divided us from one another. We recognized that we had to resist apathy and find support in networking. We also recognized that we needed to understand more fully how the corporate agenda was ruling our lives, and were challenged to imagine alternatives to our present 'economic' model. Not surprisingly, there was no consensus on what a coherent social justice coalition would look like. Our thinking seems caught up between two models of thinking about social change: the old, centred form of thinking of social change as being propelled by a single, unified movement and a new, decentred and diffuse model which has not been adequately understood. Sharing our stories and struggles, projects and possibilities, was perhaps the easiest part of the workshop. In the final part of the workshop, the facilitator invited individuals to meet in small groups, choose a favourite idea, get some tape and place it on the wall next to someone else's idea. Time was too short, facilitation absent from one large group, the issues very complex. But a flurry of ideas were generated, impetus was given to the alternative budget project, and several study action groups on community-based economic development were initiated. We ended gathered in a circle, holding hands, while long-time activist Betty Pederson led us in a 'calling forth' of these who wished to be present with us in our time of troubles and hope. This event is, in the big scheme of things, pretty insignificant – or is it? This meeting, or forum, opened up important public space for us to think together. What we don't adequately grasp, though, is that these meetings produce valuable 'social capital', contributing to the renewal of the spirit and fostering connectedness between people of diverse backgrounds and identities. If we think of our activities always in terms of remaking the whole world, then we are bound to feel constantly depressed and downhearted. So, let's start thinking differently.

In conclusion, any revitalized adult education for social justice in the twenty-first century must face this question: how can civil society be secured, sustained and invigorated in our time? The Canadian state, by withdrawing resources from the social sector in the name of deficit reduction, has not thought through the consequences of these choices. The state has abandoned the life-world. We can expect a radical increase in disturbing pathological conditions as personalities are destabilized, even more sources of meaning dry up, and communal bonds erode. A strong civil society is the prerequisite for the creation of any kind of vital (or even, in the long-run, efficient) democratic society. We are presently almost enslaved to an anti-public, anti-human way of seeing and ordering the world. Talk about deficit reduction to stimulate the 'economy' has displaced the more fundamental question of the life-world foundation of any kind of moderately equitable progress and democratic political development. A desiccated life-world or civil society will inevitably be linked with economic stagnation and political corruption. The central purpose of socially responsible adult education is to strengthen, defend and expand civil society.

Notes

1. Ontario Ministry of Intergovernmental Affairs 1991: 2.
2. Welton 1987.
3. Welton 1995: 56.
4. Welton 1996: 73–4.
5. Welton 1995: 50 .
6. Black and Chernomas 1996: 23.
7. Black and Chernomas 1996: 26.
8. McBride and Shields 1993.
9. McBride and Shields 1993.
10. Habermas 1987.
11. Cox 1995.
12. Cox 1995: 15.
13. Cox 1995: 17.
14. Black and Chernomas 1996: 23.
15. Black and Chernomas 1996: 23.
16. Parkin 1996: 6.
17. Parkin 1996: 16.
18. Parkin 1996: 17–18.

References

Black, E. and Chernomas, R. (1996) 'What Kind of Capitalism? The Revival of Class Struggle in Canada', *Monthly Review*, Vol. 48, No. 1, May.

Cox, E. (1995) *A Truly Civil Society*, Australian Broadcast Corporation, Sydney.

Habermas, J. (1987) 'Theory of Communicative Action', *Lifeworld and System*, Vol. 2, Beacon Press, Boston.

McBride, S. and Shields, J. (1993) *Dismantling a Nation: Canada and the New World Order*, Fernwood Publishers, Halifax, Nova Scotia.

Ontario Ministry of Intergovernmental Affairs (1991) *A Canadian Social Charter: Making Our Shared Values Stronger*, Queen's Printer, Toronto.

Parkin, A. (1996) 'Building Civil Society "From the Ground Up": The Halifax People's Summit', paper presented to the Centre for Studies in Democratization, February 16–17.

Welton, M. (1987) 'On the Eve of a Great Mass Movement: The Origins of the Canadian Association for Adult Education', in Cassidy, F. and Faris, R. (eds), *Choosing Our Future*, OISE Press, Toronto.

Welton, M. (1995) 'Amateurs Out to Change the World: A Retrospective on Community Development', *Convergence*, Vol. XXVIII.

Welton, M. (1996) 'Historical Perspectives on Adult Education: The Canadian Legacy', *Open Learning*, Mount St Vincent University, Halifax, Nova Scotia.

4

Women, Poverty and Adult Education in Chile

Teresa Quiroz Martin

Globalization and impoverishment

International guidelines for a market economy began to be applied in Chile in 1975. The ministry responsible, whose most influential members were graduates of the University of Chicago and disciples of Milton Friedman, believed emphatically in the need to devise an economy based upon the forces of supply and demand. Other dimensions and relations of society were held to be subordinate to this enterprise. The state refrained from intervention in business, confining its role to the maintenance of law and order, the defence of property rights, curbing inflation and opening up the Chilean economy to a global market.

Among the concrete measures applied were cuts in public spending aimed at reducing the national deficit. The major targets were budgets for social programmes and services regarded as not directly productive. At the same time, import taxes were reduced and those political elements which were seen as interfering with or hindering the relation between the economy and market were eliminated. For example, labour laws were modified substantially, with rights to minimum wages and collective bargaining particularly watered down. The right to protest more generally became subject to harsh curbs.

It was in this climate that Chile entered the global economic crisis of the 1980s, with grave consequences in both economic and social terms. Between 1982 and 1983, the national product fell by 16 per cent – the greatest contraction in all Latin America. Recovery did not begin until 1986 and even then was merely moderate. In these circumstances, unemployment during 1983 bordered on 30 per cent of the economically active population.[1] Faced with this situation, the government insisted on cutting back further on social spending. The result was that the poor had to pay for social services, particularly health and education, that previously had been provided free of charge. According to a Ministry of Planning document, 'Analysis of public spending on health as a proportion of the GNP (Gross National Product) shows a gradual decline over the decade of the 1980s, so from 3.56 per cent of the GNP in 1982 we arrive at 2.3 per cent in 1990'.[2] In simple terms, the result of such policies was that the cost of the global economic crisis in Chile fell on those least able to bear it. The extent of the burden borne by the poor is graphically illustrated by figures which show that, between 1969 and 1988, consumption in the poorest households declined from 7.6 per cent to 4.4 per cent of the national total, while consumption in the most privileged homes actually rose from 44.4 per cent to 54.9 per cent.[3]

The period 1990 to 1996 was one of restored democracy in Chile, under a government maintaining the economic strategies of the previous regime. Poverty diminished but the cleavage between the richest and poorest increased.

Feminization of poverty

In Chile, as in the rest of Latin America, it is women who are the poorest of the poor. Women more than men have had to face impoverishment when they try to meet their basic survival needs. For this reason, the number and percentage of women who have to work for an income has increased nearly everywhere in the region. According to Teresita Barbieri,[4] who notes that single young women continue to participate as workers, this new influx consists largely of women aged between 25 and 49, who are also mothers, wives and heads of households.

New jobs for women are mainly temporary and linked to harvesting and the packing of products for export. In terms of what the liberal model of production euphemistically calls 'flexibility in labour relations', the women work without contracts, with schedules and terms being imposed by the employer. Participatory research involving women temporary workers in Chile shows that these terms and conditions are extremely harsh. A day's work consists of between 12 and 16 hours and the daily wage is the equivalent of payment for 2 hours' similar work in the USA.[5]

The women do not belong to any organization or union because they are afraid of being fired, or simply because many organizations do not represent their concerns. The conditions, particularly for the pickers, are inhuman. There are no bathrooms, no places to leave small children, no places to eat. The women are frequently exposed to fumigation while they are picking fruit and the consequences include skin allergies and other toxic reactions. In January 1993, for example, 40 women from La Serena[6] had to be hospitalized after fruit was fumigated while they were working. A report about the incident was carried by the newspaper *El Diario*. The women also noted that babies had become sick as a result of contamination of their mothers' milk. A further burden carried by these women is what has been referred to as 'the double shift'. The domestic workload does not ease during the period of temporary paid work, unless there is another woman at home to share domestic tasks. A recent study[7] shows that washing clothes, cooking, cleaning, taking care of children and sick people adds over 24 hours to the weekly load. If, however, there is a daughter over twelve years old, a grandmother, sister, mother-in-law or some other woman who can help, the domestic workload borne by temporary women workers is reduced by almost half.

Another dimension emphasized by the study is the emotional stress caused to women who must worry about their major responsibility for domestic work during their period of paid work. Knowing that there are children at home and teenagers alone causes headaches, stress and general exhaustion. Indeed, there is official recognition in Chile of the fact that during this period of temporary work for mothers, there are increases in drug consumption among teenagers, in intra-family violence and in cases of child abuse. The number of women who are heads of households and must work at all cost is increasing throughout Latin America. Theirs are the poorest households in the region. In Peru, for example, the percentage of women-headed households grew from 14.1 per cent in 1970 to 22.9 per cent in 1981. In Chile, according to the 1992 census, the percentage of women-headed households increased from 23.2 per cent in 1982 to 27.2 per cent ten years later.[8]

Among the factors responsible for the poverty of women-headed households is that such households tend to have a higher percentage of small children. The result is two-fold: on the one hand, women with small children are less able to leave them at home, which limits their access to work possibilities; and on the other hand, the income of such women constitutes an important, if not the sole, source of the family income. Another reason for the poverty of women-headed households is the huge disparity between the earnings of men and women. A recent survey[9] found that the incomes of households headed by men are almost double those of women-headed households for all except the most privileged socio-economic group, where the disparity is almost four-fold in favour of males.

It is clear, therefore, that there are objective reasons for the description of the economic and political processes of the past 15 years as a feminization of poverty.

Women's organizations and adult education

From a different perspective, this calamitous situation can offer positive opportunities. These need to be identified, supported and developed through education.

As the market economy gained momentum in Chile, so did organizations for mutual aid and the defence of a better quality of life among people living in the poorer urban sectors. Similar organizations can also be found in Peru, for example, and it is likely that this rapid reaction by the people drew strength from the earlier positive experience of joining forces to improve their way of life by themselves. Indeed, this kind of self-reliance was actively promoted by the government before the coup – in 1964, for instance.[10]

Often these organizations were linked to churches, functioning either as Christian grassroots communities or as organizations aided by the churches. The churches offered the only form of available protection from the military dictatorship and established such ventures as community pots, joint purchasing units, health and housing committees, workshops and small firms, and neighbourhood day care for children. A subsequent development was a network of non-governmental organizations (NGOs) which offered financial and technical support to the church-linked groupings formed earlier.

One of the positive outcomes of this perhaps peculiar association was the linking of collective action and intellectual thought, practice and theory, in a very powerful educational activity. Based on the teaching of Paulo Freire, with the addition of methodology and techniques developed in the course of years of struggle, this pedagogical activity is called 'popular education' in Latin America. The term owes at least a small part of its being to the fact that, due to the political and economic circumstances outlined earlier, popular education developed without any connection with official policy on adult education.

The evolution of popular self-help organizations in Chile has been monitored over the years by an NGO called the Economy of Work Programme (PET). Indeed, PET has coined a term for the process: 'popular economy'.[11] A recent PET report concluded that by the beginning of the 1990s, one out of every four families in the poorer sectors was directly involved in one or other popular economic organization. A notable feature of these 'popular economy' organizations, since their aim relates directly to household subsistence, is that they appeal particularly to women. Research conducted by PET in 1992 showed that 39.4 per cent of all such organizations were 'only for women', while 7.5 per cent were 'only for men'. Of all the organization members surveyed by the researchers, 73.3 per cent were women, and 76.9 per cent of the leaders were women.[12]

These popular organizations proved extraordinarily capable in remedying deficiencies in the distribution of goods and services introduced by the dominant system. Thousands of families have been able to improve their incomes by joining productive workshops, collective bakeries or laundries, while others were able to reduce their consumer costs by sharing in community pots, health committees or community day-care.

While participation in such initiatives brings improvement, it is at the level of subsistence. Without external assistance in the form of funding, materials and technical help, popular economy groups are not able to extend their benefits to members beyond this threshold. The challenge then shifts to one of adaptation to a larger milieu. Once popular economy groups discover that they have an impact on larger dynamics than their own, they have to identify and occupy an area in those dynamics which allows them to develop, and that does not totally subordinate them or change their nature. For instance, producer organizations need to get to those areas where there is a real demand in the market for their particular products. Similarly, groups producing goods for members of the community need to join together and identify and implement the necessary development programmes.

Apart from the economic benefits they bring, popular organizations have an enormous social significance. First, they place previously invisible persons (women, the unemployed) in the public eye. Second, they place activities such as child-care, traditionally regarded as a private concern and resolved within individual households, in collective situations. Finally, they facilitate the development of individuals and communities by exposing them to situations and practices different from those to which they are accustomed.

The following comment, one among thousands of testimonials received from participants over the years, illustrates how popular organization members themselves perceive their gains.

> I think that the workshops are a very positive experience because the women, apart from learning, gain experience in other areas as well ... in the beginning I stuttered when trying to speak, but no longer have this problem. A friend who is now a good saleswoman told me that for some time when she was offering goods for sale, her heart would pound ... sure that someone will be rude to me, she thought; now she feels very confident when she is selling.[13]

Current challenges in adult education for women

From the early 1980s, NGOs involved in popular education have been accumulating experience and developing theory in relation to educational support for popular groups. However, the circumstances under which this work has taken place have militated against the creation of a thorough and comprehensive pedagogical proposal.

On the one hand, ideological opposition to authoritarian and/or neo-liberal governments has situated NGOs in an alternative environment which has made it difficult for them to think about or propose policies appropriate to a more libertarian or 'horizontal' society. On the other hand, financing systems which operate through several international co-operation agencies have pushed NGOs into competing for funds and

avoiding joint projects. Thus, despite the development of a body of critical and enlightening thought on the advantages of a holistic approach in
educational processes with adult people, NGOs are inclined towards
partial efforts concentrated unilaterally on different aspects of the same
rich popular experience. Consequently, the desired dialectic between practice and research (concentrated in different NGOs) has not been taking
place, and has not been linked to pedagogical reflection and innovation.

The challenge is to overcome this unilateral style and to develop an
integrated methodology for supporting women's efforts. The feminization of poverty, as well as the positive potential that this situation has
evoked among women, points towards methodologies that connect or
articulate – rather than separate or oppose – training (technical abilities)
and education (enlightening contents).

Similarly, the continuity between women's practical and strategic interests seems to call for an educational process directed towards meeting
urgent needs on the basis of effective, collective and sustainable action.
At the same time this should be a process informed by supplementary
information, reflection and the development of organizational abilities,
geared to equip women to act with the intention of changing supra-
everyday life contexts.

We will always have to take care to ensure that women encounter the
strategic level of this process as a dimension of the more obviously
practical and everyday world. In other words, we must avoid the trap of
theoretical discourses that have no readily evident relation to lived reality
for the majority of women. In popular education we want a response to
questions that arise from learners' everyday lives. The so-called 'gender
pedagogy' has insisted on many activities (for example, games, group
dynamics, interaction) that build up and reinforce participants' sense of
self-esteem and personal goals. There is no doubt that such activities are
of great help to women inhibited by an androcentric culture and isolated
in the confines of domestic space. For this reason, and also because it is
important to include playfulness along with concern for the person, they
should be part of the popular education process.

It is important to understand these activities not as an end in themselves, but rather as instruments for aiding and strengthening the inclusion
(not submersion) of individuals in the collective task of improving and
transforming women's lives. Personal development should not be at odds
with or move away from the task of transforming material conditions. Our
aim must be to help in actions that operate against the sensation of
incapacity that poverty and exclusion from decision-making impose.

Only in this way will we be able to escape the myth that 'personal
development' dynamics are good only for building up those partial aspects which a patriarchal society assigns to women – aspects such as
emotionality and sensitivity. By including personal development as part

of the collective task of transformation, we will strengthen both the capacity for interaction in society and those political practices which, reduced to the unilateral aspects patriarchy assigns to men, become boring, dry and eventually inhuman.

We cannot continue opposing informal education with the formal space. Such a strategy means that we give up important ground, a field of great influence in education and popular culture. Above all, it is our learners who suffer from this outmoded tactic of opposition. There are women who want and request formal acknowledgement of their participation in the courses, workshops, encounters and conferences organized by NGOs. It is true that they greatly appreciate the knowledge and experience they gain. But how can it be wrong of them to want, in addition, the official acknowledgement that will help them to work and to gain influence?

Finally, all the available information seems to indicate that the local space is the place where educational efforts must be focused. This location has been understood as a 'feminine space', where women can (for they are able to) build themselves as 'subjects', while also making use of the intended organization of their local space, for empowerment.

Local development as a fad, promoted by an official push towards decentralization, has opened up different understandings in Latin America. The challenge for organizations involved in popular education is to gain ground in this territory, to carve out a space in the dispute over the option of local power which, in its best expression, should be feminine power.

Notes

1. Ministry of Planning 1993.
2. Ministry of Planning 1993.
3. Ministry of Planning 1993.
4. Barbieri 1992.
5. Diaz 1991.
6. *El Diario* 1993.
7. Zuñiga 1996.
8. Figures quoted from here on indicate a slightly lower percentage, because the regular survey led by the Ministery of Planning for each of four years, refers to households and not to families. There are 3,817,528 families in Chile, of which 15.8% were hosted by a different family, and 52.2% of these 'Secondary Groups' are headed by women.
9. Todaro and Salazar 1995.
10. Campero 1988. 'Between survival and politics' is the central theme of the excellent work of the popular organization in Chile by the author.
11. Scholnik and Teitelboin 1988; Hardy 1988; Razeto 1984; Razeto 1986.
12. Razeto 1992.
13. Angelo 1987: 71.

References

Angelo, G. (1987) *Women are Essential,* CEM, Santiago.

Barbieri, T. (1992) 'Women and the Latin American Crisis', *Among Woman,* Lima.

Campero, G. (1988) *Between Survival and Politics,* ILET, Santiago.

Diaz, E. (1991) 'Investigación Participativa acerca de las Trabajadoras Temporeras de la Fruta', (Estudio de Casos), *Localidades de andacollo, doñihue y Mercedes,* Centro El Canelo de Nos, September, introduced and presented by T. Quiroz Martin.

El Diario (1993) La Serena, Chile, January.

Hardy, C. (1988) *Organize to Survive: Urban Poverty and Popular Organization,* PET, Santiago.

Ministry of Planning (1993) *Social Programs: Their Impact on Chilean Homes,* Mideplan, Santiago.

Razeto, L. (1984) *The Economy of Solidarity and Democratic Markets,* PET, Santiago.

Razeto, L. *et al.* (1986) *Popular Economic Organizations,* PET, Santiago.

Razeto, L. (1992) *Castaitro te Organizaumes,* PET, Santiago.

Scholnik, M. and Teitelboin, B. (1988) *Poverty and Unemployment in Poor Settlements: The Other Face of the Neo-liberal Model,* PET, Santiago.

Todaro, R. and Salazar, R. (1995) 'De mujeres sola a jefe de Hogar', in Valenzuela, M.E., Venegas, S. and Andrade, C. (eds), Sernam, Chile.

Zuñiga, Marcela Aravena Y Javier (1996) 'Mujer y Doble Jornada, Una investigación sobre Temporera de la Fruta', Tesis de grado en Trabajo Social, July, *Universidad de Artes y Ceincias Socciales* (ARCIS).

5

The State, Civil Society and the Economy: Adult Education in Britain

Keith Jackson

> The value of adult education cannot only be measured by direct increases in earning power or productive capacity or by any other materialistic yardstick, but by the quality of life it inspires in the individual and generates for the community at large.
>
> It is an agent of changing and improving our society: but for each individual the means of change may differ and each must develop in his own way, at his own level and through his own talents.[1]

This was the conclusion in 1973 of the Committee of Enquiry into non-vocational adult education carried out for the British government which became known as the Russell Report. The then Secretary of State for Education, Margaret Thatcher, arranged for the immediate publication of the report 'because of the importance of the subject, and the great interest with which the report is awaited'.[2]

Despite this enthusiasm it was twenty years before the British government introduced major legislation on adult education and training. The contrast between what happened then and the Russell Report has direct bearing on the global debate about adult education and training for reconstruction and development in the 1990s.

In 1973, the Russell Report expressed views which are argued more cogently and comprehensively in the South African context by the Reconstruction and Development Programme (RDP) of the African National Congress (ANC).[3] Most pertinently, there is the same recognition of the consequences for adult education and training particularly relating to the state, civil society and the economy. This perspective is now given major global significance by the timing of the RDP in international affairs, its origins in a powerful international movement and its quality as a comprehensive political, social and economic document.

It is instructive, therefore, to examine what has happened to the Russell Report perspective in the UK over twenty years, as an example in one country of how the values it represented have been influenced by market-driven policies in line with the global development of capital. Some may find a touch of irony within this examination in realizing that the same politician who endorsed the Russell Report became a dominant world figure in challenging the premises on which it was based.

The report contained two strong themes. First, it recognized the complex ways by which adult education contributed to the general quality of life. The report saw needs for what it called 'permanent education', which included remedial education where schools had failed, second-chance education, and also updating to keep abreast of developments for everyone, regardless of qualifications on leaving full-time education. To these it added those needs which related to personal development – artistic and personal creativity, physical and sporting activity and intellectual activity for enjoyment. Finally, Russell considered that adult education was related to the place of the individual in society, giving examples of role education concerning roles in industry or in the family and community, social and political education, community education for effective collective action, and education for social leadership.

The second theme was to emphasize how the potential for this contribution could be realized by policies which are both comprehensive and pluralistic. It proposed comprehensive planning of the 'explicit and latent demands of all kinds of adult education', which would be the responsibility of democratically elected local government. It was assumed, however, that within such plans the contribution of organizations and movements in civil society would be acknowledged and supported.

> Within our communities, there exists an enormous reservoir of human and material resources; a relatively modest investment in adult education – in staff, buildings, training and organization – could release these resources for the benefit of individuals and the good of society.[4]

This is a concept of adult education in which public policy can support what would be regarded internationally as 'popular education', expressed through social movements which are independent of the state, with the Scandinavian folk high schools as perhaps the most significant example.[5] The principle had been established in the UK when a committee appointed by the Ministry of Reconstruction after the 1914–18 war found adult education to be

> inextricably interwoven with the whole of the organized life of the community.... It aims at satisfying the needs of the individual and the attainment of new standards of citizenship and a better social order. In some cases, the personal motive dominates. In perhaps the majority of cases, the dynamic character of adult education is due to its social motive.[6]

Adult education was seen as an essential part of the reconstruction of British society then as it is in South Africa today, and in this the significance of popular education was acknowledged.

The role of the Workers' Educational Association (WEA) within the wider labour movement was given great prominence. In the Education Act of 1944 such voluntary organizations, including national women's organizations, were designated 'responsible bodies', retaining independence whilst receiving public funds.

The Russell Committee went beyond a recognition of the continuing role of established voluntary movements such as the WEA by responding to new manifestations of socially engaged adult education, in the 'urban social movements' that were increasingly reflecting the interests and concerns of the working class outside the organized labour movement. The committee welcomed examples of professional adult education breaking out of classroom modes by working within the patterns of activity of voluntary organizations and community groups and thereby widening participation. There were also examples of resources being made available to organizations involved in community action and campaigning to change public policy.

In recommending this work to the British government, the Committee imaginatively reaffirmed state support for independent voluntary and political activity, as a significant contribution to education for civil society in a period characterized by reforms to the welfare state. A key theme in these reforms was the need to increase public participation in shaping policies and services. Community development and community work created the space for popular education to open up critical debate and dialogue within the contradictions of this process.[7] Whilst radical critics reduced community development to the 'corporate management of cities'[8] it nevertheless reasserted the important principle that democracy is not merely about elections and constitutions but also requires the opportunity for responsible participation in public life at many levels.

The 1992 White Paper and its impact on adult education

Twenty years later, the Conservative government published its White Paper, *Education and Training for the 21st Century*,[9] which was a total reversal of the earlier policies and practices. Here was a wholehearted commitment to an economic dynamic rather than Russell's social dynamic. Russell's reservoir of human resources was now to be released for the good of the economy, but there was no mention of the wider society.

The main challenge to which adult education was urged to respond was the relatively low participation rate by Britain's population in post-compulsory education and training, and its low level of attainment in comparison with other countries. Initiatives such as Training and

Enterprise Councils had not met that challenge sufficiently and a new Further Education Funding Council was proposed to ensure greater responsiveness on the part of providers to the needs of learners in relation to the labour market. In contrast to the years after Russell, the government showed its seriousness of intent by committing itself to finance a 25 per cent increase in over-16 student numbers over the next three years, making this a clear priority in its spending plans.

Despite the fact that the majority of the population over 16 is adult, the White Paper dealt almost entirely with the 16–19 age group. Only two pages out of almost 100 specifically referred to the learning needs of adults. Its short chapter on Education for Adults merely said that this might be funded through the new council where there was a vocational qualification route or access to higher education. Wider educational purposes associated with the quality of individual and collective life were not mentioned, except in an assumption that local government might provide 'leisure classes' at a fee, with subsidies in deprived areas.

It was not difficult, however, to see from the outset that, in order rapidly to meet very ambitious targets, adults from a wide age range would need to be drawn into the framework. After the inauguration of the new council, the further education colleges were taken out of the hands of elected local authorities and set up as independent corporations. The mechanism of achieving targets was for these corporations to compete in a market for participants. They were able to do this vigorously by using the increased funds available to them to provide courses for adults so long as they provided one of the qualification routes outlined in the legislation. The determining factor in course design was ultimately not its suitability for participants buts its eligibility for funding as a form of vocational training or access to vocational training or higher education. There was a marked change from language and objectives relating to the quality of life and the community towards the language of the marketplace. Approaches to learning and accountability for public funds were defined in terms of quality management and quality service to customers.

The new philosophy, and the practices associated with it, had some important merits. There was by far the most serious attempt so far in UK educational policy to break down the divide between education and training, between the academic and theoretical on the one hand and the vocational and the practical on the other. The White Paper endorsed the work of the National Council for Vocational Qualifications (NCVQ) set up in 1986 to establish a national qualifications framework. Here the exclusive labour-market orientation seriously marred a valuable reform; national vocational qualifications (NVQs) were a new style of 'competence-based' qualifications, challenging purely academic criteria. But the five levels of competence were all defined in terms of work activities; a broader approach to personal competencies and social outcomes would have gained general support from adult educators and allowed for a much more creative approach to accreditation and assessment of learning outcomes for adults. Certainly there was considerable professional approval for the way in which funding in the new system was tied to clearly defined objectives and the means by which they were to be achieved.

Addressing economic needs, focusing on definite outcomes and evaluation of programmes, and integrating education and training were strengths which could have complemented Russell. Instead the concept 'value for money' – closely related to the labour market – totally displaced the concept of social value.

Adult education and the social structure

The practice of adult education and training experienced what Braverman[10] described as a rapid advance of the market in an inward direction into the territory of our daily lives and human relations as well as an outward direction to new parts of the globe. In this process, capital which 'thrusts itself frantically' into every possible new area of investment would totally reorganize society to conform to values. All activities and relationships, he argued, would thereby be transformed into commodities which can be bought and sold: caring for each other, young, old or sick, playing together, having fun and relaxing together.

Braverman describes some of the consequences clearly:

> The social structure, built upon the market, is such that relations between individuals and social groups do not take place directly as co-operative human encounter, but through the market as relations of purchase and sale. In time not only the material and service needs but even the emotional patterns of life are channelled through the market.[11]

The conviviality and engagement which characterizes popular education as we have described it are directly challenged.

The Russell Report was researched and written during the final years of the welfare state consensus in the UK, before the oil crisis of the early 1970s accelerated the reconstruction of international capital and introduced a new era when that consensus was to collapse. The new adult education and training policies of the 1990s follow the so-called Thatcher revolution of the 1980s when the British government took a leading part in introducing radical neo-liberal reforms which have become a global experience of 'structural readjustment', particularly after the collapse of the command economies within the Soviet Union alliances.

Russell treated adult education as if the economy did not exist, whilst the new policies consider training for the economy as if society does not exist. We are learning that this conceptual dualism must be abandoned;

the diametrically opposed policies ᾽associated with it do not work to achieve the objectives of either side. Contemporary facts are demonstrating what history tells us, that economics are built on the values and relations in society, and not the other way round.[12] Adult education and training in the UK now needs to deal with the problems for society created by market-driven policies as well as the need for Britain to compete in the global market.

The growing crisis in civil society

Social cohesion declined dramatically between Russell and the White Paper. Full employment, which was the cornerstone of the consensus, has now dropped off the political agenda of all parties in the UK. In fact it has become increasingly difficult to chart the precise levels and nature of unemployment because the basis of calculation has continually been changed to justify events, and also to disguise long-term consequences of structural change in the economy and the new shape of the labour market.

Companies seek to hold on to the essential core of skilled workers through good wages and conditions, but wish to retain cost flexibility by employing others on a part-time or short-term basis, or at arm's length in subcontracting, where the same employment conditions are not available. A report in the UK indicates that the proportion of the workforce employed in full-time 'tenured' or 'stable' employment fell from 55.5 per cent in 1975 to 35.9 per cent in 1993. Thus employment, short-term employment, and part-time employment combine to reduce both the income and the security of a very large part of the workforce.

Evidence of the growing gap between rich and poor in the UK has steadily accumulated. For example, the statistical monitoring unit at Bristol University reported that between 1979 and 1989 the income of the poorest 20 per cent of the population fell by 4.6 per cent while that of the richest rose by 40 per cent. The Policy Studies Institute said in 1991 that in the next 20 years the top 50 per cent of the population will increase its income fourfold, with the bottom 20 per cent increasing it only 0.5 per cent.

Alongside the social inequalities created by the market, there have also been major consequences for the institutions of civil society in the government's market-driven policies. The most dramatic examples of this have been the systematic reduction in the autonomy and influence of trade unions and local government. A radical shift in the relations between the state, the economy and civil society has been particularly significant, due to Britain's unwritten constitution, which provides no clearly defined checks and balances on the executive power. The existence of strong alternative centres of influence on policy and its implementation, rooted in civil society, has been an essential element to guard against what can otherwise be elective dictatorship. The building of consensus between central government and trade unions, pressure groups and directly elected local government, has been not only a characteristic of the welfare state but a much more fundamental feature of British parliamentary democracy itself.

Confrontations with trade unions were carefully planned and their autonomy reduced by legislation in the 1980s. Their influence, including their role in defining and developing adult education for democratic participation in civil society, steadily declined. The massive reduction in the powers of local government was less planned and was precipitated by the policies of some local councils in the major cities to resist or modify the local impact of the global market.[13] Indeed it was at local government level, particularly in major local authorities like the Greater London Council, Manchester and Sheffield, that the spirit which informed Russell and the practices which the report commended were developed in the 1970s and early 1980s.

Many local policies which had led to creative alliances between the local state and civil society, through interaction with voluntary organizations and groups representing social movements, particularly among women and the black population, were anathema to the government. Since local people consistently voted for the policies which this approach created, such as highly subsidized transport, and were prepared to pay for them, the power of local authorities to determine a local tax base was taken away, and the Greater London Council was abolished.

Market-driven policies have involved the privatization of public services with the development of quangos (quasi non-governmental organizations) composed of government appointees. These introduce the practices of the marketplace to an increasing range of public services which had previously been open to democratic scrutiny and influence. The creation of the Further Education Funding Council with its impact on adult education and training was, therefore, part of a broader programme of removing the influence of local elected authorities.

A new status of semi-citizen has been emerging in the UK, occupied by those who have little power in the marketplace and little purchase on obscure democratic processes. When the government introduced a Citizen's Charter it defined accountability more in market or quasi-market terms; accountability to the customer rather than the citizen. This is the system of relations appropriate to UK plc (private limited company), in which adult education and training is expected by government to define its objectives accordingly. Braverman's analysis of market relations, however, points to the contradictions which are leading to a return to some of the principles in the Russell Report.

A new paradigm for education and training

The need for a new approach to adult education and training which takes into account people's relations to civil society as well as to the labour market is most apparent in areas where high unemployment and industrial restructuring are reducing the quality of life and life chances most dramatically. Special programmes fund adult training programmes in some cases through the European Union's Social Fund. It is in these areas that the limitations of the UK plc model of adult education and training fails even in its own terms of vocational training.

A survey in central Birmingham[14] found that tiny proportions of the population possessed qualifications and that these proportions decreased sharply in successive age ranges after 26 years of age. The evidence suggested that people did not take formal vocational courses because they did not have the confidence or motivation to do so. Vocational qualifications are important, of course, and they are the most likely form of education to be presented effectively as a commodity since they have direct currency in the labour market. Conversely, however, people do not study for such qualifications when they perceive, accurately or otherwise, that their place in the labour market will not be improved thereby – either due to high unemployment or the low quality of much work available.[15] Thus the objectives of the new market-driven policies are themselves made more difficult to achieve by defining education and training entirely in terms of the labour market.

Braverman's analysis is relevant because education is a form of human exchange, which, if it is to be effective, requires participants to be creative partners acting individually or collectively in different circumstances and according to the interests which lead them to look for relevant learning. If the aim is indeed to increase the skills base among adults for economic reasons, we have to take seriously evidence that people who do not take up formal vocational courses because they lack confidence or motivation, can begin learning through other kinds of activities and then move on to formal learning. These are activities they undertake as people, as citizens, as members of society, not commodities in the labour market. Studies[16] on adult learning in voluntary organizations covering Health Education, Advocacy and Campaigning, Arts, Physical Activity and interests or hobbies showed that membership and activity brought a liberating sense of increased confidence. Even when formal learning and training programmes are involved in these organizations, informal learning remains significant.

As Russell recognized, in order to link personal, community and vocational interests in civil society there needs to be co-operation, collaboration and alliances across public institutional patterns and between the state and NGOs. The market model has pushed educational providers to defend institutional interests in order to compete effectively, requiring people to choose between alternative provision where a combination may be more appropriate.

Possibilities

There are significant signs of difficulties being recognized. A recent report evaluates the outcome of the whole range of programmes within the UK government's 1988 Action for Cities package.[17] It identifies failures to utilize the skills and talents of people by concentrating on purely physical and economic goals. The European Union's recent Green Paper on social policy also recognizes the problem:

> There is a high risk that the continued pursuit of present policies will lead ultimately to a dual society in which wealth creation is primarily in the hands of a highly qualified labour force, while income is transferred to a growing number of non-active people as a basis for a reasonable level of social justice. Such a society would not only become increasingly less cohesive, it would also run counter to the need for the maximum mobilization of Europe's human resource wealth.[18]

Human resource development is the global framework for those policies of community development to which Russell linked adult education and training in the UK, as the state and corporate sector seek to deal with the contradictions which are emerging. The 'reservoir of human resources' is required both for economic development and for cohesive and stable democracy. Thus, the European Union is targeting funds for 'community capacity building' to assist locally based organizations, whilst the South African RDP argues that 'the social movements ... developed in our country in opposition to apartheid oppression ... are a major asset in the effort to democratize and develop our society'.

The debate and dialogue associated with 'popular education' could again be one of the ways in which people can bring forward new ideas that point to the needs and solutions which reflect their interests. But that will depend on achieving conditions of democratic pluralism which prevail where this kind of adult education is supported by the state. It is one of the reasons why the Reconstruction and Development Programme which the African National Congress has put before the South African people offers such remarkable possibilities.

Notes

1. Russell Report 1973.
2. Russell Report 1973.
3. African National Congress 1991.
4. Russell Report 1973.
5. Borish 1991.

6. Waller 1956.
7. Thompson 1980.
8. Cockburn 1977.
9. Department of Education and Science 1991.
10. Braverman 1974.
11. Braverman 1974: 277.
12. Perkin 1969.
13. Blunkett and Jackson 1984.
14. Birmingham City Council/Heartlands Development Corporation 1989.
15. Faure 1972.
16. Elsdon 1994.
17. Robson et al. 1994.
18. Commission of the European Union 1993.

References

African National Congress (1991) *The Reconstruction and Development Programme: A Policy Framework,* Johannesburg.

Birmingham City Council/Heartlands Development Corporation (1989) *East Birmingham Survey.*

Blunkett, D. and Jackson, K. (1984) *Democracy in Crisis,* Chatto & Windus, London.

Borish, S.M. (1991) *The Land of the Living,* Blue Dolphin, California.

Braverman, H. (1974) *Labour and Monopoly Capital,* Monthly Review Press, New York.

Cockburn, C. (1977) *The Local State,* Pluto, London.

Commission of the European Union (1993) *European Social Policy: Options for the Union,* Brussels.

Department of Education and Science (1991) *Education and Training for the 21st Century,* CM 1536, HMSO, London.

Elsdon, K. (1994) 'Values and Learning in Voluntary Organisations', paper to Voluntary Adult Education Forum's Annual Conference, February, Summary Research at the Department of Adult Education, University of Nottingham.

Faure, E. (1972) *Learning to Be,* Unesco, Paris.

Perkin, H. (1969) *The Origins of Modern British Society,* Routledge, London.

Robson, B. *et al.* (1994) *Assessing the Impact of Urban Policy,* Department of the Environment, HMSO, London.

Russell Report (1973) *Adult Education: Plan for Development,* Report by a Committee of Enquiry appointed by the Secretary of State for Education and Science (UK) under the Chairmanship of Sir Lionel Russell CBE.

Thompson, J. (ed.) (1980) *Adult Education for a Change,* Hutchinson, London.

Waller, R.D. (1956) *A Design for Democracy,* Max Parish, London.

6

Globalization from Below:
The Trade Union Connections

Judith Marshall

The global relationships of Canadian workers are organized through at least three different discourses. They are the discourses of solidarity, development and, more recently, globalization. By discourse, I do not mean just a particular language, but a fluid constellation of institutions, forms, symbolic representation and practices, including language practices. These discourses organize our international relationships, and reinforce the meanings we attach to them. They also shape a repertoire of possible roles – donors, beneficiaries, victims, partners, competitors or strategic allies.

The discourse of solidarity is fundamental to the historical beginnings of the trade-union movement and a core feature of current labour identity, whether as solidarity with fellow-workers, with workers in neighbouring communities or internationally. Old practices of solidarity are challenged by global competitiveness. Workers in Northern economies face massive down-sizing in both public- and private-sector employment, with double-digit unemployment figures and a future promising 'jobless' recovery, at best. Workplace restructuring maintains only core functions in central operations while more and more is produced through outsourcing and homework. A company like Nike basically produces only the image through its core operations. For shoe production, Nike has long abandoned its original American workforce, outsourcing production in search of the lowest wage markets in Asia. The challenge for the trade-union movement is to act beyond the defence of its current members and create forms of organization and solidarity that link it structurally to the informal sector, the non-union workers and the unemployed, both domestically and further afield.

International solidarity also has a rich history. It was trade-union solidarity that brought many Chilean labour leaders imprisoned after the 1973 coup from jail cells to planes bound for Canada, Holland or Sweden.

During the long era of apartheid, leaders from the major trade unions in South Africa become familiar figures at Canadian labour gatherings. Today the South African, Chilean and Canadian unions almost yearn for the simplicity of fighting institutionalized racism and brutal dictatorships as they contend with 'global competitiveness' and the 'virtual corporation'.

The international trade-union connections organized through the discourse of solidarity are inextricably intertwined with connections shaped by the discourse on development. The standard framing of the development discourse for Canadian trade unions comes through the mainstream media, advertising and travel brochures. It is premised on a stereotypical South uniformly peopled by impoverished masses, the alleviation of whose plight rests with our charity in the 'developed' countries. Development aid is based on a flow of financial and human resources from North to South, shaping North–South power relationships into a set of donor–beneficiary roles.

During my visit to South Africa in 1991 as a representative of a labour development fund in Canada (see below), old friends in South African trade unions reflected wryly on the firm hold of this development discourse on their own behaviour. When a Northern trade-union delegation came calling, they automatically positioned themselves as beneficiaries, funding requests in hand, paternalism and dependency assumed on both sides. When a trade-union delegation from Brazil or India appeared, however, a completely different logic locked in, pushing for identification of common issues and possible areas of collaboration.

Over the past decade, yet another discourse, that of global competitiveness, has bombarded trade unionists in both North and South. This discourse urges all working people to greater 'productivity' and 'flexibility' in order to attract foreign investment. Economies in Northern countries like Canada are downsized, with jobs moving away to low-wage jurisdictions. The logic for South Africa is to make industries 'efficient' enough to compete on world markets, notwithstanding a 50 per cent unemployment rate and a population crying out for production to meet a range of basic needs from consumer goods to housing. Chile's 'economic miracle' under Pinochet is lauded as a global success, with dramatic expansion of the pie deemed more important than distribution of its pieces – 30 per cent of the population below the poverty line notwithstanding. Even eager investors in Chile's booming economy like the mining giant Placer Dome have some worries about the logic of globalization. Placer Dome's Director of International and Public Relations points to the problem:

Who benefits from our investments: is it the governing elite, the plutocrats of the capital cities, the bankers and lawyers and constructions firms? Or is it the local population in the region around our mines? Neo-liberalism, the economic model within which the great opening to mining investment in the countries of

the Cordillera has been achieved, tends to concentrate wealth rather than dis-
tribute it. Chile ... is the country in the region most keenly aware of this issue,
having succeeded remarkably in generating new wealth while witnessing the
income gap between the top 20 per cent of the population and the bottom 20
per cent widen significantly.[1]

The logic offered by global management to workers has multiple twists.
First it is a logic of workers in the North and South competing. Northern
workers are urged to a 'protectionist' stance against Southern workers,
eager to 'steal' their jobs. Collective bargaining is forced into a posture
of concessions because otherwise 'the competition' will force the company
to move production elsewhere, whether from high-wage Canada to low-
wage Mexico or from modest-wage Chile to poverty-wage Peru. The
flames of fear and racism are fanned in the process.

Another logic is 'us' – workers and management together – versus
'the competition', a logic that demands co-operation and co-management
schemes. In the early 1990s, workers for Northern Telecom in Mexico
made overtures to Canadian Northern Telecom workers, to strategize
together not about how to bargain more effectively with Northern
Telecom management but about how workers in both countries could
team up with their common managers to make 'their' company the most
competitive telecommunications company on the global market.

Living the interconnections between powerful macro forces and local
realities is by no means unique to Canadian workers. Chilean economist,
Fernando Leiva, puts it this way:

A big part of capital's success in carrying forward this strategy relates to its
relative ease in moving about to any point on the planet. Workers are rooted,
with their survival both on a daily basis and from one generation to the next,
embedded in a dense web of social relations. These are constructed in a determined time and space. Business, simply by pushing a button, can transfer
resources from Boston to Mexico, from California to Singapore, from Miami
to Santiago. A metal worker or a textile operator, however, cannot respond by
transferring the labour power grounded in his or her own body, household and
community. Conscious of this difference, transnational capital uses all its capacity
to loosen its national ties. It does so in order to increase its power and roll back
the historic conquests of workers.[2]

The 'global competitiveness' discourse also includes massive downsizing
with the need for anorexic workplaces justified by global competition.
The message to workers is about a skills crisis rather than a jobs crisis.
Get retrained and the jobs will come, is the message from management
and various government training bodies set up by politicians eager to be
seen to be addressing job creation. The reality, of course, is that alarming
levels of unemployment continue, with no likelihood of abatement without a radical change in the global economic agenda.

Labour-based development funds – a new phenomenon

Five major national trade unions have created new development funds in Canada over the past decade and begun to work more systematically on international connections through these funds. The efforts of these funds to put a distinctly labour signature to their work come just as the forces of neo-liberal fundamentalism preaching global competitiveness have intensified. There is a vast distance, however, between the simplistic presentation of global competitiveness and the complex way in which capital is now organizing production globally. Richard Barnet and John Cavanagh capture the complex moment in which these funds must learn to operate:

> In the 1990s large business enterprises, even some smaller ones, have the technological means and strategic vision to burst old limits – of time, space, national boundaries, language, custom and ideology. By acquiring earth-spanning technologies, by developing products that can be produced anywhere and sold everywhere, by spreading credit around the world, and by connecting global channels of communication that can penetrate any village or neighbourhood, these institutions we normally think of as economic rather than political, private rather than public, are becoming the world empires of the twenty-first century. The architects and managers of these space-age business enterprises understand that the balance of power in world politics has shifted in recent years from territorially-bound governments to companies that can roam the world. As the hopes and pretensions of government shrink almost everywhere, these imperial corporations are occupying public space and exerting a more profound influence over the lives of ever larger numbers of people.[3]

The pioneer was the Steelworkers' Humanity Fund, established at a policy conference in 1985 and now having operated for more than a decade. It was founded in response to the famine in Ethiopia in the mid-1980s. After it came the Communications, Energy and Paperworkers' Humanity fund, established in 1990. In 1991, the Canadian Auto Workers established their Social Justice Fund, building connections rapidly with a variety of labour and social groups. The Canadian Union of Public Employees created its Union Aid fund two years later and focused on twinning public-sector locals in Canada with their counterparts in different parts of the world. The newest fund, established formally only in 1996, is the Ontario Secondary School Teachers' Federation Humanity Fund, which will focus on links with teachers' unions in the South.

Each of the unions brought a distinct history of international connections into its development fund. The funds use a characteristic labour mechanism, the collective bargaining agreement. After one decade, close to 400 steelworker bargaining units have included the Humanity Fund in their agreements, donating a penny for each hour worked to the fund. Ten per cent of the contracts included a matching penny from management. The other funds have similar mechanisms. For the steelworkers, this means raised revenue of $800,000 to $900,000 annually which, when matched by co-funding from the Canadian International Development Agency (CIDA), becomes a sizeable development fund.

The institutional growth of the Steelworkers' Humanity Fund captures the potential of these funds to respond to globalization. As indicated above, the Steelworkers' Humanity Fund emerged at a time when people throughout Canada were inventing ways to respond to the Ethiopian crisis. If the original mandate of the fund was relief and development activities, the events during the decade of its existence have considerably broadened its scope.

After operating for this period, the Humanity Fund has built up a solid practice of development assistance with a $1.6 million programme, supporting projects of about thirty labour and community organizations in twelve countries in five regions of the world. The expectations of the organizations receiving support from the labour funds are high, whether they are trade unions or community organizations. They want the labour-based fund to take them beyond a donor–beneficiary relationship, important as funding may be, towards working links with the Steelworkers' Union as a social actor in Canada.

The Humanity Fund began offering a week-long 'development educa-tion' course in 1990. It is now offered two to three times annually at different points throughout the country as part of the broader union education programme. The week-long course is called 'Thinking North South'. It uses popular education methodology to familiarize members with the concepts of globalization, from the point of view of multiple stakeholders. Through role-play, exercises and videos, workers are en-couraged to look at their own insertion into the global economy. These activities get people thinking about the impact of globalization on North-ern workers and on Southern workers, trying to probe attitudes, attempt-ing to move beyond postures of protectionism or racism to help Northern workers feel the situation of working people in the South. The course usually begins with an exercise that has workers telling stories of their own workplaces, an activity which maps the flows of capital, resources, labour and policies. Often there are subsequent steps, going back into the mapping exercise to highlight the impact of globalization on women, the forces carrying out the neo-liberal agenda like the International Monetary Fund, or points of fight-back strategies.

The course always includes at least one resource person from the South. There are also members whose country of origin is somewhere other than Canada. The presence of real voices from Africa, Asia and Latin America, and of growing numbers of activists who can speak about real experiences during their own travel to the South, would be hard to overestimate. The course specifically challenges the comfortable relationships organized through the development discourse and reinforced by media images of North–South power relationships. A video called *Shaping the Image* which analyses how Ethiopia became a 'media event' helps members to begin to see as problematic the power dynamic of donor–beneficiary relationships which put Canadians as the 'developed' offering their resources to the 'undeveloped'. Role plays explore the differences between relationships of dependency and relationships of solidarity based on mutual interests and strategic alliances. More than 200 steelworker activists throughout the country have now taken the one-week workshop. A 'training trainers' seminar has been held to develop a shorter introductory course which member activists will facilitate in area councils and larger local unions.

Another vital component of the education programme is the linkage element. Each project supported by the Humanity Fund includes a budget line for exchanges between activists from local unions contributing to the fund and activists from organizations supported by the fund. We have resisted the tendency to make these into donor inspections, with our members seeing themselves or being seen as 'mini-project officers'. The objectives of the visits are primarily education and solidarity. The hosting organization is requested to prepare an educational process for the Canadian steelworkers. Members are asked to speak from their own strength and experience, as social activists in Canada, carrying out their activism through their unions. Often during the visit, it becomes evident that the stereotyping of the South is no worse than the stereotyping of the North. Latin American and African activists are surprised that behind the glitter of consumer society there are strong labour and social movements along with serious problems of unemployment, poverty and racism.

The linkage visits are a tremendously powerful tool for education. To date, about ninety steelworker activists have made visits and we have hosted about fifty people from the South. The visits are focused, linking labour housing activists in Canada with counterparts in labour housing in South Africa, or steelworker women involved in women's promotion and training activities in Canada with women's training programmes in Bolivia. With the growing emphasis on labour development, the specificity of the connections becomes even stronger, bringing together people who can exchange experiences on specific areas of union activity. This includes linking together workers employed by the same company in different parts of the world. Clearly these visits, like the courses, straddle 'development', 'globalization' and 'solidarity' discourses.

The emphasis of the exchange is on depth of experience, opting for more sustained contacts with a few points in the union. The hope is to create enough regularity to the North–South exchanges that the 'exotic' character wears off, allowing more serious strategic thinking to emerge.

A new emphasis on labour connections

Four of the labour funds and the Canadian Labour Congress (CLC) entered into a series of negotiations with CIDA during 1994 about funding labour's international development activities. As 'new kids on the block' with substantial capacity for raising revenue, the labour funds argued for the same right to matching funds that long-established non-governmental organizations enjoyed – and this in an era of shrinking CIDA budgets.

Another major concern of the labour funds was the increasing portion of CIDA funding going to private-sector initiatives, both through bilateral programmes and programmes like CIDA Inc. Given the historic understanding that the private sector is composed of both a labour and a management side, the labour funds put forward strong arguments for balancing CIDA's much increased support for the corporate side with significantly larger CIDA funding specifically for trade-union development in the South. The upshot of all of these discussions was the formation of a Labour International Development Committee (LIDC) made up of the four funds and the CLC, and negotiation of a $5.2 million programme with CIDA over three years. This will channel resources to Southern trade unions to strengthen their capacity to represent their members effectively and contribute to stronger civil societies.

Capacity-building takes various forms. It means support for trade-union courses on such issues as health and safety, labour rights, workplace reorganization and economic integration as well as efforts to strengthen the regional offices of the unions. For example, in Mozambique, where the trade-union movement has only recently become responsible for dues collection, regular collective bargaining and day-to-day servicing of its members, capacity-building means support for seminars with provincial officers on financial management systems. With the Authentic Labour Front in Mexico, it takes the form of support for new organizing initiatives and labour rights questions in *maquiladora* zones. Clearly the increase in direct co-operation projects with trade unions opens up many new perspectives and possibilities

Trade union connections with South Africa and Chile

The Steelworkers' Humanity Fund marked its tenth anniversary in 1995 with a level of strength and resilience in its connections with trade unions in the South far beyond its own projections. The most active links are with unions in Mexico, Chile and South Africa, where there are now multiple layers of connections weaving in and out of a variety of areas in the unions' institutional lives. This is a complex and fluid mixture of links, some fuelled by funding and others driven by similarities of outlook as we confront management – at times even the same management – and the global economy.

The increased flow of people and information between the United Steelworkers' Association (USWA) and the National Union of Mineworkers (NUM) in South Africa characterizes the new directions. Eight steelworkers have spent time with NUM, focusing on areas of common concern including housing, election monitoring, health and safety, and, most recently, member education on race and gender questions. Seven NUM members have spent time in Canada during this same period focusing on health and safety, on approaches to worker education, on housing and on organizational change. The head of the NUM collective bargaining department spent a three-month sabbatical with USWA looking at approaches to workplace reorganization and empowerment in Canada.

The most recent visit by two NUM education activists captures the interweaving of connections between the two unions. In South Africa as in Canada, the trade unions are a major force in both organization and provision of education and training for workers. The NUM has begun to bargain paid education leave into its collective agreements, which allow NUM members to book off for education. The NUM is also playing a major role in adult basic education and training and is actively working with management to promote literacy training in the workplace.

These two course developers spent three weeks in Canada soon after they had piloted their new course. While in Canada they had a chance to look at the United Steelworkers' approach to education through national, district and local levels. They were also participant-observers in the Canadian equivalents to the courses they are developing, giving them a close look at another union's approach.

Although the central focus of their visit was labour education and curriculum development, there were many strands woven into the training exchange related to broader areas, including strategies around globalization. Lunch on day one included provocative questions about the steelworkers' forthcoming unification with major unions in the US and what effect this would have on our international work. There was intense interest in how the steelworkers saw the relationship between unions and governments, from state provision of education and training to the vexing question of party affiliations by trade unions.

Two Chilean miners had arrived a week earlier to shadow local union officials in mines owned by the same Canadian mining multinationals they worked for in Chile. The South African miners immediately wanted to meet them and spoke of South African mining companies like Anglo-American that have recently made investments in Chile. They produced a document on the South Africa–Chile mining connections and speculated on the relative strengths of the labour movements in the three countries as a factor in attracting investment.

This exchange came hard on the heels of another exchange in the opposite direction. Two steelworker activists, trained as instructors in anti-racist training for the workplace, spent three weeks in South Africa where the Centre for Adult and Continuing Education at the University of the Western Cape is developing new training materials on race and gender for adult educators and trainers.

The Chile connection

Another set of connections which captures new ways of working globally and positions our operation very differently within the global economy is with workers in Chile. More than $4 billion of Canadian mining capital went to Chile between 1987 and 1993, and the pace is not abating. The attractions are evident: rich ore bodies in a country with the most liberal foreign investment policy in the world. Chile also has an abundant supply of highly skilled, cheap labour and a union movement still hamstrung by a labour code only slightly modified from the code imposed by Pinochet after the coup. Add to this safety and environmental regulation with weak enforcement capacity, little protection of native people's land rights and low corporate taxes – in short, it is a great place to do business.

What drew Chile to steelworker attention dramatically again in the 1990s was not so much Chile's needs but our own. Canadian steelworkers in the mining sector began to see a dramatic departure of mining capital and mining jobs to Chile. Entire explorations companies, like that of Falconbridge, closed up shop in Canada and moved their operations to Chile. Management studied Spanish during the lunch hour. A concerted campaign was mounted by the mining lobbies to say that Canada, and particularly British Columbia, had created a climate inhospitable to mining investment.

The need to understand what was happening in Chile was evident, and four years ago the steelworkers began to take advantage of visits to other community-based organizations in the Andean region to touch base with trade-union organizations in Chile. The logic has been to seek out unions representing workers who work for some of the same companies that we do. One of the links is with the Chilean Confederation of Mining, which represents miners in private-sector mines. The other is with Constramet, one of the metalworkers' unions. The projects include support for training activities and workshops that can strengthen the organizational capacity of the two unions.

Over a three-year period, five USWA miners and two staff representatives have visited Chile and Peru. Since health and the environment have become key factors in determining global competitiveness, the national health, safety and environment committee has begun to take on these issues as a component of its work. This committee organized an intensive month-long labour exchange which brought miners working for Cominco and Placer Dome in Chile to mines in Canada operated by the same companies.

These intensive visits to local mining communities dramatically raised awareness of the Chile connection. The Chilean miners were billeted in the homes of local members. They – and their full-time translators – shadowed local union officials through bargaining, health and safety committees, lunch-room talks, membership meetings and finally a national policy conference. The last week included discussions among labour and environmentalists from the two countries, with an active presence of South African trade unionists to build a triangular connection.

There were endless discussions about points of similarity and difference. The Chileans were struck by the civility, regularity and depth of interaction with management and the comprehensiveness of the collective bargaining agreement. There is a dramatic difference between the detailed collective bargaining agreements Canadian workers wrest from these companies, backed as they are by strong legal and research support, and the meagre agreements and protection Chilean miners enjoy.

Collective bargaining agreements have been translated and exchanged, along with all kinds of other documentation and videos. The local union in Canada has financed a fax and a modem for its Chilean counterparts while Chilean environmental activists, long-time information highway travellers, have agreed to train the Chilean unions to use them.

Monthly conference calls with the continued support of the translator have allowed the ties to continue and deepen. One such call was made at a moment of crisis in Chile. Two of the executive members were under threat, one with firing and the other with a demotion. A workplace fatality had occurred, despite union warnings to management about malfunctioning equipment, and the union had gone public.

The local union president from Canada was perturbed at what he heard – and sat down to write a letter to the company as soon as he got off the phone. He likened the stance of management in Quebrada Blanca to management postures in Canada thirty years ago and suggested that policies of union-busting and company inaccessibility to workers would be no more effective in bringing about labour peace and productivity in Chile than it was in Canada. The Cominco executive who received the letter was on the line back to Canada within two hours of receiving the fax.

Now, only a few months later, both union leaders have been fully reinstated and the union finds itself in a phase of labour peace and civility, with frequent communication with management and many problems being addressed. The Chilean unionists themselves are convinced that the letter from Canada played a key role. Meanwhile two unionists from Canada are poised for a return exchange. Certainly both unions feel themselves to be stronger in working with Cominco in their respective countries by monitoring the company's global operations.

Globalizing from below: building an alternative

We began by looking at how Canadian workers' global relationships were organized through three different discourses, each asserting itself strongly in particular moments and contexts to organize international relations. The discourses are the discourses of solidarity, development and globalization. Arguably the really interesting space being created by the labour funds is in the interface between the three all too often unconnected discourses. Our members live these interconnections in their daily lives, caught between powerful macro forces of multinational companies and international institutions like the General Agreement on Tariffs and Trade and the North American Free Trade Agreement, and the micro realities of their fights for jobs and communities and social wages and a future for their children.

The challenge for us as unions is to use the institutional space these new funds create to promote new kinds of labour connections, a renewed sense of civil society and a new practice of global solidarity. Basically this means challenging the kind of corporate globalization presently on offer by getting better at globalizing from below. Jeremy Brecher and Tim Costello[4] liken the power of the transnationals and the neoliberal agenda to the marauding Gulliver as seen by the tiny Lilliputians. In the same way that the Lilliputians tackled Gulliver by immobilizing him in his sleep with hundreds of tiny threads, they argue that trade unions and other popular organizations and movements need to connect their actions and energies.

In this new era, then, workers will either be haplessly played off against each other as rights and standards fall to the lowest common denominator, or find ways to work in concert to level rights and standards upwards. This means strengthened institutional capacity, both in the North and the South, to globalize from below, working together to invent alternatives that create jobs and communities, affirm equity and diversity, and promote sustainable development.

Notes

1. Cooney 1995: 7.
2. Leiva 1992: 2.
3. Barnet and Cavanagh 1995: 14.
4. Brecher and Costello 1994.

References

Barnet, Richard J. and Cavanagh, J. (1995) *Global Dreams: Imperial Corporations and the New World Order*, Touchstone, New York.

Brecher, Jeremy and Costello, Tim (1994) *Global Village or Global Pillage*, South End Press, Boston.

Cooney, James (1995) 'Managing Political Risk in the Americas: The Role of the Exploration Geologist', paper presented at Conference on Geology and Ore Deposits of the American Cordillera, Reno, Nevada, 13 April.

Leiva, Fernando (1992) 'The Other Face of the Chilean Model', *Porta Voz*, No. 32, September, ILSA (Latin American Institute of Alternative Legal Services).

7

Feminist Popular Education in the Light of Globalization

Linzi Manicom and Shirley Walters

In the mid-1980s, after years of hovering on the sidelines of the adult education field and on the margins of the women-and-development movement, feminist popular education started receiving some gratifying endorsement. Reviews of the Decade for Women were showing that the conditions of women's lives around the world, far from improving, were deteriorating absolutely and in relation to men's. It was not enough for women to be merely visible in the development process; they needed to be 'voiced', too. Feminist Popular Education was promoted in this regard, most notably by Gita Sen and Caren Grown[1] in their now classic articulation of the popular development approach of the Development Alternatives with Women for a New Era (DAWN) collective.

If development was to address the basic needs of the poor majority of the world in ways that were sustainable, DAWN argued, the current top-down, North-centric, male-biased perspective had to be replaced with that of poor, Third World women. Their critical role in the provision of households' livelihoods, and as reproducers of life more broadly, dictated that they be fully and actively involved as planners and decision-makers, not as mere executors of the development agendas of others. Feminist Popular Education, as a participatory, action-oriented process of organization-building, consciousness- and confidence-raising, was essential to the methodology of what became known as 'the empowerment approach' to women-and-development.

The valorization of women's knowledge, starting from and building upon what women already know in their everyday lives, is a central tenet of Feminist Popular Education. Feminist Popular Education was thus equally pertinent to the focus on 'sustainable development' that subsequently assumed importance in development circles, particularly in the period around the 1992 United Nations Environment Conference in Rio de Janeiro. A central plank of the environmentalist platform is the argument that local indigenous knowledge of the environment, particularly that of women farmers and food-providers, is the soundest basis upon which to plan development projects that conserve, rather than destroy, natural and precious resources, amongst them human lives.

What of the compatibility and relevance of Feminist Popular Education to the current debates within development discourse? Talk today is of 'good governance and democracy', of 'building capacity within non-governmental organizations' (NGOs) and 'strengthening civil society'. But this discourse takes place against the background of an increasingly taken-for-granted neo-liberal promotion of marketization and export-orientation, and diminishing authority over the economic policy of nation-states. Women, in these debates, tend to be confined to the marginal place of 'women's organizations within civil society'; the more profound implications of gender for the reconfiguration of relations between state and civil society and the democratization of relations within state and civil society slip too quickly out of the frame. Yet it is precisely these shifting sets of relations that are a primary and critical area of concern for Feminist Popular Education.

There are three other areas in which the political landscape for Feminist Popular Education is currently being redrawn:

- the gendered process of global economic restructuring and the feminization of poverty;
- the rising influence of nationalist, fundamentalist and ethnic movements with distinctively conservative gender ideologies; and
- the growth and institutionalization of global feminism.

Paralleling these phenomena have been significant developments within feminist intellectual work which provide for the more sophisticated and culturally sensitive theorization of feminist practice and pedagogy. Though some of these conceptual shifts will be referred to in passing, space does not allow for elaboration.

The objective of this chapter is to explore, in very broad brushstrokes, the implications of these four global trends for the politics, priorities and the methodology of Feminist Popular Education. By Feminist Popular Education we are referring to the characteristic form of educational work with and for grassroots women which has been developing in local contexts around the world over the past decades. The term 'popular education' is associated with the concept of 'conscientization' and the work of renowned Brazilian educationalist Paulo Freire. Feminist popular education is defined by its broad objective of empowering women to gain more control over their lives and transform oppressive relations, particularly, though not exclusively, those organized by gender. The term Feminist Popular Education does not resonate in all regions. What is remarkable, however, is the degree of commonality in the forms, principles and practices of educational work with women in very divergent contexts. Yet, Feminist Popular Education is not a prescribed, universally applicable toolbox of methods. It is an essentially localized practice. Its objectives, form and process are shaped by and respond to the immediate exigencies of women's (and men's) lives; the cultural, economic and political context. Therein lies the basis of Feminist Popular Education's strength, particularly for those sectors of the community, such as poor women, which have been excluded from decision-making. But therein also lie the limitations of Feminist Popular Education; for unless the localized process is informed by an appreciation and analysis of the broader developments that are refracted in local milieux, constraining and shaping local possibilities, its potential to effect and consolidate substantive changes in women's lives is diminished.

This complex, layered relationship of local and global is mirrored in another traversing set of dimensions within Feminist Popular Education, the pedagogical and political. Like local and global, the pedagogical and political are not dichotomous or mutually exclusive terms but are rather mutually defining formations with shifting, merging boundaries. Pedagogical choices reflect political context and implement political objectives.

In an earlier article in which we reviewed critical accounts of Feminist Popular Education experiences, we abstracted their common themes. A central motif was that of 'starting from the place of women', whether this be the quotidian concerns of their lives, their emotions, their sexuality, or their bodies. All of these are points of experience, reflection and analysis that can begin to yield insights about the potential and strategies for change.[2]

Another strong metaphor of Feminist Popular Education is that of 'breaking silence' and 'giving voice', connoting the process of women gaining the confidence to articulate publicly previously private concerns. We also identified the dilemmas that confront feminist popular educators: how to balance the validation of women's experience and knowledge with the introduction of expertise and specialized skills; whether to have an open-ended, exploratory process or one more orchestrated, object-oriented and controlled; how to work constructively with the power differentials between educator and learners, between participants of different genders, racial and ethnic groups, regions and access to resources; and how to introduce feminist analysis in ways that do not impose, as authoritative or universal, Western feminist discourses which derive from different political imperatives and cultures. These dilemmas and debates about pedagogic choices and learning strategies are being reframed, given new emphases and urgency by the broader, contemporary political dimensions of Feminist Popular Education that we focus on in this article.

One of the factors prompting us to review the global context of

Feminist Popular Education is what we experience as the misappropriation and devaluation of the currency of international development discourse. Terms like 'empowerment', 'participatory development' and 'indigenous knowledge' that previously were associated with grassroots, people-centred development approaches now trip lightly out of the mouths of the World Bank/IMF set, who argue their validity in terms of the greater 'efficiency' such approaches can deliver. Insistence on the 'participation of women' in the development of projects is now a standard funding criterion. While seemingly a commendable objective, 'participation' is rarely on women's own terms, nor always for the benefit of the women themselves, for whom it can mean yet another task added to their overloaded days.[3] We also find 'popular education', 'gender- and diversity-training' practised in corporate seminars as a managerial strategy, a deployment of the methodology very far removed from its original revolutionary intention. Even the presently favoured phrases of aid politics – 'strong civil society' and 'capacity building' – are deployed equally by the international financial institutions, the UN family of organizations and the international and national NGOs.

How do we distinguish between the empowerment of women as authored by the World Bank and the empowerment of poor women through a popular education process? It is clearly time for some rethinking, realignment and perhaps reaffirmation of the radical tradition of Feminist Popular Education that explicitly locates itself within broader struggles for social transformation.

Global reconfigurations

There is wide acknowledgement that the economic restructuring which has been taking place – characterized by deregulation, trade promotion and state cut-backs, and imposed on many Third World indebted countries through IMF-designed structural adjustment programs – has had the most devastating effects on poor women. It has been the back-breaking expansion of women's daily labour and the ingenuity and doggedness of women's survival skills that have held households together – barely. The costs of adjustment on health, nutrition, education, personal relationships and the general quality of life of women and children around the world are now well and shockingly documented. But it also needs to be emphasized that the forms of labour which have essentially underwritten the neo-liberal version of economic globalization are feminized ones: the global assembly line is 'manned' by women workers in free trade zones; subcontracted industrial homeworking is performed at kitchen tables by women who 'have time on their hands'; home-based teleworking is carried out by women who can't afford day-care costs and are grateful to have paid work.

As formal jobs fade permanently from the employment scene, the range and volume of income-generating and micro-enterprise activities swelling the informal sector reflect both the desperation and the entrepreneurial skills of women. The growth of the international sex trade must be seen in this context too. In fact, the overall 'flexibilization' and casualization of labour through which global capitalism has managed to sustain its profitability depends upon the survival needs, the vulnerability and lack of choice, as well as the desire for economic autonomy and independence of poor women around the world. It depends too on the mobilization of gender ideology; defining the new forms of labour as 'women's work' immediately lowers the wage bill and confirms the precariousness of the work.

These two broad consequences of global economic restructuring – the feminization of poverty and the feminization of labour – produce a compelling agenda for Feminist Popular Education. The critical economic situation of growing numbers of households around the world – particularly female-headed ones – prioritizes the devising of survival strategies. Emphasis is placed on the development of practical, marketable and entrepreneurial skills. Building confidence and esteem to enable women to enter new domains of social life is especially important where gender culture has previously secluded women. The raising of feminist consciousness under these conditions is more pertinent when linked to the recognition of ways in which gender relations constrain women's capacity to secure a livelihood, rather than to abstract notions of the moral injustice of women's oppression.

Feminist Popular Education must recognize and work with the incredible physical and emotional stress of poor women's lives, the often increased domestic violence and volatile personal relationships, and of course the paucity of women's time to engage in any activity that does not produce positive and concrete results. The slow, creative, consolidating process that is the ideal in the Feminist Popular Education process has become a luxury in these times, one that must be revamped and streamlined in accordance with the stark realities.

A central challenge for educators is the development, with women learners, of a gendered analysis of global restructuring, but one that is not overwhelming and defeating in its bleakness. As Elson[4] maintains, moments of crisis are at the same time moments of opportunity. Educators could emphasize the contradictory character of the new feminized forms of labour to build on the positive possibilities while acknowledging the extent to which women's labour and survival capacities are being exploited by global capitalism. Nadeau[5] discusses how she grappled with this particular problem by working on ways of renewing the energy and resolve of women confronting economic hardship as they simultaneously increased their understanding of its global dimensions.

Along with activists and organizers, popular educators face the question of finding organizational forms that are more effective and appropriate to the times. Traditional factory-based labour organization cannot reach many of the women induced, by the new forms of production, into the labour force. In free trade zones, there are strict prohibitions against unionization and homeworkers are too separated and vulnerable. Activists are experimenting with new ways of organizing women workers, including working with women in their places of residence and providing social and support services rather than focusing on work issues.[6] A critical aspect here is the organization of women into transnational networks, to create the possibility for women to gain a global perspective on their local experiences of economic restructuring.[7] In the past decade, enormous experience and proficiency has been gained by grassroots women and popular educators in building micro enterprises, credit schemes, and producer co-operatives. They have built collective consumer and support groups, such as soup-kitchens and burial organizations in areas with high AIDS fatalities.[8] These schemes often involve the revival and adaptation of local cultural traditions, a prime example being the communal savings schemes that are prevalent amongst women in numerous places. Such forms address women's survival needs while at the same time building solidarity and support.

Another element of the global economic context affecting Feminist Popular Education is the dramatic reduction in funding to the NGOs that have been involved in organizing women over the past two decades. This places a responsibility on feminist popular educators to provide training for local women in management, accounting and productivity – aspects of organization-building that were often left unattended in the days of subsidized NGO personnel and operating costs in women's projects.

The second major global trend is the rise of identity-based political movements, particularly those of nationalism, fundamentalism, neo-traditionalism and ethnicity. It is, in many ways, inappropriate to lump together what are in fact distinct political movements. However, our interest here lies in what these tendencies have in common, namely, their development in conditions of economic upheaval and insecurity,[9] their reclamation and reassertion of strong cultural identity and, most significantly for Feminist Popular Education, their explicit and central gender ideologies which position women primarily as 'mothers' and 'keepers of the tradition'. Again, there are both positive and negative implications and possibilities for women and for Feminist Popular Education.

Aggressive ethnic and fundamentalist movements have been responsible for devastating armed conflict, genocidal offensives and massive refugee plights in recent years, situations which have affected women in specific ways. In many of these identity-based movements, the constructs of 'woman' are extremely conservative, extolling women's virtues and invaluable cultural role but also seeing them as vulnerable to corruption, justifying the reimposition of extreme forms of seclusion and social constraint and feeding an anti-feminist sentiment.

But there is another side to identity and culturalist politics more broadly conceived, one that has had a salutary influence on Feminist Popular Education in two ways. First, it has provided a place on the international and national feminist agendas for the perspectives of previously excluded, minority and marginalized women – black, indigenous, ethnic minority, Moslem, lesbian, immigrant – who have increasingly challenged the hegemony of narrow, North Atlantic, 'equality feminism' and the assumption that gender is the only or the most salient category of women's oppression. In Feminist Popular Education, this has translated into debates on 'working with difference', to refinements of educational work on anti-racism and cultural diversity.

Secondly, of particular practical significance to feminist popular educators, identity politics has stressed the importance of paying attention to and working with cultural constructions of gender which, in many communities, centre on familial identities and responsibilities. The challenge for feminist popular educators is to work from and with the gendered constructs that are central to women's identities, respecting difference and valuing the political initiatives and leverage that derive from those identities as, say, 'mothers' or 'Moslem women'. At the same time, as feminists, we cannot condone or concede to reactionary politics and cultural arrangements which, under the guise of 'tradition', limit the choices and capacities of women. Relatedly, assertions of identity often work to occlude class and power differences within culturally defined communities. Feminist Popular Education has clearly to confront relations of power and exploitation – or more positively, of resource redistribution – in its grappling with the complexity of issues of political identity. A direction for Feminist Popular Education emerging from the lessons of failed development projects, from deeper understanding of collective household strategies for survival and of the more complementary rather than competitive constructs of gender found in Third World communities,[10] is that of working with women and men together as a sounder basis for the transformation of gender relations. The assumption that women-only educational processes are necessarily the most advantageous for women has to be reassessed. Educators have to develop skills in facilitating mixed-gender groups[11] and learn to consider when an integrated process might be more effective.

The globalization of activist feminism is the third contemporary social force with consequences for Feminist Popular Education. The extensive international women's conferencing, networking and collaboration of the past decades have enormously strengthened and legitimated women's politics around the world. Of course there are vast numbers of women who remain isolated and marginal to this development, but certainly, for Feminist Popular Education, the transnational exchange of experiences has been an invaluable and enriching support. The down-side of this globalization is the uniformity it tends to impose on the framing of issues and the discourses of national feminism – the 'Beijingization' of feminism, it could be called. What gets downplayed in this process is the differential power of regions, nations and classes to shape the priorities of the international women's agenda. Local women's issues, the fabric of Feminist Popular Education, are so decontextualized and diluted in the process of translation into common, global issues, that they no longer depict grassroots women's concerns. The discourses of international feminist politics with relevance and relation to Feminist Popular Education have shifted over the past decade. Most significant has been the disappearance of the political reference point that internationalist socialism provided for an earlier generation of feminist popular educators who worked hard to insist on the immediate, non-deferrable relevance of women's and gender issues to the revolutionary goal.

The 1980s saw international feminism couched mainly in terms of 'woman and development', and there, as we discussed earlier, Feminist Popular Education was associated with the empowerment approach of Third World poor women. Since then, dating particularly from the testimony of women at the 1993 Vienna Tribunal, the representation of 'women's issues' as women's rights within a human-rights and liberal-democratic framework has been ascendant. Where Feminist Popular Education stands in relation to rights discourse within global feminism is an issue for more extensive debate.

The politics of rights has much to offer women generally in fighting legal and constitutional discrimination, and in challenging gender-based persecution. Popular feminists have pushed for rights to be inclusive and substantive, to address basic needs like shelter, safety from violence and reproductive choice, and it is obviously this more encompassing strategic approach to rights that is most congruent with the political orientation of Feminist Popular Education. But where 'rights' remain narrowly conceived, where the procedures of litigation needed to mobilize their effects are formal, costly, slow and dependent on a high degree of literacy and juridical knowledge, the quest for women's rights can come to exclude poor, marginal women and constitute a distraction from the broader popular objective of redistributing the world's abundant resources to those desperately in need. The pedagogical question for Feminist Popular Education is whether and when and with which issues it is useful to reframe the preoccupations of local women in the terminology of 'rights', to claim its moral and international clout.

Finally, we return to the theme of the reconfigurations of state and civil society. Neo-liberal policies, as mentioned above, have had the effect of cutting off state services for women and resources for women's NGOs. In many national contexts the loss of funding has weakened women's organizations. On the other hand, it has pushed NGOs into becoming more efficient and viable on the market, in some situations undertaking the local distribution of social services on behalf of the state, at best delivering them to poor women in less bureaucratic, patronizing ways.

A related tendency, one that derives from the global force of feminism and the pressure of the UN on national governments, is the institutionalization of women's issues within the state itself. The establishment of women's machinery and the formal representation of women on policy-making bodies, though often a mechanical form of 'state feminism', potentially creates a space for organized women's groups and coalitions to intervene in national politics.

If grassroots women's voices are to have any impact, Feminist Popular Education is faced with the challenge of developing the political skills and capacities amongst local women's groups to engage effectively with state bureaucracies,[12] of working to transform state processes so that they are more friendly to the concerns and style of women's politics, and of building women's organization nationally and transnationally.

Conclusion

This sweeping, rather than exhaustive, review of the ways in which globalization is challenging and provoking Feminist Popular Education suggests, first, that Feminist Popular Education has a critical role to play in empowering grassroots women in this global moment of extreme constraint as well as flickering opportunity. It also suggests, however, that this role will best be served not by blindly and blithely concurring with the apparently progressive and pragmatic discourse of neo-liberalism and democracy, but rather by delineating and defining a specifically feminist and popular take on these global trends. A recuperation of the radical tradition of both popular education and feminist politics is, we would argue, in order. This involves a deep immersion, through Feminist Popular Education practice, in the local contexts of women's lives and the local discourses of gender – but with a constant appreciation of how the local is configured, now more than ever, by global trends. It also involves a constant assessment of the appropriateness and effectiveness of pedagogical practices and learning strategies, honing them to reflect the reorientations and refinements of the politics of feminism and social transformation.

Notes

1. Sen and Grown 1987.

2. Walters and Manicom 1996.
3. Mayoux 1995.
4. Elson 1992.
5. Nadeau 1996.
6. Heng 1996; Dagg 1996.
7. Mitter and Rowbotham 1994.
8. Daines and Seddon 1993.
9. Moghadam 1994.
10. Puar 1996.
11. Friedman and Cousins 1996.
12. Patel 1996.

References

Dagg, A. (1996) 'Organising Homeworkers into Unions: The Homeworkers' Association of Toronto, Canada', in Boris, E. and Prugl, E. (eds), *Homeworkers in Global Perspective: Invisible No More*, Routledge, New York and London.

Daines, V. and Seddon, D. (1993) 'Confronting Austerity: Women's Responses to Economic Reform', in Turshen, M. and Holcombe, B. (eds), *Women's Lives and Public Policy: The International Experience*, Praeger, Westport, CT.

Elson, D. (1992) 'From Survival Strategies to Transformation Strategies: Women's Needs and Structural Adjustment', in Beneria, L. and Feldman, S. (eds), *Unequal Burden: Economic Crises, Persistent Poverty and Women's Work*, Westview Press, Boulder, CO.

Friedman, M. and Cousins, C.C. (1996) 'Holding the Space: Gender, Race and Conflict in Training', in Walters, S. and Manicom, L. (eds), *Gender in Popular Education: Methods for Empowerment*, Zed Books, London and CACE Publications, Bellville.

Heng, C. L. (1996) 'Talking Pain: Educational Work with Factory Women in Malaysia', in Walters, S. and Manicom, L. (1996) *Gender in Popular Education: Methods for Empowerment*, Zed Books, London and CACE Publications, Bellville.

Mayoux, L. (1995) 'Beyond Naivety: Women, Gender Inequality and Participatory Development', *Development and Change*, Vol. 26, pp. 235–58.

Mitter, S. and Rowbotham, S. (1994) 'On Organizing Women in Casualized Work', in *Dignity and Daily Bread: New Forms of Organizing Among Poor Women in the Third World and First*, Routledge, London and New York.

Moghadam, V. (1994) *Identity Politics and Women: Cutural Reassertions and Feminisms in International Perspective*, Westview Press, Boulder, CO.

Nadeau, D. (1996) 'Embodying Feminist Popular Education Under Global Restructuring', in Walters, S. and Manicom, L. (eds), *Gender in Popular Education: Methods for Empowerment*, Zed Books, London and CACE Publications, Bellville.

Patel, S. (1996) 'From a Seed to a Tree: Building Community Organisations in India's Cities', in Walters, S. and Manicom, L. (eds), *Gender in Popular Education: Methods for Empowerment*, Zed Books, London and CACE Publications, Bellville.

Puar, J.K. (1996) 'Nicaraguan Women, Resistance, and the Politics of Aid', in Afshar, H. (ed.), *Women and Politics in the Third World*, Routledge, London.

Sen, G. and Grown, C. (1987) *Development, Crises and Alternative Visions: Third World Women's Perspectives*, Monthly Review Press, New York.

Walters, S. and Manicom, L. (eds) (1996) *Gender in Popular Education: Methods for Empowerment*, Zed Books, London and CACE Publications, Bellville.

8

Women on the Global Assembly Line

Chan Lean Heng

Towards the end of the 1960s many of the developing Asian countries shifted their strategy of economic development to export-oriented industrialization (EOI) to provide a new engine of growth to their economies. This coincided with the industrial redeployment of labour-intensive manufacturing industries from the high-wage advanced capitalist countries to the relatively low-wage production sites in the South. These shifts brought an unprecedented rural–urban migration and employment of female labour. The phenomenal expansion of these off-shore activities and the integration of women into the global production systems were the most dramatic developments in these countries in the 1970s.

A corollary to these developments is the suffering of women recruited as labour for these factories. To woo foreign investment, host governments set up free trade zones (FTZs) and offer foreign-owned transnational corporations (TNCs) the advantage of fiscal incentives, tariff exemptions, market opportunities, subsidized land and infrastructure, less restrictive regulations and cheap, 'disciplined' labour. In many countries, even labour enactments have been amended to meet the demands of these off-shore industries.

It is well known that the growth of TNCs and FTZs is based on the exploitation of cheap and docile female labour.[1] This is blatantly illustrated through the investment promotion campaigns of host governments. In a brochure the Malaysian government says: 'The manual dexterity of the Oriental female is famous the world over. Her hands are small and she works with extreme care. Who, therefore, could be better qualified by nature and inheritance to contribute to the efficiency of a production line than the Oriental girl?'

This chapter describes the experiences of women on the global assembly lines. In particular, it tells of the lived experiences of emotional subordination of Malaysian women workers. It argues for the importance of addressing these experiences and reconstructing subjectivities in and as educational work with women workers.

Malaysian women factory workers

Malaysian women workers, like other global assembly-line operators, work in tedious, repetitive, menial tasks as non-unionized, unskilled shift-workers. They are subjected daily to rigid discipline, pressure, verbal abuse and intimidation from supervisors and male co-workers. Their work environments are both hazardous and stressful. In fact, gender relations at work are a common source of subordination and work-related stress for the women. Corporate welfare activities, apart from obstructing and negating the development of gender- and worker-consciousness, reinforce feminine stereotypes and prejudices.

The way in which women have been integrated into the global industrial workforce makes them most vulnerable to technological, economic and industrial change. They are the first to lose their jobs in times of recession. For example, during the 1985 recession in Penang, Malaysia, when Mostek retrenched 1,500 workers, the government told the workers not to be choosy about jobs because 'there were people who could not even find a job'. They were further told to '*balik kampung* [return to the village] ... *tanam jagung* [plant corn] ...' even though government officials knew that the women did not have the necessary skills as they had been working in the factories for many years. At the time, the acting Chief Minister made a public call for workers to be self-reliant. He said, 'Those who can write can earn money as free-lance journalists, and those with electrical skills should open up small electrical businesses!'[2]

Malaysian women factory workers are also at the bottom of the social hierarchy. In general, it is understood that factory girls are the ones who obtained poor grades in their public examinations, often stigmatized as 'stupid girls who failed the exams'.[3] Hence the stereotype of academic failure is associated with factory work. Many factory women are still ashamed to acknowledge openly that they are production operators. A monthly-paid office job from eight to five o'clock is still regarded as of higher status, even though the take-home pay may be much less. Most factory workers are ashamed of their job and aspire to office jobs.

They are also regarded as immoral and sexually promiscuous. They are silent victims of abuse, derogation and sexual harassment. They are made to feel responsible for and shamed by the harassment inflicted on them. Such incidents are endured in silence and accompanied by feelings of inferiority because of the shame and blame they bring. Since the establishment of the FTZs they have been ridiculed with labels such as *Minah Karan* (meaning 'hot stuff') or *jual murah* (cheap stuff). Most of the women workers are migrants from rural areas, first-generation industrial workers to the city. Many of the host community residents are very suspicious and hostile towards them.

For many of the women workers, the endurance of this humiliation is one of the most degrading experiences of factory life, a stigma which many of them recount bitterly. The social injury, brought about by society's definition of them, has been and still remains a factor in their feelings of inferiority and shame. Like other Malaysian and Asian women in general, they are socialized into accepting patriarchal values and practices. They are expected to be respectful and obedient to male authority and domination. Cultural and religious norms demand their unquestioned subservience.

After well over twenty years of industrial development, numerous changes have taken place, even improvements in the material conditions and economic standing of the women. However, certain subjective experiences remain much the same, in particular the prevailing experiences of subordination and denigration by men.

Talking pain

In order to convey the women's emotional sufferings, I present direct words from women shared during educational workshops which I have held with them:

> People look down on us. They see us with only one eye. Society looks disparagingly at us. They say factory girls are cheap. They fall for any man in the street.... All this talk makes us feel inferior. Even when they are not saying anything I can feel their belittlement from the way they gawk at us.

> Young men whistle as we alight from the factory bus: 'Look, they go day and night like prostitutes.' How to retaliate? You know what kind of characters they are! All creeps! If I retaliate back they may bring their gang to tackle us – we have to use this road everyday. We just pretend not to hear.

> Even my own family feel embarrassed with my factory job. I avoid my neighbour so as not to be asked insinuating questions. One day she asked: 'You came back almost at midnight yesterday and left again so early this morning. What do you actually do?' All I could say was work ... I felt ashamed, defensive, actually disgusted ... I am not what she may be thinking.

> We are petrified all the time. You can literally see some jerking when shouted at, stammering and shivering. You can imagine the kind of tension we work in. I do not know any more how to think, only anticipating when I will be shouted at.

> It is very difficult to tell anyone about hurts from your own family. Outsiders cannot know how it hurts. Five years ago, in my first annual leave, I had a quarrel with my brother. He hit my niece over the head for playing in the sun. I tried to stop him but he only shouted at me, 'Who are you to control me? Is this what the factory has taught you?' My mother, instead of appeasing us,

reproached me. Such is the fate of girls in Indian families. This brother is much younger than me. Yet I have to obey him and get his approval for everything since my father's death. Maybe if I were an office clerk I would have a better say.

My husband derides me until I am not worth a cent. Not only does he prevent me from participating in neighbourhood activities, he tells others that I am a stupid useless woman, that anything I do will bring chaos.... How not to feel mad but if I retaliate I am no longer a good wife! More ammunition for him to run me down. Better to ignore him than invite more attacks.

The effects of emotional subordination

Daily experiences of emotional subordination generate feelings of shame, guilt, inadequacy, self-doubt and inferiority. The cumulative effect of these experiences is to ingrain a deep sense of helplessness, fear, ineptitude and incapacity. Minds become blank and dulled over time, as the women I worked with narrated. Their emotions and reactions numbed, inhibiting the potential of development. Devaluations are not only dehumanizing and demeaning. They disable and maim confidence and self-esteem. They affect not only how the women feel about themselves but also their self-image and sense of their capacities – their subjectivities and agency.

Subjectivity constitutes the individual's sense of self, thoughts, emotions, modes of understanding the world; the sense of individuality, uniqueness, identity and continuity; and the reflexive awareness of these things.[4] It refers to the conscious and unconscious thoughts and emotions of the individual, her sense of self, and her ways of understanding her relation to the world.[5]

Subjectivity is a dynamic analytical concept to understand the silenced dimensions of internalized intimations of subordination, and its effects upon the various aspects of the person. Because of its contradictory and continual nature,[6] the concept also provides a framework for change, for reconstitution. Hence, the problematic potential of reconstructing existing subjectivities that are paralysing.

Experience, feelings and subjectivity are inextricably linked. Subjectivity embodies lived experiences and experienced feelings. Experienced realities and their effects construct subjectivity, and at the same time subjectivity structures the person's psyche and sense of agency. As much as subjectivity is being constructed by experiences inflicted by others which impact on the self, it is also self-constructing and open to redefinition. The resultant subjectivity can regulate or constrain the agency and autonomy of the person, as in the case of psychological oppression and the intimations of emotional subordination.

Subjectivities are not fixed and immutable. They are constantly being reconstituted in discourse each time we think or speak.[7] Thus they are open to reinforcement or revision and reinterpretation. Usher noted that subjectivity can be re-constructed through practical and discursive encounter and engagement.[8] Subjects can recreate themselves in discourses which are oppositional to currently dominant discourses. Thus subjectivities can be sites for contestation and reconstitution for the recovery of an authentic self-reconstructed subjectivity through self-definition. It is such an understanding that allows the possibility of reconstitution from the devastating effects arising from emotional subordination of the individuals concerned.

Reconstructing subjectivities

Emotional sufferings and their effects, when unprocessed and repressed, are disabling. In the situation of women on the global assembly line, we have seen how, through the case of Malaysian women factory workers, they have been subjected to constant denigration. They have internalized the various negative definitions, stereotyping and abuses at great personal emotional cost and incapacitation. A process which allows the reconstruction of a woman's experience from her own standpoint, in which a new subject position is reconstituted to see anew and make sense of her situation, a situation which makes her the subject rather than the cause of the contradictions and pain she is experiencing, is fundamental to consciousness-raising.

The debilitating effects of internalized oppression, commonly depicted as powerlessness and learned helplessness, have been a core concern of the women's movement.[9] The problematic potential of lived experiences of subordination as a source of oppositional knowledge, has been the revolutionary core of feminist transformation.[10] Feminist practice emphasizes the need to address the emotional welfare of women, whether in feminist therapy,[11] in organizing,[12] in popular education[13] or programmes for women's empowerment.[14]

Various approaches have been experimented with, to facilitate the healing and recovery from experienced injuries and reconstitute women's subjectivities.[15] Story-telling-sharing has been used extensively and effectively as a tool for consciousness-raising and mobilization in the women's and indigenous movements.[16]

Consciousness-raising is practised as a healing and recovery process which begins with renaming reality according to personal standpoints and experienced realities. This involves rejecting names and definitions that are not grounded directly in one's own experience, but because they have been adopted, have the effect of containing, controlling and constructing what one is or what one does.

Women's consciousness-raising groups have been a means for overcoming some of these psychological obstacles,[17] exploring feelings as a 'critical way of knowing' or 'inner knowing', the source of true knowledge of the world for women living in a society that denies the value of their perceptions.[18] Collective discussion of personal problems, often previously assumed to be the result of personal inadequacies, leads to a recognition that what have been experienced as personal failings are socially produced contradictions and inflections shared by many women in similar situations. The power of redefining and naming feelings and experiences from one's own standpoint has been proven to be powerful in helping to change perceptions and subjectivities. This process of discovery and recovery leads to a reinterpretation of one's experience and self-definition instead of allowing the self to be constructed by others.

Within feminist discourse, voice and speech are metaphors for women's self-definitions,[19] countervailing the constructions of others. Indeed, moving from silence to voice has been shown to reclaim what has been denied and dismissed. It is to assert opposition to the dominant discourse. It is an act of profound personal and political significance, reinstating the suppressed or submerged knowledge and subject of the marginalized.[20]

I have used story-telling-sharing as education in small groups to evoke repressed voices for reconstructing subjectivities:[21] the recollection and articulation of feelings and thoughts associated with experienced subordination for the purpose of recovery, self-definition and self-reconstitution. Narration of lived experiences of anguish and pain, which the women who had been victimized had suppressed, was encouraged. In this informal conversational mode, connections, new meanings and understandings emerge through listening, questioning and reflecting on each other's stories, and it is this process that contributes to the recovery of the women's authentic realities as they themselves have experienced them.

In conclusion

Education for women workers on the global assembly lines must address the material–objective conditions as well as the subjective–affective dimensions. Most often educational work with women workers tends to focus only on their objective–material conditions related to employment and their class position as worker. It is essential that silenced experiences of emotional subordination, powerlessness and inferiority are taken on board in and as educational work. Educational methodologies and strategies of action that can unpack, challenge and reconstitute women's sufferings of subordination and their subordinated position are vital. It is essential to address conscious and unconscious thoughts, unexpressed feelings and emotions that make up their sense of themselves, their relation to the world and their inability to act. Although emotional suffering is only one dimension of women's subordination, it is a critical aspect.

Although the focus has been on Malaysian women workers, addressing internalized effects of subordination and reconstructing subjectivities to facilitate women's recovery from hidden injuries of subjugation does not apply only to women workers in Malaysia. This aspect of educational work is essential to any other subordinated group whose voice and sense of self are muted, especially women toiling in other industrial zones. Given the impact and trend in global capitalist industrial development, many more millions of women will no doubt join the global assembly lines and will continue to need this kind of educational support.

Notes

1. Froebel, Heinrichs and Kreye 1980; Elson and Pearson 1981; Lim 1983.
2. Lochhead 1988.
3. Ackerman 1984.
4. Usher 1989.
5. Weedon 1987.
6. Weedon 1987.
7. Weedon 1987.
8. Usher 1989.
9. Steinem 1992.
10. Lourde 1984.
11. Krzowski and Land 1988.
12. Dominelli and Mcleod 1989.
13. PERG 1992.
14. Gutierrez 1990.
15. Barry 1989; Collins 1990; Davies 1992.
16. Christ 1979; Buker 1987.
17. Butler and Wintram 1991.
18. Weiler 1991.
19. Collins 1990.
20. Daly 1978; Christ 1979; Rich 1975.
21. Chan 1996.

References

Ackerman, S. (1984) 'The Impact of Industrialisation on the Social Role of Rural Malay Women', in Hing Ai Yun *et al.* (eds), *Women in Malaysia*, Pelanduk Publications, Kuala Lumpur.

Barry, K. (1989) 'Biography and the Search for Women's Subjectivity', *Women's Studies International Forum*, Vol. 12, No. 6.

Buker, E. (1987) 'Storytelling Power: Personal Narratives and Political Analysis', *Women and Politics*, Vol. 7, No. 3.

Butler, S. and Wintram, C. (1991) *Feminist Groupwork*, Sage Publications, London.

Chan, L.H. (1996) 'Talking Pain: Educational Work with "Factory Women" in Malaysia', in Walters, S. and Manicom, L., *Gender in Popular Education*, Zed Books, London and CACE Publications, Bellville.

Christ, C. (1979) 'Spiritual Quest and Women's Experience', in Christ, C. and

Plaskow, J. (eds), *Woman Spirit Rising: A Feminist Reader in Religion*, Harper & Row, San Francisco.

Collins, P.H. (1990) *Black Feminist Thought: Knowledge, Consciousness and the Politics of Empowerment*, Unwin, London.

Daly, M. (1978) *Gyn/Ecology: The Metaethics of Radical Feminism*, Beacon Press, Boston.

Davies, B. (1992) 'Women's Subjectivity and Feminist Stories', in Ellis, C. and Flaherty, M. (eds), *Investigating Subjectivity: Research on Lived Experience*, Sage Publications, London.

Dominelli, L. and Mcleod, E. (1989) *Feminist Social Work*, Macmillan, London.

Elson, D. and Pearson, R. (1981) 'The Subordination of Women and the Internationalisation of Production', in Young, K., Walkowitz, C. and Mccullagh, R. (eds), *Of Marriage and the Market: Women's Subordination in International Perspective*, Case Books, London.

Froebel, F., Heinrichs, J. and Kreye, O. (1980) *The New International Division of Labour: Structural Unemployment in Industrialised Countries and Industrialisation in Developing Countries*, Cambridge University Press, Cambridge.

Gutierrez, L. (1990) 'Working with Women of Color: An Empowerment Perspective', *Social Work*, March.

Krzowski, S. and Land, P. (1988) *In Our Experience: Workshops at the Women's Therapy Centre*, The Women's Press, London.

Lim, L. (1983) 'Capitalism, Imperialism and Patriarchy: The Dilemma of Third World Workers in Multinational Factories', in Nash, J. and Fernandez, K. (eds), *Women, Men and the International Division of Labour*, State University of New York Press, Albany, NY.

Lochhead, J. (1988) 'Retrenchment in a Malaysian Free Trade Zone', in Heyzer, N. (ed.), *Daughters in Industry*, Asia Pacific and Development Centre, Kuala Lumpur.

Lourde, A. (1984) *Sister Outsider*, Crossing Press, Trumansburg, NY.

PERG (1992) *Women Educating to End Violence Against Women*, Popular Education Research Group, Toronto.

Rich, A. (1975) 'For a Sister', in *Poems: Selected and New (1950–1974)*, W.W. Norton, New York.

Steinem, G. (1992) *Revolution From Within: A Book of Self-Esteem*, Little, Brown, London.

Usher, R. (1989) 'Locating Experience in Language: Towards a Poststructuralist Theory of Experience', *Adult Education Quarterly*, Vol. 40, No. 1.

Weedon, C. (1987) *Feminist Practice and Poststructuralist Theory*, Basil Blackwell, Oxford.

Weiler, K. (1991) 'Freire and a Feminist Pedagogy of Difference', *Harvard Educational Review*, Vol. 16, No. 4.

Part II

Adult Education and Training Strategies

This section raises the possibility of a greater *rapprochement* between adult education and training, as economies are opened up to global competitiveness. The demarcation lines between the market's emphasis on human-resource development and traditional adult education's humanistic concern for democratic, holistic approaches to people's education are blurring to some degree. The analytical approach of starting with people's daily lived realities, used by Moshenberg in his chapter, helps to encourage a more integrated view of adult education and training that is relevant to people's lives.

The integration of adult education and training is tackled directly by Lugg, and by Gamble and Walters. Lugg describes aspects of the debates in the construction of a national qualifications framework in South Africa, which is to be a mechanism to achieve integration and also greater equity. Gamble and Walters point out the very different understandings of integration. The integration debates point to the tension inherent in the creation of a complex technical instrument to achieve democratic educational and social goals. Michelson warns of the conservative outcomes that are possible in strategies like the recognition of prior learning. Moshenberg argues that the focus on technical solutions is wrong: the only way to achieve democratic outcomes that will favour the majority of people, who are women, is to start by sitting down and listening to them.

The role of education and training in economic development is the focus of the chapters by Murphy, Minty, and Winterton and Winterton. The Wintertons discuss critically multi-skilling as a strategy to improve productivity and worker satisfaction. Minty in turn assesses the elaborate plans for the economic regeneration of Newfoundland and Labrador in Canada, and the role of adult education and training. Murphy describes a person-centred, vocational education strategy for women that is designed to develop women's potential to shape the change needed in Northern

Ireland. The programme combines personal, political and professional aspects to achieve an integrative, holistic approach. All recognize the importance of broad and active participation by those involved if there is to be any chance of improving prospects for economic and personal development.

A strategy to improve the possibilities for the integration of education, training and development is described by Gamble and Walters, who tell of the construction of the education, training and development practitioner (ETDP) in South Africa. They question whether a generic practitioner who can cross traditional boundaries and 'live in the gaps' is a passing fad or new identity. Several of the chapters attempt to rethink adult education and training strategies that challenge the dominance of human-capital free-market perspectives.

9

'Sit Down, Listen to the Women!'

Daniel Moshenberg[1]

> It is the knowledge of man's bad faith which makes women wiser about
> the limits of a solidarity that pretends to be neutral to gender. The rounded
> unitary world of kinship can never be the same for her again: 'soiled and
> humiliated' she has recourse to an *alternative solidarity* – a solidarity of
> women.[2]

We are trying to locate adult education and training in the context of
national reconstruction and development. Where is adult education and
training positioned? To whom does it speak? Outside of the community
of adult education and training promoters and providers, formal or informal, who actually talks about it? When we talk about adult education 'on
the ground', which ground are we thinking of? On which and on whose
map does it appear?

In a preliminary fashion, I want to construct this map in two ways:
through the written representation of invitations, taken and missed, to
adult education; and in what might be called the popular text of adult
education, what 'we' talk about when we talk about adult education, and
who, in so doing, we become. In both approaches the map-making is a
textual and contractual construction and negotiation of land and people.
To think through the problems of adult education in 'its real complexity
rather than its mythical depth',[3] we must see the ground, the map, the
land, the people, and struggle with temptations towards metaphor and
towards abstraction, even and especially in the construction of appropriate theoretical apparatuses.

As an example of the written representation of invitations to adult
education, I turn to an article entitled 'Whites Evict Black Farmers in
South African Land Conflict' that appeared on the first page of the *New
York Times*, Saturday, 14 October 1995, written by Suzanne Daley. The
article opens with the scene of instruction interrupted:

First, the police went to the local school and took the children from their classrooms. Then they stood by as a crew tossed the Khulu family's meagre belongings into a truck and drove off with them. After that, the white land-owner, Andrias Scheepers, hitched his tractor to a chain he had strung around the family's mud and cow-dung huts and pulled them down.

This is a terrible, and terribly complicated, story with innumerable strands; I will follow only two. The first is the beginning. The story, and its version of the action, begins in school. We do not know the location or the identity of the 'local school', which given the location of the farm and the history of farm schools, seems a bit curious. Nevertheless, the point is that eviction is not an act of removal but rather, as its etymology indicates, an act of conquest, not an act of marginalization but of sub-jugation. In the 'politics of space',[4] eviction is extermination: all traces must be removed. If the family is to be 'relocated' to a site a mere couple of kilometres away, why must the children be removed from school? The next day, those children should be going back to the same school. What is the social meaning of school in this encounter among poor, black African tenant farmers: the state – in the persons of police and school personnel, and the white farmers? Why begin with the children? How does this interruption of children's education refer to the articulation of poor, black tenant farmer adulthood by the state and by the farmers? What would an adult education and training programme, and specifically an adult literacy campaign, look like in the context of the eviction cam-paign described, one that establishes and locates adult social ontology in family networks that it designates through destruction? If education is viewed as a critical intervention, then an educational programme must be seen in the context of countervening and competing modes of interven-tion. In this case, eviction.

The reporter Daley describes at some length the situation of tenant farmers, 'among the poorest of South Africans', predominantly 'illiterate'. The only person quoted is Geoff Budlender, a special adviser to the Minister of Land Affairs. Budlender is quoted because the 'real' story begins many kilometres away from the farm, in Parliament, where a bill pending would allow tenant farmers the right, power and opportunity to purchase the land they, and their forebears, have worked. This new leg-islation would also protect tenant farmers from malicious or retaliatory eviction.

Where exactly does that story, in its complexity rather than depth, really begin? From the special adviser and the situation of tenant farmers, the article takes a curious turn to gender. This turn is the heart of my argument. Daley describes the family, 'a few days after being evicted in September', as still living on the side of the road. They have lost all their meagre possessions and savings, to fire and tractor. Their livestock had been confiscated for trespassing. The Khulu family lives in a small box, made of scavenged corrugated tin and tarpaulin. While we do not know how many are in the family, the report stated that eight grandchildren are living in that box.

Then the turn to gender, which takes place in two parts: 'None of the Khulus knew about the legislation. Asked why they had been evicted, Mrs Khulu, a frail, barefoot woman, said she thought it was because they had asked Mr Scheepers to pay $3 a month for the labour of the children, so they could buy soap. "We had not refused to work," she said. "We had just asked for money. Everything would have been all right if we had not asked for the money."'

The article continues:

> Nomsa Musuku, who lives on another tenant farm that belongs to Mr Scheepers, said he was a very hard man. Ms Masuku is among the six women working in his modest home, which in any American suburb would be called a tract house. They work from 6 a.m. to 6 p.m. seven days a week except for a few hours off on Sundays. There is no cash wage. They get one meal a day, she said; they share half a plastic milk carton of porridge, which each women dips into with her own spoon because they are not given bowls. When the farmer's wife recently tried to give them tea, Mr Scheepers got mad and would not let her speak to them anymore.

This article is 36 paragraphs in length. The turn to gender occurs in the eleventh paragraph. At the head of the article is a photo, three columns wide, of 'Mrs Albertina Khulu with part of her family at her destroyed house...' We see Mrs Khulu at the outset, her strong face framed in the empty window sash of the free-standing wall, all that remains of her house, but we do not hear from or about her until well into the article. And when we do, she appears as a frail, plaintive, misinformed rural black woman.

As an adult educator, I am interested in Suzanne Daley, especially in the context of Nomsa Musuku and that woman who inhabits a curious double world of anonymity and nomenclature, 'the farmer's wife' whom we assume would be identified as Mrs Scheepers, but who is not. The farmer Scheepers understands clearly that on his farm, tea is never just tea. It is communication, dialogue: dialogue being the premium vehicle of education – social, political and technical. People obviously must come together in a shared construction of space, time and purpose. What is not obvious, what is actively repressed as it is evoked, is the history of Mrs Scheepers's desire to offer her domestic workers tea. Was this the first time? Or was it the first time the farmer noticed? Or was it the first time as one identified not in her own right but exclusively as 'the farmer's wife'? How exactly does 'Mr Scheepers not let her speak'? Women struggling against male and patriarchal suppression of woman-to-woman speech is a rallying cry around the world.

The situation to consider here is the way in which we find out about this silencing. Were it not for the eviction of the Khulu family, as social metonym for all the black farming families evicted or 'under eviction', we would never hear about the repression of the farmer's wife and those domestic workers who remain. Again, eviction is not about removal. It is a politics of extermination and is understood as such by all.

So, Mrs Scheepers and the domestic workers go on with their stories untold. But this story of prohibited speech follows directly, and curiously, upon an account of misinformed or 'naive' speech. Mrs Khulu knows nothing about any impending legislation giving tenant farmers the right to tend the lands they have worked. She thinks this is about wages; unpaid labour, labourers' requests (hardly demands) for modest, instead of decent or living wages; and the desire for soap.

What does Suzanne Daley do? Does she accept the historical invitation to dialogic education? She finds herself by the side of the road with Albertina Khulu and her people. These are people who have literally nothing to lose and everything to gain. They have, according to Daley, no basic or essential information. They are metonymically wrapped into the 'frail, barefoot' body, the name and the speech of Mrs Khulu. If Daley tells Mrs Khulu what the legislation is, what the reasons for her eviction are, what might happen in all of South Africa? Contextually, what is that legislation? As social text, how do we read its distributive geographies of dissemination and silencing? Why does Suzanne Daley tell me, thousands of kilometres away, and not Mrs Khulu?

If we conceptualize adult education and training as accepting the invitation of those 'under eviction' to develop access to basic and essential information, what might occur? How might Suzanne Daley be encouraged, be 'couraged' 'to try to give her tea'? This is a structural issue, not a desire to see a thousand gardens blossom. In *A Bed Called Home*, Mamphele Ramphele asks, 'At what point do individuals assume responsibility as active agents of history? Can an outsider intervene meaningfully in the face of the politics of space as played out in the hostels?'[5] I pose similar questions, and also believe they are part of a politics of that much beleaguered word, empowerment, and see the politics of empowerment in specifically gendered and women's terms.

In Daley's article, the elements for a national policy and practice of adult education concern first a focus on contested local sites, actual physical spaces; woman-to-woman communications in which information and social contact are intimately enmeshed; analysis of and resistance to domestic and intimate patriarchy; and an almost deconstructionist analysis of the status of insider and outsider. When 'outsider' police come to evict the Khulu family, whose family and whose people have traditional claims to the land that predate those of the Scheepers, who then is outsider and who is insider? If Suzanne Daley were to educate Albertina

Khulu, what would happen to the geo-political discourse and practice of inside/insider and outside/outsider? When Mr Scheepers prohibits his 'officially unnamed' farmer's wife from serving tea or even talking to the help, among whom is numbered the named Nomsa Musuku, who is insider and who outsider, and what is it people, as individuals and as members collectively, are inside or outside of? Who draws this map?

Finally, how is the construction of this map a narrative of nation-state? Specifically, how does the eviction of the Khulus repeat the former apartheid state's eviction of all those who could be Khulus? Surely, we acknowledge farmer Scheepers' radical lack of originality in this context; he does not write the story so much as is written and authorized by it. Generically, how does Scheepers's eviction of Albertina Khulu replicate relations between nation-state and women?

I suggest that we, as agents committed to the role of adult education and training, draw a map that begins with women's autonomous conversations and women's constructions of information networks and bases. This means seeing education and training as a campaign against evictions and silencings, against the removal of bodies and the repression of speech; it means beginning one's analyses of educational practices and programmes in the constrictions of so-called domestic space and the constructions of gender. It means understanding the phrase 'meaningful intervention' as both 'significant' and 'significative'. It means listening.

So, let's listen. How do people talk about adult education? What is its popular articulation? Instead of offering a focused ethnography, I offer two popular South African sayings.

The first comes from 'generic' South Africa: 'Educate a man and you educate an individual. Educate a woman and you educate a nation.' According to Carolyn Newton, those enjoined to educate a woman, educate her as mother and as teacher, but not as a woman, not as individual, and certainly not as citizen of a nation of women.[6] This woman is the space across which nationhood via education passes. As Cheryl Walker notes: 'mother of the nation' often has very little to do with tangible benefits.[7] Penny Enslin further specifies: 'The ideal of the mother of the nation is an idealized notion which does not accord with the extension of democracy to women. The logic of nationhood with its universalist assumptions is a logic of exclusion, which will not be conducive to the growth of democratic gender politics. How can we redirect the pursuit through education of democratic, non-sexist politics?'[8] How can we describe not only the education of women but the education of 'a woman' in the context of both common sense and good sense without interpolating mother, and mother of the nation?

Second, the famous line sung by over 20,000 women on 9 August 1956, at the steps of the Union Buildings in Pretoria: 'Now you have touched the women, you have struck a rock, you have dislodged a boulder, you will be crushed.' As you know, these women were protesting the 'new' policies of a Dompas[9] for women. This is the principal motif of women's national education and training, this scene in which thousands of women organized, spoke and sang and moved as one, in which, as the dompas made them 'visible invisible', they asserted their visible presence and became 'threatening'.

I have an obvious and simple question: in both sayings, who are 'you'? You who 'educate a women and educate a nation', you who have 'touched the women'? How are subjecthood, agency, subjugation and gender connected in these common insights? This is about the political economy and historical narrative of national map-making, as conducted in the people's culture, as it concerns the historical juncture in which the map-making becomes a part of the self-reflexive historical and social construction of gender. The specification of gender is crucial in any analysis of the language used to describe actual and universal teaching, training, educational and learning practices and cultures, especially when one considers the gender of the nation's teachers, almost exclusively female at the pre-primary and primary levels. What about at the adult levels? Who teaches adults to be a nation, to crush? At what point do women and women's culture 'enter into' and 'engage with' map, map-making, map-makers? Where do we start drawing a map of this nation of contested and contesting women and men and 'you'? Who will you become when tea is served?

To begin to answer that question, I want to tell you a story from my neighbourhood. *The Washington Post* of 26 August 1995 describes the kinds of work women of colour in the United States are required for, women's languages and national literacies. It is about what poor and oppressed working women of colour say when they are told by the conjuncture of State and Capital to shut up ... or else. It is about eviction.

For nine years, Victoria Romero and Maria Granados scrubbed bathrooms, made beds and vacuumed rugs at the Sheraton National Hotel in Arlington. The pay was low and the pace was demanding, but the Salvadoran immigrants said they were grateful for steady jobs. Then, in late July, both housekeepers were fired without warning. They said that after they were informed that their work had failed inspection, they were told to leave the building immediately. To make sure they did not cause trouble, the two middle-aged mothers were escorted from the hotel by guards. 'I never had a complaint in all the time I worked there, and I was never insulted like that in my whole life,' said Romero, 43, her eyes filling with tears as she recounted the episode last week in her Alexandria apartment. 'I just cried and cried.' ... Latino workers at the Sheraton National and two other Northern Virginia hotels ... said they have to contend with a host of humiliations on the job.... More than 75 per cent of the kitchen and housekeeping staff at these hotels are Latinos. Of about 20 workers interviewed from the three sites, virtually all asked that their full names not be used, saying that they feared losing their jobs. After some hesitation Romero and Granados agreed to be identified, but both women, who are immigrants with temporary work permits to work in the United States, expressed concern that public exposure could jeopardize their pending applications to become permanent US legal residents.

As with Albertina Khulu's family, this story is about public eviction. Why must these women leave immediately? What danger do Victoria Romero and Maria Granados pose to the public weal and health, such that they must be bodily, forcibly and immediately removed? Its general logic is twofold and simple: its ethics is the exercise of power; we do this because we can. Its ethos is the spectacle: it relies on the power of the public insult and abuse to hurt people, to make them cry and to make them weary and worn.

The manhandling of Victoria Romero and Maria Granados was a function of their becoming women workers of colour, and specifically women-of-colour workers, in the political consciousness of hotel managers and owners. As political agents, you must retain the following image in your head: you must see two middle-aged Latino workers at work. A white male comes up to each, since they work individually and alone, and tells her, in English, that she's fired. Without notice or delay, two male guards grab each by the arms and forcibly remove her. This story, as with all evictions, is not original; it repeats the dominant foundational narrative of nation-statehood in the United States today, that of deportation of the dangerous, unwanted, undocumented, illegal resident, and especially the women, and specifically Central American and Asian working women.

The scene of eviction is also a scene of refusal to educate and of competing literacies and enforced illiteracies. Allegedly, the hotel had received word from its parent company that it had failed 'cleanliness inspections'. Neither these inspections nor their reports were ever made available to the workers. Instead, workers were informed by memo that the management would be conducting random and unannounced room inspections. Again, this was declared, never negotiated.

Finally, allegedly, despite years of complaint-free labour, Victora Romero and Maria Granados undergo a room inspection, fail, and are never given instruction. Why are they removed instead of trained and educated? Surely, from a 'purely' educative perspective, it makes more sense, and costs less, to train and to teach someone with nine years' experience in the actual work site than to train someone completely new to the environment? We must start talking about literacy as access to information in the context of structured cultures of violently refused, denied and prohibited access to information.

As educators and formulators of educational policy, we must see the physical removal of Albertina Khulu's body, of Victoria Romero's body, of Maria Granados's body, as a multilayered social act of instruction.

What kind of literacy might disrupt and counter a culture of contempt in which women's forcibly invisible work and bodies are 'translated' into the public domain, only to be articulated as erased? In the masters' plan, Victoria Romero and Maria Granados, Albertina Khulu and the 'the farmer's wife' only appear in public when they are being picked up and thrown out. As Granados says at the end of the article: 'It's so unfair. Most of us are humble women who barely speak English, and they just take advantage.' Here Maria Granados provides the basic materials for an adult education and training programme at the community level.

We have to begin critically looking at unfairness and injustice. How do we know what is unfair or fair, what is unjust or just? The first stage of instruction is our own sense of injustice and justice and our own inquiry into their interrelatedness. We then have to move on to one's collective and individual social identity and history because who we are is a matter of political geography. The question is not who are we; the questions are who are we *here*, *how* are we here? As workers, women, people, why do Salvadorans come to the United States to the hotels? Why are most of these workers women? Why, after nine years of consistent labour at a hotel, do they describe themselves as 'barely speaking English'? This is the second stage of instruction: our own sense of identity. The third stage is the analysis and critique of the dominant order. In the case of the Latino workers, a history of hotel owners and managers, involving research and analysis, involving training in research skills, in numeracy and literacy, in English. The last stage is the refusal and transformation of the rejection, to refuse the historical verdict of having been thrown out like garbage, of having accepted one's position and positionality as such.

Which twentieth-century post-colonial or post-independence state has successfully educated its adult masses, and according to whom? Cuba? Perhaps. Instead of lamenting the failure, or catastrophically partial success of nation-states, and specifically post-colonial nation-states, to act as providers of adult education and training, perhaps we could ask a better question. Is the nation-state better at constructing adult education or at dismantling and destroying adult education? Instead of conducting a global survey, I suggest we look at definitions of basic needs in the context of women's leadership development, women's politics of need interpretation, and women's stories. Practically, this entails two simple, concrete proposals for adult education and training.

Proposal one Any policy document concerning adult education must have a preliminary section in which the politics of needs interpretation is elucidated and interrogated, specifically from the perspectives, and preferably from the text and textualities, of working women, rural, peri-urban, urban. In each 'nation', we must study together the ruling minority, the unruling minoritized. In so doing, adult education must first address its own problematical political economies. Politically, adult education and training must focus on those adults who are treated, formally and informally, as sub-adults: women.

Proposal two Adult education and training, understood as women's education and training, as a women-driven programme, should take as its models current and historical women's mobilization. That legacy should provide the framework for formulations of principles as well as everyday educational praxis. For adult education and training as women's literacy/ leadership development, that story could 'begin' with the South African women's anti-pass laws campaigns, which reached their most public and famous expression in the march to Pretoria in 1956. Although dompasses were instituted, the women's anti-pass campaign never died. The traditions of women's political mobilizations provide curricular and pedagogical materials for a national adult education and training programme. How did those women organize themselves? What cultural traditions specific to those particular women were operative in mobilizations? What skills were required? How do our learning situations relate to these struggles and concrete practices? How did and do they sustain their struggles from 1956 to today? What are the lessons of women's sustainable empowerment?

We ask these questions as we study the anti-pass law campaigns of South Africa and try to link Victoria Romero and Maria Granados with Albertina Khulu and 'the farmer's wife'. South African activist and writer Ellen Kuzwayo[10] encourages us to sit down and listen. We try to heed their teaching. We attempt to sit down and listen in the context of our women's pedagogies of women's leadership formations and cultural and political practices of women's 'literation'. Re-write the adage: study women's literation, and we engage in national liberation. Sit down and listen.

Notes

1. This version was practically co-authored with You-me Park; everything good in here she contributed. The final copy belongs to Maoboy.
2. Ranajit 1987: 106.
3. Macherey 1978.
4. Ramphele 1993.
5. Ramphele 1993: 106.
6. Newton 1994: 2–3.
7. Walker 1990.
8. Enslin 1993/94: 13–25.
9. The Dompas was a pass book issued to all black people to allow them access to white areas during the apartheid era in South Africa.
10. Kuzwayo 1994.

References

Enslin, P. (1993/94) 'Education for Nation-Building: A Feminist Critique', *Perspectives in Education*, Vol. 15, No. 1.

Kuzwayo, E. (1994) *Sit Down and Listen*, David Philip, Cape Town.

Macherey, P. (1978) *A Theory of Literary Production*, RKP, London.

Newton, C. (1994) 'Editorial', *Agenda* 21.

Ramphele, M. (1993) *A Bed Called Home: Life in the Migrant Labour Hostels of Cape Town*, David Philip, Cape Town.

Ranajit, G. (1987) 'Chandra's Death' in Guha, R. (ed.), *Subaltern Studies V: Writings on South Asian History and Society*, Oxford University Press, Delhi.

Walker, C. (1990) 'Review: Woman-Nation-State', *Agenda* 6.

10

Personal, Professional and Political Development for Women

Pauline Murphy

People's participation in social and political transformation can only be achieved through the establishment of societies which place human worth above power and liberation above control.

'In this paradigm, development requires democracy, the genuine empowerment of the people. When this is achieved, culture and development will naturally coalesce to create an environment in which all are valued and every kind of human potential can be realized.'[1] This belief was expressed by Aung San Suu Kyi, one of many brave women who have been inspiring role models to women all over the world, encouraging them to put an end to the culture of silence.

Clearly, she understands the importance of getting rid of the legacy of silence, which in the Northern Ireland context has been a feature of society for many decades. She would agree with bell hooks who wrote:

> Moving from silence into speech is for the oppressed, the colonized, the exploited and those who stand and struggle side by side, a gesture of defiance that heals, that makes new life and new growth possible. It is that act of speech, of talking back, that is no mere gesture of empty words, that is the expression of our movement from object to subject – the liberated voice.[2]

Participation and power

Recognition that people's participation in social and political transformation means inclusion of women as well as men is a first step in the process of change. It is a reminder that needs to be articulated frequently and widely. Participation must lead to change in gender power relations; to change in the management, use and ownership of resources. Empowerment must mean change in decision-making processes, in policy-making, in the ownership of knowledge and control of information. No country or region can develop socially, politically and economically if half of the population – women – do not have opportunities for participation at all levels and in all spheres. 'Change will come about only if women at all levels, fully aware of their rights and responsibilities, express their convictions collectively.'[3]

A healthy civil society will have strong communities which encourage interactive learning through action. Community and adult educators have a major role to play in the reconstruction and development of Northern Ireland, as hopefully the two communities emerge from violent conflict and move towards the creation of a new democratic model where 'men and women have an equal chance to make their contribution and find their creativity in a society which neither owns and both can share'.[4]

The Northern Ireland context

Northern Ireland was created in 1921, when six counties of the nine-county Irish province of Ulster were partitioned off from the rest of Ireland. For the first fifty years of its existence, it was administered by a parliament at Stormont and since 1972 directly by the British parliament at Westminster. Of the current population of approximately 1.62 million, 50.2 per cent define themselves as Protestant and 38.4 per cent as Catholic.

Unemployment differentials

Between 1971 and 1991 male unemployment in Northern Ireland rose from 10 to 16 per cent and the number of men recorded as economically inactive rose from 5 to 16 per cent. Combining these figures shows that the proportion of men without work doubled in that period from 15 to 33 per cent. But this increase was not experienced equally by the two communities.

Currently much political activity and lobbying centres on efforts to bring about change in the statistics quoted above. Legislation, inward investment, creation of small and medium-sized enterprises, increased funding from the USA and from the European Union (EU) are geared towards regenerating the economy, thereby increasing employment.

However, whilst the male unemployment differential has become and remains centre stage, not so much attention is claimed for the position of women. Inez McCormack writes:

> The position of women remains undervalued and under-resourced, particularly in areas of high disadvantage. For large numbers of women, caring for their families and elderly relatives means giving up educational and employment opportunities. For large numbers of young women, after-school experience consists of training schemes and a choice between early marriage and unemployment.[5]

Many women are in part-time, poorly paid, fixed-term or casual employment which makes the difference between chronic financial insecurity and extreme poverty. A recent research report for the Equal Opportunities Commission Northern Ireland (1995), confirms that the differences between women's jobs and men's jobs are substantial: women are concentrated in a smaller range of jobs and carry out work of lower status and lower pay; they hold the majority of part-time posts and opportunities for promotion are limited. It also reveals another differential, which is that Catholic women's economic activity is markedly lower than that of Protestant women; the proportions in work are lower for Catholic women for both full-time and part-time work; and Catholic women are consistently more likely to be unemployed than are Protestant women.

Given the patterns of segregated living, the above findings have implications for the provision of adult education and training for women in Northern Ireland. The case study section of this paper will illustrate how the Unit for Personal and Professional Development for Women at the University of Ulster, Jordanstown Campus, structured the design and delivery of courses to enable women from both communities to overcome barriers.

Women in power structures and public life

'There is little visibility of women indigenous to Northern Ireland in the political system and none among the political representatives of Northern Ireland in either the British or European parliaments. At local Council level, less than 13 per cent are women and of these, 50 per cent have either no women representatives or just one.'[6] Boards appointed by the British Secretary of State for Northern Ireland were introduced in the 1970s and are responsible for housing, health, education, training and enterprise. Women now make up 32 per cent of these boards – a political success story after extensive and vocal lobbying by women's groups and associations during the past three years.

This paucity of women in decision-making is not, of course, peculiar to Northern Ireland. Demands for the inclusion of women in decision-making have been a feature of international conferences in the 1990s. Calls for all government and non-governmental organizations (NGOs) of the world to comprise no more than 60 per cent, no less than 40 per cent of either sex; for women to win greater representation in existing power structures in order radically to reform them; and for non-acceptance of current economic models that link development with economic growth at the expense of human well-being, have been made by Women's World Congresses in Miami, Dublin and Athens. 'All were agreed that as half of the human race, women have a right to demand leadership and control of a new kind of economics that puts life and quality of life for all first.'[7]

Strategies for change

It would be difficult to disagree with the recommendations of Stacey and Price[8] that if women wish to change the societies in which they live, they must 'seek and achieve power positions. It is essential that women should enter the political arena since the societies are male dominated and men cannot be relied upon to initiate or carry through the necessary changes.'

Ruth Lister[9] maintains that there is a twofold challenge for politics if current political systems are to enhance the citizenship of half the adult population. 'The conduct of politics has to be transformed – to become less adversarial, sitting at civilized hours and providing child care for those with young children.' In addition, 'the relationship between "strong" and "weak" forms of politics needs to be reconstructed so that the former is made more accountable to the latter.' She makes a distinction between 'strong' and 'weak' polity according to whether or not decision-making as well as opinion-forming is encompassed. Her analysis suggests that women's under-representation in formal politics is partly a function of institutional and discriminatory barriers and of the constraints imposed by the reality of women's lives – lack of time, mobility and money on formal political participation – as well as of women's perceptions of the nature of politics in the 'strong' polity.

Coote and Pattullo[10] focused on the 'sense of exclusion from and aversion to the language and form of politics with a big P'. In contrast, the community-based political activities in which many of the women they interviewed were active, were more accessible and more enjoyable. Participation in community-based organizations or social movements can also be more immediately empowering. Nevertheless they concluded that 'no matter how successful women were at organizing at grassroots level, their power was limited while they remained outside the circles where key policy decisions were made and implemented'.

The effectiveness of women's community action in introducing women to methods of challenging acceptance of a secondary role is not doubted.

> The values underlying ways of organizing emphasize local control and au-
> tonomy, local social and cultural activities, relating theory to practice,
> encouraging procedures and leadership styles, which make participants feel
> confident and involved and recognize that differing views about tactics and
> strategy may be rooted in real experience and are worth listening to and
> discussing.[11]

Drude Dahlerup acknowledges the effectiveness of the women's movement in stimulating women into action and maintains that,

distant national structures over which you feel little control, formal procedure which does not seem to achieve anything, rigid notions of the correct line which suppress hesitant disagreement and questions, theoretical debates which do not shed light on practice, solidarity based on abstractions with little commitment to each other – none of these could have moved women to cast off their passivity and self-subordination.[12]

Evaluation of the Personal, Professional and Political Development Courses at the University of Ulster indicated that, for Northern Ireland women, community activism at local level was an important first step in agency in civil society.

The European dimension in Northern Ireland

The recent cease-fire (now ended) in Northern Ireland opened up unprecedented opportunities for introducing new forms of decision-making, an inclusive style of discourse and the chance to formulate policy at many levels in society. To demonstrate its support for the peace process, the EU has allocated a generous additional fund of more than 300 million ECU over three years, with a promise of more to come. Five priorities have been identified in this Initiative for Peace and Reconciliation, namely Employment; Urban and Rural Regeneration; Cross-border Development; Productive Investment and Industrial Development; Social Inclusion.

Numerous consultations and meetings have been held with business people, academics, trade unions, local government and a wide range of community and women's groups involved in community action (Ruth Lister's 'soft' polity). The growing confidence of the NGO sector prompted the EU to suggest that instead of funding being channelled through government agencies, global grants could be used and made available to intermediaries designated by the EU. Such intermediaries could include women's groups and community groups, which would be responsible for selecting and assisting projects.

The idea of community or area partnerships has also been accepted with 26 partnerships, formed with membership from district councils, NGOs, trade unions and the private and statutory sectors. These initiatives provide a unique chance to experiment with a participative democracy which involves a whole variety of expertise in finding solutions to local and regional problems.

Training as a catalyst for change

The EC Commission White Paper[13] *Growth, Competitiveness, Employment* stresses the role of education and training in stimulating growth and restoring competitiveness and a socially acceptable level of employment in addition to their fundamental task of promoting the development of the individual and the values of citizenship. The countries with the highest levels of general education and training such as Germany or Japan are least affected by problems of unemployment. In combination with other measures in industrial and trade policies and research, education and vocational training could play a significant part in the emergence of a new development model in the EU in the twenty-first century – but only if the systems of education and training are suited to the task.

Life-long education with universally accessible advanced vocational training is recommended as the overall objective for national communities. Greater co-operation between universities and business is stressed. The emphasis should be on the role of universities in training and retraining teachers, trainers, middle and senior management as well as on research to anticipate skills needs, to identify developing areas and anticipated economic and social functions.

A new 'information society' is emerging in which management, quality and speed of information are key factors for competitiveness. The changeover towards an information society has placed severe demands on the adaptability of education, training and employers.

The risk of exclusion as a result of inadequate skills or qualifications and the emergence of a two-tier society is not to be underestimated. The Northern Ireland Economic Council has pointed out that Northern Ireland has the lowest proportion of students of any UK region studying science and technology, and emphasizes the need for developing human resources and skills levels as both an economic strategy and a means of avoiding social exclusion.

Case study: the Women's Projects Unit, University of Ulster, Northern Ireland

A research report[14] found that girls and women during primary, secondary and further education in all areas did not have equal access to knowledge, attitudes and skills necessary for their personal, professional and political development to enable them, as fully functioning human beings, to fulfil their potential in the private and public spheres of employment and civil and political society.

Discussions with the women centred on the need to have clear and accurate information accessible to them in their local areas. Because of internalized sexism and past negative experiences in education and training women suffer a substantial lack of confidence about their ability. Many women stressed the importance of knowing, not only the range of relevant options from which to choose, but also the possible consequences of decisions taken.

At that time the Northern Ireland Community Education Association, with branches in rural Northern Ireland as well as in Belfast, embarked on a process in local communities to assess the human potential in disadvantaged areas, in partnership with the then Department of Adult and Continuing Education, University of Ulster. They organized outreach courses for women in towns and communities.

A personal development course entitled 'Time For Me' was the start of the programme of courses for women which included vocationally oriented courses such as Telematics, Telecommunications, Management and Enterprise. Partnerships with other countries in Europe were created in the design, delivery, validation and evaluation of these programmes. All courses lead to University of Ulster qualifications.

Holistic person-centred ethos

A distinctive feature of all of the courses, from pre-vocational to certificates in Information Technology, Management and Supervisory Skills, Diplomas in Information Technology, Telematics/Telecommunications and Management is the integration of all modules and the holistic person-centred approach.

To reach women psychologically to facilitate this growth, they need to interact with empathetic tutors equipped with interpersonal as well as technical skills. To reach women geographically demands a realistic reappraisal of the recruitment and selection procedures. It is necessary to provide access progression routes to ensure participation by women in Catholic and Protestant communities.

All of the courses have their own specific objectives, some including acquisition of a foreign language, but the broad aims of all the programmes are:

- To provide education and training in the acquisition of new knowledge and skills in information technology, management and enterprise creation, which will facilitate professional development and enable the women either to continue their education to a higher degree level, or to gain employment preferably at middle management or supervisory level, or to generate self-employment and start their own business.
- To facilitate personal development, resulting in increased self-confidence, a more positive self-image, improved assertiveness, group work and communication skills, greater political and European awareness and the development of qualities of leadership.
- To develop critical consciousness of political, economic and social systems and structures, and of their own potential to participate in changing and shaping these systems.

Vertical and horizontal integration for women in the labour market is the ultimate aim. The word 'training' is not often used. The word 'development' is. Permeation of the boundaries between education and training is continuous. The need for an integrated approach to training is realized by many educators; for instance Gelpi[15] maintains that it will not be possible to continue making a distinction between training for workers, education of the citizenry and education of the human being. It is indispensable for society that these forms of education should be unified.

The confidence factor

The holistic person-centred design of the courses is premised on the realization that women's educational and training needs are different because their socialization, experience and status in society is different. If it is accepted that the inequality that women experience in an androcentric society is due in some measure to the internalization of the values of the privileged, i.e. men,[16] whether this is the internalization of 'appropriate' female behaviour or the belief that autonomy, power and independence are not so important for women, then it is necessary to consider the type of learning framework which facilitates growth of self-esteem. The development of such empowerment is essential, if society itself is to reap the benefits of involvement of all potential female citizens as well as the liberation of individual women within their own lives.

Extensive research into obstacles facing women returners in Northern Ireland has continuously placed lack of self-confidence at the head of the barriers identified by the women.[17]

In addition to a pedagogy and support structure designed for women, research began with the Certificate in Information Technology Studies. In an evaluation report on a three-year study of the progress of women attending the course, it was shown that the course had been effective in developing self-confidence and leadership skills.[18]

In 1993 research with students of a pre-vocational training course for women in urban and rural areas of Northern Ireland further examined this confidence factor.[19] The results showed an increase in personal growth for all students. In addition, two quantitative measures were used.[20] It was postulated that if the personal development elements had been effective and the experience of learning new skills had made students feel more competent, then students would have a more internal locus of control and higher self-esteem scores.[21]

In addition, a survey of obstacles to women living in rural areas returning to education was carried out, based on the trainees on the Management Development/Supervisory Skills course in Northern Ireland and a comparative study undertaken with transnational partners in Germany.

On completion of the course it was found that the level of confidence was significantly higher at the end than at the beginning of the course. Many women were held back from returning to education or training by anxiety which made them doubt their worth and ability. It was the experience of the women on the course that through participation and due to assertiveness training they rebuilt low levels of self-esteem and self-confidence. There is a close correlation between high levels of assertiveness and high levels of self-esteem, self-confidence, self-concept, self-efficacy, internal locus of control, self-actualization and self-empowerment.[22]

Students found that their locus of control altered significantly, showing greater personal control which indicates a higher level of self-assertion. 'Women's behaviour is often characterized by a pattern of waiting: waiting to grow up, to be asked to dance, for a proposal of marriage, waiting for a child to be born, to grow up, to leave school and leave home; always waiting, waiting for something to happen first.'[23]

Assertive power on the other hand means choosing. Women interviewed all confirmed their ability to assert themselves and were conscious of increased confidence. 'The principle of equality is one of the most important hallmarks of assertive behaviour.'[24]

The overriding purpose of these courses must be to help redress the imbalance for women as compared with men in employment by building confidence as well as providing the essential skills to succeed. 'Under-representation of females in the professions has been attributed to low self-confidence, fear of success, fear of loss of femininity, non-conscious sex-role ideology, differential values and orientation and low independence.'[25]

Conclusion

The holistic person-centred approach adopted on all courses in the Projects for Women Unit was successful, not only in the achievement of growth in self-esteem, but also in terms of outcome for the women in terms of employment and higher education at degree level and in increased participation in community activism and regional politics.

An evaluation report[26] came to this conclusion that

> it is without doubt that the course has achieved the objectives which it has set out to achieve. The high success rate of women finding jobs after participation is only one measure of its success. In economic terms, the success can be measured in relation to the number of previously-unemployed women who found jobs. In relation to human resource problems in the region – disadvantages facing women in the labour market, difficulties of existing training – the course has been remarkably successful.
>
> The number of women gaining commendations and obtaining jobs and the high standards achieved are all the more remarkable given that the women were recruited mainly from areas of high unemployment and most hold few or no formal educational qualifications. The low drop-out rate reflects the careful selection procedure and this supportive environment which enables the women to complete the course, despite considerable obstacles.

Notes

1. Aung San Suu Kyi 1994.
2. hooks 1989.
3. De Lourdes 1996.
4. President Mary Robinson of Ireland, inaugural speech.
5. McCormack 1995.
6. Beijing Ad Hoc Group Northern Ireland 1995.
7. Murphy 1993.
8. Stacey and Price 1981.
9. Lister 1993.
10. Coote and Pattullo 1990.
11. Murphy 1993.
12. Dahlerup 1990.
13. EC White Paper 1994.
14. By the Northern Ireland Department of Education Working Party on Guidance for Adult Learners, 1986.
15. Gelpi 1996.
16. Mansfield 1993.
17. Murphy and Mullan 1989; Murphy and Kelly 1995.
18. Murphy and Mullan 1989.
19. Murphy and Mullan 1993.
20. Rotter's Locus of Control (1966) and Rosenberg's Self Esteem Scale (1965).
21. Murphy and Mullan 1993.
22. Health Education Authority Northern Ireland (1990).
23. Phelps and Austin 1975.
24. Dickson 1982.
25. Eccles 1985.
26. Of the first three-year WIT project prepared for the European Centre for the Development of Vocational Training (Cedefop), Berlin, by the Policy Research Institute Belfast, 1989.

References

Aung San Suu Kyi (1994) 'Democracy, the Common Heritage of Humanity', Address to Unesco's World Commission on Culture and Development, Manila.

Beijing Ad Hoc Group Northern Ireland (1995) 'Women in Northern Ireland: Working Towards Equality, Development and Peace', Unpublished Report, Presented at Beijing by the Northern Ireland Group.

Coote, A. and Pattullo, P. (1990) *Power and Prejudice*, Weidenfeld & Nicolson, London.

Dahlerup, D. (ed.) (1990) *The New Women's Movement: Feminism and Political Power in Europe and the USA*, Sage Publications, London.

De Lourdes, P.M. (1996) *Caring for the Future: Report of the Independent Commission on Population and Quality of Life*, Oxford University Press, Oxford.

Dickson, A. (1982) *A Woman in Your Own Right*, Quartet, London.

EC White Paper (1994) *Growth, Competitiveness, Employment: The Challenges and Ways Forward into the 21st Century*, EC Publications Office, Luxembourg.

Eccles, J. (1985) 'Sex Differences and Achievement Patterns', in Sonderegger, T. (ed.), *Psychology and Gender*, University of Nebraska Press.

Gelpi, E. (1996) 'Power and Education in International Relations', in Hinze, H.

(ed.), *Development Oriented Adult Education, Adult Education and Development Journal*, No. 46, IIZ/Dvv, Bonn.

hooks, b. (1989) *Talking Back: Thinking Feminist, Thinking Black*, South End Press, Boston.

Lister, R. (1993) 'Tracing the Contours of Women's Citizenship', *Policy and Politics*, Vol. 21, No. 1.

Mansfield, S. (1993) 'Consciousness Raising in Women's Groups', in Murphy, P. (ed.), *Women on the Move. The International Journal of Community Education*, Vol. 1, No. 4, Community Education Development Centre (CEDC), Coventry.

McCormack, I. (1995) 'A View from the North', in D'Arcy, M. and Dickson, T. (eds), *Border Crossings, Developing Ireland's Island Economy*, Gill and MacMillan Ltd, Dublin.

Murphy, P. (1993) 'Women in Action: The Tide is Turning', in Murphy, P. (ed.), *Women on the Move. The International Journal of Community Education*, Vol. 1, No. 4, Community Education Development Centre (CEDC), Coventry.

Murphy, P. and Kelly, G. (1995) *Overcoming Obstacles for Women Returners,* Evaluation Report of an EU-funded Transnational Action-Research Project, Northern Ireland and Germany, University of Ulster, Jordanstown.

Murphy, P. and Mullan, T. (1989) 'Time for Women', in *IT Interim Evaluation Report of EC Women and IT Project*, University of Ulster, Jordanstown.

Murphy, P. and Mullan, T. (1993) *Evaluation of EC Action Research Project, Pre-Vocational Training for Women*, University of Ulster, Jordanstown.

Phelps, S. and Austin, N. (1975) *The Assertive Woman*, Impact, San Luis, Obispo, CA.

Stacey, M. and Price, M. (1981) *Women, Power and Politics*, Tavistock, London.

11

From Economic Dependency to Regional Self-reliance

Mildred Minty

The province of Newfoundland, Canada, is undergoing major economic restructuring. This chapter describes the concerted approach which integrates education and training with bottom-up economic plans.

Economic background

The province of Newfoundland is a land of rugged alpine barrens. It comprises both the Island of Newfoundland and a vast piece of the Canadian mainland called Labrador. Original settlers came in search of codfish stocks in the sixteenth century. They stayed, without permission, building temporary dwellings along the cliffs which characterize the coastline.

Economic development followed the typical path of many resource-rich parts of the world. Abundant fish, forest and mineral resources were extracted and transported elsewhere for secondary processing and profits went largely to absentee landlords. In the first quarter of this century, Newfoundland came close to bankruptcy and turned to Britain to replace its government with a Commission, which pulled it back sufficiently far from the brink that, with an extra boost from construction of American military bases during World War II, it entered confederation with Canada with accounts balanced in 1949.

Confederation with Canada brought levels of social benefits which Newfoundland and Labrador had never enjoyed before. The federal government of Canada, by virtue of its constitution, was committed to equalization and the reduction of regional disparity. (In Canada, provinces which do not have large enough taxation bases to generate sufficient income to maintain social, health and education services on a par with the Canadian average receive equalization payments from the federal government.) Canada brought to workers in Newfoundland and Labrador the safety net of unemployment insurance. Given the climate, much employment is seasonal in nature, and this safety net was welcomed. When it was extended to include fishermen's unemployment insurance, the majority of the population was spared the hardships which earlier generations had endured.

Working in paid employment for part of the year to receive federal transfer payments during the remainder became a standard, and accepted, employment pattern. Although many people became unemployed for part of every year, as illustrated by our perennially high unemployment rates, seasonal workers incorporated government income support into their perception of themselves as self-reliant people. While economists coined the term 'transfer dependency', and the statistical picture of our per capita income appeared dismal, in reality many people were far better off than their mainland counterparts because their seasonal employment left leeway for growing vegetables, hunting, cutting wood and building houses.

In 1992, the catastrophic decline of the staple northern cod stock, and the federal government's subsequent declaration of a moratorium on the cod fishery, dramatically escalated the province's dependency upon federal fiscal support. The timing could not have been worse. Canada is operating under a large financial deficit, as are most of the industrialized nations, and federal government impetus is toward cutting costs. According to Welton, 'Balance the budget is the neo-conservative mantra, chanted over and over again in corporate boardrooms and political backrooms.'[1]

The province has:[2]

- the highest unemployment rate in the country;
- the lowest personal disposable income per person;
- the highest illiteracy rate;
- nearly the greatest proportion of undereducated unemployed people;
- the greatest dependency on federal transfer payments as a source of provincial revenue and personal income.

Given this state of affairs, it is not surprising that a sense of urgency has arisen in the province toward evoking economic development. In 1992, the provincial government produced a strategic economic plan entitled *Change and Challenge*.[3] As does most recent global economic development rhetoric, it proclaimed human resource development, through education and training of a technologically adept and competitive work-force, to be 'key' to prosperity. In fact, there is good reason for concern about educational attainment in our population. In 1989, the Survey of Literacy Skills Used in Daily Activities[4] reported that 'Newfoundland registers the lowest estimated skill levels. Almost a quarter of its adult population has limited reading skills and only 39 per cent have skills sufficient to meet most everyday requirements. This compares to 16 and 62 per cent of the national population respectively.'

Under-education of the province's population is due to two main factors:

• Rural residents traditionally worked in the fishing sector, where high educational attainment was not required to gain employment or make a substantial income. Thus education has not been valued as a tool for survival.
• Lack of diversification in the economy has resulted in a high rate of out-migration among the province's best educated young people.[5]

The 'new' regional economic development planning: economic restructuring

Government structure in the province comprises three levels of operation: federal, provincial and municipal. (It does not include a regional level of authority.) Consequently, government economic development intervention has been conducted to varying degrees at these three levels. In addition, non-governmental organizations, including some 58 Regional Development Associations, received public funding over the past three decades to work at a local or community level. The result of this mix has been a plethora of non-integrated, largely un-coordinated programmes and projects, all intended to evoke economic development within the province. While there have been many success stories, the results have not been as impressive as the amounts of money spent.

In the 45 years since confederation, Newfoundland and Labrador have been assimilated into the Canadian welfare state, with Ottawa (the federal capital of Canada) situated firmly as the source of transfer payment and developer of programmes aimed at solving our economic problems. The locus of control has been very much 'top-down'. According to Welton, overall in the country ordinary people and communities were transformed into clients who required their needs, experiences and life problems to be interpreted for them.[6]

A shift in this approach started when the 1992 provincial Strategic Economic Plan introduced a new concept for economic management of the province – the establishment of zones of economic planning. Inspired by the government's Strategic Economic Plan to non-governmental 'umbrella' organizations, the Newfoundland and Labrador Rural Development Council and the provincial Federation of Municipalities jointly requested the Community Economic Development (CED) Task Force's intervention in 1994. Through a public hearing process, the task force consulted widely throughout the province. Its report[7] made various recommendations regarding the establishment of the economic zones. The government largely accepted those recommendations and a process is now under way to make the zones operational.

That process is very much intended to be a 'bottom-up' approach, as is characteristic of community economic development. The recommendation of the CED Task Force, derived from feedback from the community development organizations and agencies in the field, was that an interim structure, or 'provisional board', be formed from existing groups and agencies to determine the structure of the permanent Regional Economic Development Board (REDB) in each zone. The provisional board comprised representation of the lead community-based organizations, education and training institutions, women's groups, youth, labour and other key stakeholders appropriate to the characteristics of each zone.

By May 1996 eighteen of these Provisional Boards had formed and identified the structure of their respective permanent REDBs, and the democratic process by which they were to be selected, based on the following principles (recommended by the CED Task Force):

- to recognize existing regional development groups, with their accumulated experience and committed volunteers;
- to include municipalities, with their democratic legitimacy, local taxation and regulatory powers, and human and physical resources;
- to encourage and support business and labour representation to link regional development to enterprise development and commercialization;
- to integrate education and training institutions with zonal approaches;
- to recognize the principle of gender equity.

These permanent REDBs have been mandated the following leadership functions:

- to develop and implement zonal strategic economic plans;
- to co-ordinate business development support for small investments;
- to support organizations and communities within the zone;
- to co-ordinate all social and economic initiatives relating to regional economic development in the zone;
- to promote public participation and community education.

The REDBs will negotiate performance contracts with federal and provincial governments to improve efficiency and flexibility, while assuming local control and accountability.

Integration of education and training

Concurrent with the establishment of the economic zones, the former Economic Recovery Commission (now subsumed in the new Department of Development and Rural Renewal) developed a 'postsecondary education and training strategy for economic development', entitled *Education and Economic Zones: Partnerships in Self-Reliance*.[8] That document

put forth an action plan for integrating education and training interventions into economic restructuring through the zonal process. Long-
term job creation will require economic diversification and sectoral growth.
These, however, will be contingent upon the development of human and
physical capital through the investment of time, effort and money in a
climate where there is an expectation, will and commitment to change.

The vision of the education strategy was stated as 'sustainable economic development by individuals who have the knowledge and skills,
and are empowered, to participate collectively in attaining the self-reliance
of their communities'. This was to be achieved through three primary
goals which focus upon democratic participation, employment and entrepreneurial culture, stated as follows:

- a population empowered and possessing the skills to participate democratically and collectively in achieving the self-reliance of their communities;
- an entrepreneurial base from which regional development opportunities can be realized through new business growth in new sectors and
  value-added growth in the traditional sectors;
- a workforce with the full spectrum of workplace skills from basic
  employability skills and technological literacy to technological excellence
  and innovation, matched to the economic development objectives of
  the province and its regions in the context of a global economy.

It is not surprising for adult educators that adult literacy and community education are identified as routes to public participation in regional
economic development. This is consistent with what Welton terms the
social-democratic tradition of adult education, committed to 'the notion
that individuals belong together as sharers of a common fate'. The other
two goals are more in keeping with what he terms the 'learning for
earning bandwagon'.[9]

Though none of the strategic goals, objectives, targets or action items
is individually surprising or strange, what is unique to our situation is the
process we recommended for connecting education and training to strategic regional development through government-supported zonal activities. In 1996–97, the democratically selected REDBs, on which education
representatives are voting members, will develop strategic economic plans
for each zone. These REDBs and their strategic plans will provide the
means by which new partnerships can be activated to provide services
and stimulate economic growth. Representation and participation of the
education and training system in development and implementation of
strategic economic plans will make the task of identifying local skills gaps
a more straightforward event than it is presently, and will allow educational institutions to be more responsive and flexible in their approach to
skill building. Of even greater significance is the inclusive, participatory

nature of the strategic planning process itself. Empowerment for demo-cratic participation in collective visioning and planning is a key area where adult educators can, and indeed must, contribute in this province.

The province has a well-developed post-secondary (tertiary) education system, comprising a university, five colleges of applied arts, technology and continuing education (which are about to be amalgamated into one multi-campused institution) and numerous private training institutions. In addition, the fisheries union operates adult learning centres with various community-based volunteer literacy programmes. This system has the capacity to provide training for new economic growth areas and regional economic development. Until now, however, that training has been deliv-ered on an ad hoc basis with no guarantee that it will result in employment. Although training and retraining have been promoted as an adjustment mechanism to displaced fisheries workers, a question commonly asked is, 'Training for what?' – there are no jobs. The rural economy, which relied heavily upon the fishery, is not sufficiently diversified to employ graduates of the many training opportunities which exist in the province. Education and training activity, from basic skills to advanced training programmes, has been preparing people more adequately to leave than to stay. It has been focused upon altering the labour supply by increasing skill levels, in the absence of interventions to alter the demand for skilled labour.

However, one hopes that zonal strategic planning will permit the training of individuals to be connected to the collective economic aspirations of the zone via work experience, job creation and business development programmes. If zonal plans call for sectoral diversification, new training programmes can be developed involving the appropriate industrial stake-holder in the design phase. There is the potential for work experience, job creation and self-employment programmes to be used to support students and graduates to make workplace transitions in line with planned eco-nomic activity. Educational institutions could even establish training busi-nesses and co-operatives to provide work experience in support of planned development. Business development programmes could make support contingent upon appropriate training. The REDBs' mandated role in co-ordination of social and economic initiatives related to regional economic development in the zone make them ideal counterparts for other agencies with provincial mandates and regional responsibilities. Here also is an venue for adult educators to deal with the challenge Welton identifies – of figuring out 'imaginatively and creatively, how we can transform the meaning of "job" ... into "worthwhile activity" (producing goods and services for others that sustain life and foster solidarity)'.[10]

Fulfilling their mandated functions in strategic planning, co-ordination of social and economic initiatives and promotion of public participation and community education will involve the REDBs in several sets of activities which pertain directly to education and training:

- Given the need for a zonal strategic plan, the Boards will have to assess readiness and availability of local expertise to prepare the zone's plan, and if there is sufficient expertise, create strategic economic plans (or refine and consolidate plans already made);
- if there is insufficient expertise, or if residents are not ready, start where people are, arrange for community development work, arrange training of planners, and then plan.
- The Boards will create zonal strategic economic plans which focus on the full range of activities and human resources required to allow sustainable development and community/regional prosperity.

Given these regional strategic plans, the Boards will have to:

- identify the human resource development requirements to achieve their goals through projects outlined in the plan;
- develop an inventory of the human resources which the zones presently have;
- identify gaps in human resource capacity;
- ensure the availability of appropriate training to fill these gaps, given the needs of the individuals who are available and recruited. A full range of training, from basic skills and academic upgrading to technological training may be required and various sources of training will have to be considered;
- link work experience, job creation, business development funding (and support) and education such that transition from training to work is smooth, swift, co-ordinated and consistent with the zonal plan.

However, the REDBs will have to function within the context of provincial and federal government structures. While these volunteer, community-based zone boards will provide the ideal opportunity and mechanism for integrated action, they will not be able to accomplish it without the co-operation and support of government agencies. Direct support to establish and set up operations is being extended to the REDBs through the Department of Development and Rural Renewal (DDRR), supported by a federal-provincial Co-operation Agreement on Strategic Regional Diversification. DDRR support includes information dissemination, facilitation, performance contract development, workshop delivery and liaison between various stakeholders. Within DDRR, staff have been allocated specifically to support the type of zonal connections and education linkages put forth in the education strategy.

The long-term success of economic management at the zonal level is contingent, however, upon the support and co-ordination of central government structures. Each provincial agency has been asked to examine the way it does business, and to adopt policies that will facilitate the operation of the zones and effectively support regional economic development.

Evaluation

Measuring the contribution of education and training to regional economic development cannot be straightforward because of the multi-dimensional nature of the relationship. While clear objectives were stated for the education strategy, there are many variables outside the control of the education and training system which can influence attainment of those objectives. However, DDRR is in the process of setting up an evaluation framework for monitoring the performance of the zones. It will include:

- collecting aggregate economic development data to portray the state of the province's and each zone's economy;
- tracking 'inputs' identified by government and REDBs to implement zonal strategic plans;
- tracking 'outputs' or strategic activities proposed in zonal plans; and
- determining 'outcomes' of those strategic activities reflected by their effectiveness in attaining the goals and objectives put forth in zonal strategic plans.

This four-tiered evaluation framework should yield rich qualitative and quantitative data to increase our understanding of the role of education and training in regional economic development. We feel that the relationship between education and other components of regional development is more likely to be synergistic than 'cause and effect', with the total impact of our integrated approach being greater than the sum of the individual parts.

Aggregate economic development data

We are in the process of identifying indicators which should be observed over the long term. Given the increasing sophistication of geographic information management capacity within the province, we will be able to analyse a composite statistical picture on a zonal basis. Quantitative indicators which are likely to be followed include measures of growth, capacity development (individual, community and business), and entrepreneurship development, such as earned income per person, employment–population ratio, unemployment rate, quality of human resources (e.g. labour costs), cost of production input (e.g. energy costs), job creation, competitive level of firms (e.g. profit margins), enterprise creation, self-employment, propensity to export, capital formation, application of new technologies, infrastructure development, rate of small business growth, primary/elementary/secondary education attainment, adult literacy rate, tertiary (post-secondary) attainment, graduate follow-up, employment in field of study, migration by education level and age, and skill shortages.

Inputs

The role of REDBs and government in supporting the development and creation of zone strategic economic plans will be defined through performance contracts negotiated between the two parties. In negotiating the contract, both parties will identify what they will contribute toward implementing the zone's strategic economic plan. If an event fails to happen as planned, the monitoring and evaluation process should be able to identify whether either of the parties did not contribute their planned share.

Outputs

The performance contracts will identify up-front the outputs, or short-term results expected from each input. Where low education levels and/or skill shortages are targeted for action in zone strategic plans, associated inputs and outputs are likely to be identified.

Outcomes

Each of the strategic activities or economic initiatives identified in a zone's strategic plan is to be evaluated in terms of its long-term effectiveness in achieving the objectives and goals identified in the zone's plan. As each activity is initiated, its evaluation is to be designed as an integral feature of the development process. The process will likely comprise identifying goals and desired outcomes; then assessing process, actual outcomes and long-term impact. Appropriate instruments will be administered to the stakeholders involved. Such evaluations are to be conducted not only by funding agencies, but also by the communities in which they have occurred, so that both parties can make use of the information in the ongoing monitoring and evaluation of zonal strategic economic plans. Where training or development of adequate skill levels is a contingency in the success of such initiatives, information on the relationship between education or training and economic development will be revealed by the evaluation process.

Conclusion

There is no doubt that this small, peripheral province faces unheralded change. The present economic crisis can be interpreted as disaster or as opportunity. By embracing change, one can seize the opportunity. This paper has described the attempt to build on the strengths in new ways, suited to new times. Never has the need for concerted action been so clear.

Notes

1. Welton, Chapter 3 in this volume.
2. Statistics Canada 1994.
3. Government of Newfoundland and Labrador 1992.
4. Statistics Canada 1991.
5. Statistics Canada 1993.
6. Welton, Chapter 3 in this volume.
7. CED Task Force 1995.
8. Economic Recovery Commission 1995.
9. Welton, Chapter 3 in this volume.
10. Welton, Chapter 3 in this volume.

References

CED Task Force (1995) *Community Matters: The New Regional Economic Development, Report of the Task Force on Community Economic Development in Newfoundland and Labrador*, St John's, Newfoundland.

Economic Recovery Commission (1995) *Education and Economic Zones: Partnerships in Self-Reliance*, St John's, Newfoundland.

Government of Newfoundland and Labrador (1992) *Change and Challenge: A Strategic Economic Plan for Newfoundland and Labrador*, St John's, Newfoundland.

Statistics Canada (1993) Catalogue 93–322.

Statistics Canada (1994) Catalogues 13–213, 71–220.

Statistics Canada (1991) *Adult Literacy in Canada: Results of a National Study*, Ottawa: Ministry of Industry, Science and Technology.

12

ETDP: Passing Fad or New Identity?

Jeanne Gamble and Shirley Walters

Liberated from the shackles of the apartheid era, South Africa has joined
the global quest for the simultaneous achievement of social equity and
economic development. Our labour movements are arguing for growth
through redistribution, our employers are arguing that redistribution will
only occur though growth, whilst amongst policy-makers there is a
heightened awareness of the complex interface between political, social
and economic issues. Whichever way round the argument is made, all
are in agreement that general education and training are essential
developmental ingredients. An integrated approach to education and
training has become the cornerstone of education and training policy,
with a proposed National Qualifications Framework (NQF) as the
operationalizing instrument.

None of this is particularly new or unique to South Africa. Global
conditions of increased knowledge production and wider and faster knowledge dissemination have shifted power relations and problematized the
rules of knowledge production so that it is no longer the precinct of the
academy or of specialist cadres. Users or consumers of knowledge are
now participants in the production process, albeit not as technical ex-
perts but as those to whom knowledge-makers are accountable in social
and political terms. The collapse of mental/manual divides and shifts in
the social distribution of knowledge are also leading to increased
massification in the demand for educational and training opportunities.

What is perhaps unique to South Africa is the momentum given to
transformation by the collapse of the apartheid state. It is not only driven
by state initiatives such as the Reconstruction and Development Programme (RDP) and private-sector determination to enter global markets;
it also draws on the energy of millions of people who suffered under
apartheid and who fought for its demise. That energy has not dissipated,
the memory of the power of mass mobilization is recent and the stern

agendas facing policy-makers in all terrains need to meet both social and economic expectations.

In the next sections we will briefly sketch one of the key policy processes. We will present examples of different ideological interpretations before considering the implications for education and training practices, and for the preparation and development of those who mediate the learning of others.

Moving towards 'integration'

One of the initial policy forums functioned under the auspices of a state structure called the National Training Board.[1] The process which began in 1993, a few months before the first election of a Government of National Unity, was initially located within a training (or vocational) context. Four stakeholder groupings, of which two were accustomed to bargain against each other in an industrial relations framework, entered the process with sets of concerns relating to their constituencies.

Given the particular moment in the history of our country, the state grouping was a particularly complex configuration. The official state representatives represented the 'old' state, while the shadow state representatives came in under the ANC–Cosatu alliance.[2] While the latter grouping therefore did not officially represent the state, their concerns (many of which were shared by the official state representatives) were a dominant agenda. Any new training strategy should address the twin concerns of economic reconstruction and growth within globally competitive markets, leading to active labour market policies, while at the same time correcting past injustices and inequities in the domain of learning provisioning. Employers shared the concern about economic growth and the capacity for global competitiveness, with particular emphasis on the need to improve productivity through worker training.

Labour concerns (driven by Cosatu representatives) revolved around the need for employment security and employment growth for their members, as well as the need for career paths that would be opened up by access to training and development opportunities. They strongly articulated a need for the provision of Adult Basic Education as the foundation for further formal or accredited learning.

Education and training providers were concerned about the fragmented nature of learning systems that prevented the possibility of continuous learning pathways, as well as the impact that an integrated approach would have on curriculum shifts and the competence of the people currently teaching or instructing learners.

These four sets of concerns interacted in both complementary and contradictory ways to shift the debate from a concern about vocational training, to a broader conception of vocational education and training, to an integrated approach to all activities and systems currently classified as education and training. A National Qualifications Framework was proposed as the integrating and regulatory mechanism that would bring cohesion to current learning systems and practices, and simultaneously transform these systems and practices.

Even in the conceptual stages it was recognized that the training of trainers would be an important aspect of any transformation attempt. A committee was given the task of developing a strategy to improve the quality of training provision by recommending measures to improve the competence of trainers.

As the argument for an integrated approach to education and training started to unfold, it was no longer possible to talk only about trainers. A concept was required that could cover the educators/trainers/teachers/ facilitators/instructors in industrial and commercial workplaces, non-governmental organizations, community-based organizations, technical schools and colleges, community colleges, industry training boards, regional training centres, state departments, technikons and universities.

The tongue-twisting term Education, Training and Development Practitioner (quickly reduced to ETDP) was coined for a number of reasons:

- It made it possible to talk to and about a broad range of people who mediate learning in some form or other, without giving offence to any particular grouping.
- It intended to signal inclusivity rather than exclusivity.
- It reflected the policy-makers' intent of bringing about articulation of different forms of learning provision in one coherent system.
- It referred to something new, something emergent, something future-oriented.

Those responsible for making the term held the view that each field of practice contains sufficient elements of the other to enable these elements to be brought into closer proximity. This would establish a common base for practitioner progression and development, although it was recognized that there would never be a total overlapping of fields. They argued for a baseline of core competence in three areas:

- occupational or subject-matter expertise;
- broader contextual understanding;
- expertise in education, training and development and the facilitation of learning.

These were more crudely framed as the *what*, the *why* and the *how*, with further role specialization across ten common roles, namely administrator, assessor, designer of learning experiences, developer of learning materials, evaluator, facilitator of one-on-one learning, facilitator of group learning, manager, needs analyst and strategist.[3] The model made provision for full-time practitioners and those who perform ETD work as a part-job activity, as in the case of community workers and workplace mentors.

Perhaps not unsurprisingly the notion of an ETD practitioner found immediate ideological and market currency. Some people started referring to their practices as ETD practices and calling themselves ETD practitioners. Some provider institutions re-labelled their courses as certificates, diplomas or degrees in ETD. Some people smiled sceptically and ignored the debates. Many have not heard of the term.

Are boundaries so easily crossed?

The coining of a term does not change the ways in which social meanings are generated. The worlds of education, training and development have traditionally been far apart. Although there are many 'form' similarities at the level of activity, these practices are institutionally apart; they have different social functions and purposes; they are subject to different pressures and constraints; and they are embedded in different philosophical traditions.

At a colloquium hosted by the Centre for Adult and Continuing Education (CACE) of the University of the Western Cape in 1994, these differences came to the fore when four speakers gave their views on what 'integration' meant to them.[4]

Zweli Nokhatywa comes from an adult education centre based in an impoverished, sprawling township which lies on the outskirts of Cape Town. He works part-time in a poorly resourced 'night school' which provides school equivalent classes for adults in the evening. He spoke about the needs of his learners.

> People should also get skills to be independent and self-reliant.... There needs to be a centre which will offer skills training, including things like spray-painting, sewing, typing, business skills, mechanical skills, running meetings and so on. We need to be able to improve our contributions at home, work, and at meetings.

He emphasized the need for formal school-equivalent education, vocational skills training for the informal and formal economy, and skills for community management. He was acutely aware of the fullness and complexity of poor people's lives and that 'integration' should mean taking account of people's education and training needs at home, at work and in the community. He was particularly concerned with redress for the apartheid past and economic survival.

Ralph Alexander is a trade unionist who works in a textile factory. He identified the need for workplace education and training to enable workers to have greater career mobility. The recognition of prior learning was important, as few workers had high levels of formal schooling; but he also argued that formal schooling opportunities for families of workers was crucial. His presentation also reflected concern with issues of redress, social equity and economic competitiveness.

> We need people to participate in the development of the country and we must have realistic requirements and find ways of accrediting people for the skills they already have. We also need to look at paid time for education ... People have families and that has to be taken into account, and training should happen at times appropriate for workers.

From the side of the employers, Peter Riches of the Clothing Industry Training Board outlined some of the philosophical assumptions that underlie their commitment to 'integration'.

> Any industry that wishes to stay in business must achieve a state of international competitiveness, and to do this they must have skills to put a product on the market at the right place, time, etc. The primary reason is to increase profits, but a secondary reason is to increase economic growth and improve the living standards of everyone in the country. The purpose of working is to enjoy a standard of living – we wish to raise it for all. The RDP is geared to that.

Chris Winberg, an educator from an Adult Basic Education and Training (ABET) NGO expressed a more elaborated view on 'integration' when describing a course for ABET practitioners which she and her colleagues were piloting, using the ETD practitioner model outlined as a framework.

They attempted to answer the question: What do a literacy teacher, a health educator and a clothing industry instructor have in common? They identified nine areas of competence required of all ETD practitioners regardless of their work sites. These areas were: learning skills; language and communication skills; theorizing adult learning; contextual understanding; administrative skills; teaching/facilitating skills; assessment skills; evaluation skills; and subject/content knowledge. They argued that outcomes or areas of competence did not operate independently of one another and that each comprised affective, cognitive and practical or behavioural aspects.

While the last example focuses on curriculum issues and the previous three on the outcomes of learning, differences in discursive framing emerge clearly. When one asks a general question about effectiveness, without distinguishing that which makes a practice qualitatively meaningful, criteria for evaluation become generic in nature and unlocated in either a site of practice or in a system of learning, such as ABET, technical training or health education. Effectiveness thus becomes decontextualized in a professional sense.

As soon as one asks the 'effectiveness for what?' question, the generic utopia starts to crumble and different social functions of learning, as indicated by the first three speakers, come to the fore. While practitioners from a diverse range of practices may well engage in similar role activities, one cannot argue that a practice is a practice is a practice. Practices do not fulfil the same social functions, nor are they accountable to the same norms and values. Practices are embedded in institutions which enact or represent philosophical or moral traditions and values developed over time. Such traditions provide the institution with a set of identities that enable continuity and stability, and provide principles for 'good' practice. They also constitute that which is deemed worthy of protection or retention. Changes facing institutions may be in harmony or in conflict with historical traditions and practices, and may therefore be strategically embraced or resisted.

It becomes clear that a term such as ETDP cannot suddenly be inserted into restructuring debates like a magic wand which will transform pumpkins into coaches, as in a fairy tale that some of us remember from childhood. The term may carry symbolic value for some, but it is clearly a construct with both transformative and obfuscating potential.

Yet, before coming to the gloomy conclusion that this particular reform initiative is doomed to failure, we need to consider the structural conditions of the future. Two major areas of change lie ahead: institutional change and labour market shifts.

Institutional change

All providers of learning opportunities are faced with some of the following:

- An increasing demand for formal value in the form of accreditation and therefore a requirement for formal assessment.
- New forms of (multi-)accountability in response to demands for participation by broad and inclusive stakeholder groupings as well as demands for a downward devolution of authority to provinces, regions, localities, institutions and communities.
- A shift in learner groupings with a greater demand for access and greater emphasis on foundational education, perhaps better expressed as a demand for greater social distribution of the ETD 'product'.
- The impact of information systems technology and the possibility of larger classes with a combination of modes of delivery, for example, 'dual modes' or a combination of contact teaching and independent study; 'mixed modes' where an integration of contact teaching and distance education means less teaching and more self-study materials and tutorial support.

- Greater rationalization of resources. Some institutions and organizations are privatizing or closing down their ETD practices. Others are growing and centralizing or specializing.
- Shifts in job and role demarcations. Certain jobs and functions are disappearing and others are emerging.

Labour-market shifts

It is a well-known reality that jobs are becoming scarcer. Practitioners are increasingly seeking to cross from one ETD sector to another. ETD practitioners are usually employed in one of four types of jobs:

- Permanent full-time jobs with annual notch and merit salary increases and subsidized fringe benefits, such as medical aid and pension. Progression is often equated with promotion on an institutional hierarchy ladder. Promotion may offer scope for job enhancement.
- Temporary full-time jobs on a contract basis, either within existing salary and conditions of service policies or by individual negotiation. Incumbents of such positions are not eligible for promotion and job continuity is uncertain and usually dependent on funding considerations.
- Short-term specialized contract jobs in a piece-work system. Practitioners may work as professional consultants, or they may simply try to make a living by taking on whatever they can find.
- ETD work as a part-job activity. This occurs when teaching or facilitation of learning entails a passing on of accumulated knowledge or wisdom gained in the primary or encompassing role. Examples are: an artisan or supervisor who is also a trainer or coach; a manager who is also a mentor; an administrator who is also responsible for staff development; an academic who also teaches.

Global trends increasingly forecast a reduction in the permanent workforce and a shift to peripheral and occasional or seasonal work. It is reasonable to assume that the ETD fields will not escape these labour-market shifts, despite the emphasis on life-long learning and continuing education. Teaching (in many sectors) is increasingly being framed as part of another job or role or identity, with the exception perhaps found in the university sector where certain forms of teaching are becoming specialized and detached from research. A remedy is required if we are not to become extinct as a species.

These two sets of structural conditions bring a new generic ETD identity within the realms of possibility. While conditions of uncertainty do not eradicate differences in social goal and function, they become decisive factors in themselves. Flexibility across boundaries of established knowledge domains is what is required. Being specialized under the authority claim of a particular discipline or field of expertise is no longer sufficient. Flexibility requires individuals to be proficient across a wide range of knowledge and skill areas, thus increasing capacity to deal with unpredictability. 'Professional status', as a power mechanism, has the capacity to bestow authority and legitimacy on threatened occupations. The pervasive claim to professional status linked to an increased demand for flexibility may well provide the conditions under which the ETDP may flourish and grow, despite the very real differences in both the form and function of different ETD practices.

As long as we do not attempt to collapse the boundaries between practices or fall into the trap of believing that generic competencies are a universal panacea, we may well succeed in developing a cadre of practitioners who can 'live in the gaps' between traditions and sectors of education, training and development. New conditions of alignment will emerge, calling for multiple identities. At times ETDPs are likely to align themselves professionally, at times politically and at times sectorally. The ETDP may well turn out to be, not a passing fad, but an identity that meets the structural requirements of late modernity.

Notes

1. It should be borne in mind that the National Training Board process was only one of many processes that were taking place simultaneously or in succession.

2. We refer here to the tripartite alliance between the African National Congress (ANC), the Congress of South African Trade Unions (Cosatu) and the South African Communist Party (SACP).

3. In the conceptual model these roles were listed in alphabetical order to avoid a hierarchy that poses administrative work as a lower order activity and management or strategic work as a higher order. It was also recognized that the roles are inter-related and seldom performed in isolation.

4. CACE 1995.

References

CACE (1995) *Integrating Adult Education and Training: Possibilities and Constraints*, CACE Publications, UWC, Bellville.

13

The NQF, Reconstruction and Development

Rosemary Lugg

Since 1994, in South Africa, there has been intense discussion about the establishment of a National Qualifications Framework (NQF). While the argument has been that it is an important mechanism in the attempt to achieve equity and redress, there is a counter-argument that this will not be possible. The questions thus remain. Can the NQF be a progressive educational instrument to achieve equity and redress, or is it by its nature conservative and exclusive? Will it work for or against reconstruction and development? There are ongoing debates amongst South Africans as they grapple with international practices and relate them to their own conditions.

This chapter describes important issues and one of the initial attempts towards the construction of the NQF. In general, there is increasing acknowledgement amongst educators and trainers that the NQF can work for or against reconstruction and development. It is not inherently radical or conservative but is a social construct which can be shaped in a variety of ways. The development of the NQF is being approached in a holistic way to cover general education and vocational training. In many countries, the NQF has a narrow vocational orientation.

In passing the South African Qualifications Authority (SAQA) Act (1995), the South African government has made provision for this new qualifications framework, anticipating that it will enable the transformation of the education and training systems through the redistribution and recognition of knowledge and skills.[1]

The SAQA Act provides brief, broad definitions for a few specific aspects of the proposed framework, but responsibility for the detailed development of the NQF lies with SAQA. Even so, various documents have already explored ideas around how the NQF might eventually work.

During South African education and training policy development processes, the role of an NQF in reconstruction and development gained support from various, often competing, discourses, as demonstrated by the collaboration of different interest groups in, for example, the National Training Strategy Initiative process and the Human Sciences Research Council (HSRC) process. McGrath, who has used a 'series of discourses' to interpret the 'development of education and training policy and practice since the 1994 elections' states that:

> it appears that there is a large amount of apparent convergence around a series of themes. Included amongst such themes are the prevalence of rapid and transformatory technological change; the need to move towards a high skill economy with multi-skilled workers; the need for career paths for lifelong learners and the need for an integrated approach to education and training. However, the use of the framework of discourses through which the data has been viewed points to the different meanings and potential implications many of these consensus terms display.[2]

He goes on to suggest that:

> Whilst the official discourse seems to reflect an uneasy and potentially unstable alliance between interventionist and fast capitalist discourses, it is evident [that] market-orientation and legitimization crisis accounts remain as counter-hegemonic visions which, for good or ill, have the potential to challenge or even derail elements of the official vision as it seeks to become inscribed in practices.[3]

The implication of McGrath's warning is that as SAQA moves from policy development to implementation, the superficial nature of the consensus around the form and function of the NQF is likely to become evident, and could derail the vision of the NQF as a tool for transformation. Consequently, careful deliberation about the models that are proposed for the NQF will be necessary. SAQA will have to work to understand the implications of the superficial consensus around terminology, to ensure that the models proposed are appropriate to South African learning contexts and that they will, in practice, actually embody the vision of the NQF. Furthermore, we need to consider how particular models might constrain learning and the recognition of learning. That is, we need to be concerned about the forms of knowledge that could end up excluded from, and subsequently marginalized by, the spaces created by the NQF.

This paper explores some of the ideas that came out of one particular NQF-oriented process which resulted in the HSRC document entitled *Ways of Seeing the National Qualifications Framework*.[4] The HSRC document examines how constructs of the NQF might aid or retard reconstruction and development. It argues that adult educators will be crucial in ensuring that the NQF is able to make a difference in people's lives. Educators will be charged with turning the ideals of the NQF into real learning and assessment experiences for people.

Some proposals for the NQF

The Human Sciences Research Council workshops based their work on
the proposals outlined by the national Department of Education[5] and the
National Training Board,[6] and drew heavily on the experiences and ideas
of the workshops participants as well.

Levels

The NQF is envisioned to constitute eight levels, with the first level
being equivalent to a school-leaving certificate after ten years of schooling.

Given that many children and an estimated 15 million adults fall below this level of formal education, an NQF that begins with the General
Education Certificate leaves out the majority of the South African population. Debate within SAQA[7] has been intense, but the current compromise seems to be that level 1 may be made up of three 'sub-levels' for
adult basic education and training (ABET).

The NQF levels have been approximately linked to current levels in
the education system, across three broad bands: General, Further and
Higher Education and Training.[8]

Qualifications

The SAQA Act states that the NQF will register national standards and
qualifications.[9] The HSRC document has proposed that the combinations
of units that make up a qualification should be informed by agreed
understandings of quality learning and the purposes of the learning initiative, so that qualifications can support the NQF objective of improving the quality of learning.

Standards

The SAQA Act defines standards as 'registered statements of desired
education and training outcomes and their associated assessment criteria'.[10] This suggests that a person could gain recognition for a national
standard through demonstrating the desired outcomes during a formal
assessment.

Given that the NQF is committed to facilitating access to the learning
system, it is suggested that standards should not indicate where the learning must happen. This allows for an open learning system and the Recognition of Prior Learning (RPL) assessment processes as strategies to
enable access to the learning system.[11] The NQF cannot contribute to
reconstruction and development if people do not have access to learning
and assessment opportunities.

An integrated qualifications framework

The NQF is intended to 'create an integrated national framework for learning achievements',[12] and to achieve this through common approaches to accreditation. A single approach to accreditation could enable learning credits to be portable across the previous systemic divides in education and training, making learners far more mobile within the education and training systems. Second, integration with increased mobility could open up more diverse learning pathways for learners. Third, integration could make more sense from a 'knowledge construction' perspective, as people would gain access to learning opportunities in which both content and skills were developed. Finally, integration is advocated as one way to remove the historical gap between 'masters' and 'slaves' perpetuated in our society through separating education (for thinkers) and training (for workers).[13]

The challenge of developing an integrated approach to the national framework for learning achievements (the NQF) could start with exploring a new understanding of learning. It may be that such an understanding of learning could even challenge the claim that we can articulate diversity in learning experience and encourage mobility and progression, through a single accreditation system with its fascination 'with the false sciences of measurability, predictability and standardization of individual skills development as the means to dynamic, innovative and creatively new learning processes'.[14]

The NQF and the risk of separating assessment from learning

Given that the NQF will register 'education and training outcomes and their associated assessment criteria',[15] it will be an accreditation framework that is based on the assessment of learning outcomes. Usually assessment involves the judgement of some kind of performance that is demanded of the person seeking accreditation. By seeking to recognize 'learning achievements',[16] but by setting these as outcomes demonstrated by performance, the NQF creates an uneasy tension.

Why should we attempt to hold the tension? It is argued that in an outcomes-based approach, learning to perform is an issue to consider in curriculum development. The role of the NQF is to accredit expert or competent performance; responsibility for developing the learning pathways that will lead to these outcomes is allocated with curriculum developers and educators.[17]

It is critical to balance the tension between learning and performance within our conceptualizations of the NQF itself. This balance is essential if the NQF is to achieve its own aims of integration of education and training, improved quality of learning and of progression for learners through learning pathways,[18] particularly since outcomes-based approaches have tended to become narrow and reductionist forms of learning in the past.

Marginson warns that frameworks which are concerned with measuring observed performance only serve the interests of those who demand the performance, for example assessors or employers. He describes the conflict as being between

> the view that the student is the learning subject with the goal of empowering the student and the view that the student is the object of education with the goal of meeting the needs of employers. By establishing a work-based competencies framework, and adhering to the vocational orientation through the measurement of performance and a ladder of standards, competency-based education resolved this conflict decisively in favour of the needs of employers and the student-as-object.[19]

Marginson's comments suggest that a mono-purpose, performance-based approach to the NQF cannot serve the interests of the learners as well.

Removing responsibility for learning from the NQF undermines completely the principles of progression and portability that are claimed for the NQF. Learning abilities make it possible for learners to progress through the NQF pathways; without their own control of these abilities, people could get stuck at their current level of learning.

> Transfer happens in the activity of learning itself. It relies on learners becoming aware of how and why they are employing different abilities during task performance. It also relies on learners being able to read the contexts within which any task or activity is located, and understanding the differences between those contexts.[20]

The crucial question then becomes, 'How can we support learning in plans for an outcomes-based NQF?'

Building a framework that supports learning to perform, as well as performance

The ideas described in the HSRC document suggest that the NQF could support learning in several ways:

- through the understanding of performance developed within the NQF;
- through the formulation for a qualification;
- through the formulation of a unit standard;
- through the notion of levels.

Describing performance

The document describes an understanding of performance that includes reference to the learning processes that may underpin that performance.

Performance is described as evidence of: communication and social interaction; tool usage or dexterity. However, the performance also includes
other, less visible dimensions including:

- the information or content that the performer is using;
- the mental or cognitive abilities (such as problem-posing, analysis and
  synthesis) that are employed to engage with the information;
- the performer's particular value orientation;
- the learning abilities that the performer gained in the process of
  learning how to perform this activity;
- abilities which may be used to transfer the learning to the assessment
  task.[21]

This understanding of performance may offer a model that could
articulate a common accreditation framework, within which both expert
performance and the process of learning to perform could be accommo-
dated. It may also enable a genuinely integrated approach to the NQF.

The identification of both information and tool usage/dexterity within
this description of performance – the stereotypic perceptions of the domains of education and training respectively – begins to move towards an
understanding of an integrated approach for the NQF. However, more
meaningful integration may come from the recognition of the role of
cognitive abilities in performance. The development of cognitive skills is
one of the purposes educators claim for learning. Equally, the workplace
claims to need thinking and flexible workers, and seeks to reform training to achieve this. So it may be that the common concern for cognitive
abilities could provide some common ground in an integrated approach.

There is a significant difference between a common concern for
cognitive abilities across contexts and the comparable use of those abilities
across contexts. The identification of cognitive abilities may serve to
facilitate bureaucratic coherence within the NQF, may indeed support
the learning purpose of the NQF and may encourage an integrated approach to the NQF. However, the use of abilities as 'common currency'
across contexts needs to be cautioned – we cannot easily claim that the
identification of the use of cognitive abilities in different contexts suggests easy mobility for learners across these contexts, or has any meaning
as an indicator of comparability across the contexts.

Wolf warns against making too many assumptions about the transfer-
ability of cognitive skills across contexts. She argues that whilst we may
wish to encourage the development of problem-solving in the workplace
and problem-solving in maths, we cannot assume that the way we solve
maths problems is transferable to workplace problems. 'Drawing
comparisons, thinking about how to encourage problem-solving in a given
context, does not thereby give the construct independent, measurable
life.'[22]

Learning qualifications

The smallest entity that can be assessed and registered on the NQF is the unit standard.[23] Qualifications could support current understandings of quality learning through the combinations of unit standards that have to be met in order to be registered on the NQF. Current proposals for qualifications suggest that they could be made up of units from an appropriate spread across different areas of knowledge. The spread could include areas of learning that are thought to support further learning, that are appropriate to different contexts, as well as those that are specific for the role or context in which the learner is specializing.[24]

The HSRC document has also suggested that in order to qualify, a learner could be required to undertake an integrated assessment activity. The nature of the integrative activity would depend on the qualification sought, but could be something like a portfolio of work, a thesis, or the completion of a crafted masterpiece, such as the creation of a piece of furniture. The integrated assessment should provide the opportunity for the learner to draw on and integrate all the capabilities that he or she has developed through the units that comprise the qualification.[25]

The HSRC document has suggested a format for unit standards, with the intention that a single format could provide coherence in the accreditation system and, through its construction, could facilitate an integrated approach.

Learning and the unit standard

Performance outcomes

Performance outcomes are descriptions of what a person would need to demonstrate in order to gain credit for a unit. It is a description of the communicative and manipulative activities associated with the required performance. Examples of performance outcomes given in the HSRC document include: start, stop, and conduct other equipment-related procedures or operations (industrial context); collect, organize and analyse information (communications field).[26]

The performance outcomes are the manifestation of the NQF as a performance-based framework: these are the particular, desired performances that the NQF sets out to recognize and accredit. Performance outcomes could be selected because they are believed to facilitate economic growth, or the implementation of development projects, or people's participation in political, social and cultural activities. Thus, the NQF might contribute to the reconstruction and development of society through recognizing and valuing particular activities. Inevitably, the relevance and credibility of the standards will be determined by both the composition of the standard-setting bodies and the nature of the standard-setting process. Learners and educators will need to be represented to ensure that the performances that are selected are relevant to their constituents' needs and act in their interests.

Recognizing broader and deeper aspects of performance

In attempting to avoid narrow, reductionist forms of performance outcome, the HSRC document suggests that the unit format deliberately incorporates the more subtle aspects of performance, such as underpinning cognitive skills and underpinning knowledge.

Educators may be able to help standard-setting groups to identify the relevant underpinning knowledge in particular activities, but must be enabled to do this without blindly repeating known syllabi.

Assessment criteria as a source of contextualized abilities

Assessment criteria provide information about the level and kinds of performance that are regarded as acceptable to gain the standard. Often, assessment criteria select aspects of the performance that are indicative that the required standard has been reached, or that are desirable in some way, for example performance accuracy to certain specifications, or within time constraints, or drawing on specific information that is considered significant in that field or subject.

Assessment criteria often have a strong backwash effect on curricula, as knowing the assessment demands can influence how people learn an outcome. Conversely, people often perform better in assessment situations if the assessment processes relate closely to the ways in which they have learned. In recognition of the close link between learning and assessment and a concern that the NQF should be a 'mechanism for the accreditation of assessed learning performance',[27] the HSRC document proposes that assessment criteria could include statements of appropriate contextualized abilities.

Examples of these kinds of assessment criteria are:

- job requirements determined from applicable documentation;
- calculations relating to inputs completed;
- procedure for job planned;
- evidence of systematic problem-solving to rectify common production-related faults during the course of setting up and running;
- information is analysed and organized in a way which is consistent with the performance.[28]

SAQA should explore different understandings of assessment criteria as it may be that different forms of learning or performance need different kinds. The development of assessment criteria is likely to require the participation of people who have an understanding of the learning and performance contexts, of the use of cognitive abilities that are assumed to be involved in the performance activities, and of appropriate assessment processes. A considered approach could enable the NQF to encourage the development of innovative and transformative approaches to assessment.

Range statement

The NQF is intended to ensure that learning credits are portable within the system,[29] but real portability of learning implies transfer. People will only be able to transfer their learning if the learning process is deliberately designed and implemented to support the development of skills that are specific to and necessary for transfer.

Marginson proposes that there are skills specific to transfer itself: 'These skills are generic and include an awareness of context, the capacity to move between different viewpoints, languages and systems of knowledge (which produces flexibility), self-reflection (which encourages adaptability), self-regulation and learning how to learn.'[30] But Marginson notes a concern about assuming transfer and quotes Perkins and Salomon's research:

> To the extent that transfer does take place, it is highly specific and must be cued, primed and guided; it seldom occurs spontaneously. The case for generalizable, context-independent skills and strategies that can be trained in one context and transferred to other domains has proved more a matter of wishful thinking than hard empirical evidence.[31]

If the NQF is intended to support mobility and transfer of learning across contexts, this cannot be achieved merely by noticing that 'the same' cognitive abilities are identified in different contexts and in various unit standards, or that similar performance outcomes are written in different contexts. To assume transfer from the superficiality of neat bureaucratic formats will again disempower learners.

The range statement provides information about the kinds of context in which a particular unit standard might be appropriate. It also gives information about the level of complexity to which this unit standard might be applied and the scope of the unit standard. If range statements are to be used to support the transfer of learning between contexts, range statements must be developed with an understanding of how transfer happens, when and where. This understanding of transfer and of the unit range statements would then need to inform curriculum development and the design of assessment events, in order to impact on learners' development of transfer skills, if the notion of portability is to have meaning.

Implications for adult educators

The implications of the proposals for the NQF for adult educators will be profound. A new accreditation approach is likely to bring with it the need for new curricula and probably new teaching and assessment approaches.

Participation in NQF processes, research and development

Simply developing the NQF and then informing educators about it will not bring about changes in their practice nor in the quality of the learning system. Burns and Hood argue that: 'One of the critical factors in the successful implementation of curriculum change is the systematic involvement through research and professional development of the practitioners who will inevitably play a major role in the delivery of the curriculum.'[32] They go on to cite Fullan who 'warns of the need for ownership of the change by those who are required to implement it and of the need for change to evolve through successive phases of implementation'.[33] The quality of the ultimate learning experiences associated with the NQF will depend, in part, on the involvement of educators in the research, implementation and development phases.

If educators are to engage with and be a part of the developing debate and research that will shape the NQF, their participation will require government advocacy, the allocation of resources and structures, and their professional development for full and informed participation. It will also require the educators' commitment to the processes involved.

Professional development and new roles

Burns and Hood state that a 'top-down' imposition of new curriculum frameworks or guidelines is particularly inappropriate where the educator has had 'little or no previous contact with, or understanding of, the theoretical bases implicit in the documents and is given little or no professional support for their implementation in the classroom'.[34]

For many South African educators the theoretical bases underpinning the proposals for the NQF are unfamiliar and unexplored. Clearly, professional development is essential for educators if they are to engage fully with new proposals, participate in the policy development process, and collaborate in action research throughout implementation. This is particularly important given Burns and Hood's observation that the educators in their study 'draw in significant ways on their own underlying theories, principles and beliefs about teaching and learning in their efforts to develop effective strategies to implement competency-based programming, and to take into account the ... needs of their learners'.[35]

Burns and Hood stress that 'organizational support for research and professional development which is intimately associated with classroom implementation, are crucial factors in achieving effective curriculum change and ultimately educational quality'.[36]

The professional development of educators will be critical as the development of new, integrative approaches to learning will bring new roles and responsibilities for educators. Integrative approaches might require educators to extend their current expertise, to work together in teams or with other kinds of educators – such as mentors, workers, learners – in new ways. It is likely that the assessment demands of the NQF, including recognition of prior learning (RPL), will require educators to also perform assessor roles.

Concluding remarks

Proposals made in the HSRC document have drawn on global trends in education and training but have also tried to resist some of the negative consequences that these trends have had elsewhere. Whether these adaptations will be adequate, or are even appropriate, remains to be seen. Whilst there is currently broad consensus around the NQF at a rhetorical level, the tenuous nature of the shared understandings is likely to become apparent as SAQA moves from policy to practice.

The models developed for the NQF will ultimately be translated into people's learning and assessment experiences by educators. Consequently, whether the NQF can fulfil its transformative role will depend in large part on the skills, preparedness and commitment of educators.

The unit standard format has been proposed as one organizing mechanism for the NQF. The concept of, and proposals for a format need to be interrogated by SAQA, by pilot standard-setting projects, by stakeholder bodies and by educators. The format's role in shaping the nature of learning and whether it is possible to stretch an outcomes-based approach to include learning considerations through the way standards are formatted needs to be explored. We need to consider whether building a learning-achievements framework for reconstruction and development on a performance-based model, largely imported from vocational training models in the developed English-speaking world, will, in fact, end up asking the impossible of South African educators.

Notes

1. African National Congress 1994: 62; RSA 1995: point 2.
2. McGrath 1995: point 14.
3. McGrath 1995: point 14.
4. Human Sciences Research Council 1995.

5. Department of Education 1995.
6. National Training Board 1994.
7. Department of Education 1995: 26.
8. Department of Education 1995: 26.
9. RSA 1995: No. 1v.
10. RSA 1995: No. 1x.
11. Human Sciences Research Council 1995: 12.
12. RSA 1995: No. 2a.
13. Gustavsson 1994.
14. O'Connor 1995: 3.
15. RSA 1995: No. 1x.
16. RSA 1995: No. 2a.
17. Human Sciences Research Council 1995: 29.
18. RSA 1995: 2.
19. Marginson 1995: 109.
20. Human Sciences Research Council 1995: 52.
21. Human Sciences Research Council 1995: 43.
22. Wolf 1991: 195.
23. RSA 1995: No. 1v.
24. Department of Education: ABET 1995: 9; Human Sciences Research Council (HSRC) 1995: 66–7.
25. Human Sciences Research Council 1995: 67.
26. Human Sciences Research Council 1995: 78–9.
27. Human Sciences Research Council 1995: 50.
28. Human Sciences Research Council 1995: 78–9.
29. RSA 1995: 2b.
30. Marginson 1995: 112.
31. Perkins and Salomon 1989: 19.
32. Perkins and Salomon 1989: 19.
33. Burns and Hood 1994: 78.
34. Burns and Hood 1994: 78–9.
35. Burns and Hood 1994: 85.
36. Burns and Hood 1994: 79.

References

African National Congress (1994) *The Reconstruction and Development Programme: A Policy Framework*, Umanyano Publications, Johannesburg.
Burns, A. and Hood, S. (1994) 'The Competency-Based Curriculum in Action: Investigating Course Design Practices', *Prospect*, Vol. 9, No. 2, September.
Department of Education (1995) *White Paper on Education and Training*, RSA Government Gazette No. 16312, Cape Town.
Department of Education: ABET (1995) *A National Adult Basic Education and Training Framework: Interim Guidelines*, Department of Education, Pretoria.
Gustavsson, B. (1994) 'Life Long Education: International Perspectives', *Integrating Adult Education and Training: Possibilities and Constraints, Report of a Colloquium*, CACE, Cape Town.
Human Sciences Research Council (HSRC) (1995) *Ways of Seeing the National Qualifications Framework*, HSRC, Pretoria.
Marginson, S. (1995) 'Is Competency-based Education a Good Enough Frame-

work for Learning?', *Critical Forum*, Vol. 3, Nos. 2 and 3, April.

McGrath, S. (1995) 'Accounts of Learning Policy Reform in Post-Election South Africa', unpublished paper, University of Edinburgh.

National Training Board (1994) *A Discussion Document on a National Training Strategy Initiative (NTSI)*, NTB, Durban

O'Connor, P. (1995) 'A Spanner in the Works: Workers' Cultures and Learning', paper presented to the 5th National Workshop on Vocational Teacher Education, Tasmania, September 1995.

Perkins, D. and Salomon, G. (1989) 'Are Cognitive Skills Context-Bound?', *Educational Researcher*, Vol. 18, No. 1.

RSA (1995) *South African Qualifications Act*, Act 58 of 1995 RSA Government, Cape Town.

Wolf, A. (1991) 'Assessing Core Skills: Wisdom or Wild Goose Chase?', *Cambridge Journal of Education*, Vol. 18, No. 1.

14

The Politics of Memory:
The Recognition of Experiential Learning

Elana Michelson

The recognition of prior (experiential) learning (RPL) began in the USA as a way for universities to evaluate academically equivalent knowledge. As accomplished adults returned to higher education in ever-increasing numbers, a technique was needed for assessing expertise that had not been gained through formal academic study and for avoiding the absurdity of forcing people into classrooms to relearn what they already know. At the time, RPL was part of an attempt to make university study more widely accessible – in the USA, by reducing the time and money necessary to complete a degree and later, in Britain, by serving as an alternative to class-bound academic entry routes. RPL's function at the time was broadly consistent with liberal traditions of education that stressed equal opportunity, meritocracy and the role of education in social mobility.

In the past twenty years, RPL has transcended its original university setting and has become enmeshed in workforce development policy across much of the English-speaking world. In Britain, Ireland, Australia and New Zealand, the assessment of undocumented workplace learning has become an important aspect of national schemes of vocational qualifications. Here, the stated aim is fourfold: to provide individual workers with employment credentials; to enable employers to identify appropriately skilled workers; to help government and educational institutions identify needed areas for training and re-training; and to enhance the nation's economic edge at a time of global competition and technological change.[1]

As the emphasis has shifted from the academic to the vocational, assumptions that RPL is sociallly beneficial have continued to be the norm. Credentialling schemes are broadly portrayed as a value-free, 'win–win' situation: companies can identify appropriately skilled workers, and workers are empowered, as the current rhetoric goes, to attain the jobs for which they are qualified. Thus all 'partners in the learning enterprise' are presented as gaining from the introduction of national schemes for recognizing work-based learning:

> Employees ... gain an up-to-date cumulative record of skills achieved ...; increased flexibility in utilizing these skills; ... [and] self-esteem from having a tangible record of achievement...
>
> Employers ... gain verification of employee skills ...; increased flexibility in utilizing these skills ...; and better information on which to base short- and long-term personnel decisions.
>
> Industries ... gain the definition of skills to match current needs ...; skills resource data to identify potential locations for new industries; and rapid response to the skills demands of new occupational categories.
>
> Unions ... gain protection of occupational status ..., equal opportunity for equal skills .... [and] assistance in linking salary levels to skill levels.[2]

This formulation is interesting, in part, for its erasure of any potential conflict among the 'partners' in economic development – over 'salary levels', for example, or 'industry relocation' – and, within that, for the continued association of RPL with 'equal opportunity'. As individuals from less privileged social categories are given an alternative framework for entry and promotion, the examination and recognition of their expertise is seen as providing concrete aids to equity and social mobility. While in South Africa this is a question of social justice for a majority non-white population, the relationship of RPL to the aspirations of indigenous peoples as well as immigrants has been articulated in Canada, New Zealand and Australia. Paul Zakos of the First Nations Technical Institute in Ontario, for example, explicitly ties RPL to 'a growing demand and an urgent need for improved access to education and employment opportunities for aboriginal Canadians and newcomers from other cultures' at a time when 'the mosaic of the Canadian population is undergoing significant change' and the non-white population of Toronto is approaching 50 per cent.[3]

The association of RPL with equal opportunity is not without justification. RPL clearly discourages some of the more blatant forms of race and gender bias and is beneficial to some groups of workers – immigrants with foreign credentials, for example – who have no other means of corroborating their expertise. More broadly, the separation of the content of knowledge from its context – what one knows rather than where one learned it – challenges the rationales both for 'old school tie' snobbery and for sexist, racist and classist assumptions about the kinds of people who are likely to know specific kinds of things.

In a number of countries, an attempt has been made to concretize the relationship between RPL and social justice. In Britain, for example, the National Council for Vocational Qualifications has committed itself to a lack of discrimination in both standardized performance criteria and in the specificity of competencies[4]. Qualifications schemes must be 'free from barriers which restrict access and progression ..., free from overt or covert discriminatory practices with regard to gender, race and creed, and designed to pay due regard to the special needs of individuals'.[5]

Administered carefully and supported by explicitly anti-discriminatory policies, RPL can indeed contribute to movements for greater social mobility. RPL, however, is both more radical and more conservative than this implies. As a technique for naming and rewarding socially useful knowledge, RPL is inevitably deeply embedded in how a society apportions status and visibility. It can't help but be a site in which the social order is mediated, in which differentially powerful groups and institutions struggle towards a vision of human society.

On the other hand, RPL fosters radical social transformation because it destabilizes the divisions between 'intellectual' and merely 'manual' labour and thus undermines the hierarchies of class, race and gender that support and are supported by that divide. RPL recognizes that knowledge is gained in concrete human activity, not in socially isolated contemplation. Moreover, it challenges the monopoly of knowledge that is the hallmark of the traditional academy. The distinction between the liberal and the servile arts, for example, was predicated on the disdain for productive and life-maintenance activities and the perceived superiority of those whose lives could be devoted to 'higher' pursuits.[6] RPL makes the claim that historically devalued lives – those of workers, of women, of non-Europeans – are locations from which valid knowledge can be created, thus positing the experience of the non-elite as an alternative authority.

The radical potential of RPL has been given greater immediacy through its introduction in South Africa. Mokubung Nkomo has argued that the post-apartheid dispensation will require profound social, political, and economic transformation, but that 'perhaps more daunting' will be the task of challenging the epistemology of apartheid, that is, its embedding in formal and informal knowledge structures that were then used as justificatory strategies.[7] In challenging traditional divisions of knowledge and, with them, divisions of labour and of power, RPL is potentially an important tool in deconstructing that epistemology. Because RPL insists, first, that socially useful knowledge is gained through active engagement with the world and, second, that work is our primary means of engagement, it recognizes workers as creators of knowledge and thus encourages what Nkomo calls 'a reconceptualization of the knowledge–power relation'.[8]

At the same time, and in spite of this radical potential, RPL has evolved both academically and vocationally within quite conservative constraints. While recognizing alternative sources of knowledge, academic RPL has never challenged the university as the sole legitimate arbiter for what is or isn't accreditable. It has therefore not proved an opportunity to enrich academic learning with alternative ways of knowing or to value knowledge for its difference from rather than its similarity to academic expertise. Academic RPL in most institutions is on a 'course-equivalent' basis; the process students undergo consists of 'analysing and document-ing [their] learning' and then 'matching that learning to ... University courses'. The portfolio of learning thus assembled is 'then submitted to appropriate faculty members who evaluate the learning to determine if it matches what they teach'.[9]

It is ironic, therefore, that little attention has been paid to the shift from university to corporation as educational authority. At a time when the privatization of funding sources has brought universities under the ever more explicit control of the private sector, RPL has participated in the redefining of national educational needs in terms of corporate re-quirements. To remain effective and viable, it is argued, providers of tertiary education must

> find ways of supplementing their funding ... while pursuing policies designed to increase and widen participation. That means evolving imaginative forms of collaborations with industry and commerce ... And often at the heart of those discussions there is the tension between using both APL [Assessment of Prior Learning] and APEL [Assessment of Experiential Learning] for personal development and as a component of liberal education and seeing them as part of the provision for Vocational Qualification.[10]

> Business sees many benefits of RPL: increasing the numbers of employees with qualifications, increasing individuals' self-esteem and confidence, promoting partnerships with education providers, upgrading skills, reducing the cost of training, providing opportunities for advancement, reducing the time away from the job.[11]

Whatever its associations with social equity, then, RPL is arguably complicitous with inequalities of economic and institutional power. Be-cause categories of vocational skills are typically defined by management, they can be seen as 'reproducing and reinforcing the old divisions in the labour market that are the basis of inequality'.[12] The divisions of labour and power at the workplace are built into qualifications grids which, far from enabling social transformation, reinforce the status quo. Moreover, the rhetoric of 'empowerment' and 'employability' at a time of shrinking job markets and weakened trade unions in many countries has placed the onus of unemployment on individual workers and implicitly blamed lack of national competitiveness on the inadequacies of employees. Finally, the systematical use of assessment differentials makes employment seem a function of worker/worker competition rather than one of national industrial policy or, for that matter, the conflicting interests of workers and management.

This last point is related to an additional conservative feature of RPL as currently practised, namely its emphasis on the ideology of individual achievement. RPL perpetuates traditional Western assumptions that both experience and knowledge are individual products, that cognitive development is tied to personal autonomy, and that knowledge is to be used for individual advancement and individualistic goals. Focused on the assessment of the knowledge of individuals, RPL has not concerned itself with the relationship between the historical experience of the community and the personal experience of individuals, or treated knowledge as a social product that humans make collectively. According to the current understanding of RPL, justice lies in the recognition of individual achievement. Thus, equity is defined within the value system of bourgeois individualism: free choice and a level playing-field.

The implicit conservatism of RPL has been the grounds for its rejection by some adult educators who are otherwise committed to experiential learning. For these educators, as Weil and McGill point out, it would be 'anathema' to have the knowledge of historically oppressed communities evaluated and accredited by a formal institution. 'Learning is borne out of a struggle to examine experience from new perspectives – not those embodied in dominant values, structures, and institutions of societies.'[13] The formal assessment of experiential learning is contrasted to such experiential learning practices as Freirean pedagogy and feminist consciousness-raising, in which the collective exploration of experience is part of a strategy to understand one's own oppression and to make links between personal and social history.

The political embeddedness of RPL does not justify its rejection. On the contrary, precisely because RPL always enacts a specific relationship between knowledge and power, it can be an important venue for negotiating economic prerogatives and social visibility. The development of a structure for RPL is an occasion to ask and demand answers to fundamental questions about the ways in which a society apportions power:

- What will the relationship be between knowledge and access to power?
- Whose knowledge will be seen to 'count'?
- Who will judge whom, and on what basis?
- What ways of knowing will be legitimated, and what will that mean for historically marginalized groups?
- How will the boundaries be negotiated for what is -- or isn't – seen as socially useful knowledge, and whose interests will those boundaries serve?

As a way of examining the relationship between RPL and these larger issues, I'd like to consider developing an assessment policy for the traditional American craft of quilting. First, how will the qualifications of a given quilter be measured? By how warm her quilts are, or how beautiful? And according to what system of aesthetic values will that beauty be gauged? Secondly, who should be given the authority to assess a quilter's expertise? Another quilter? An art historian? A cultural anthropologist? In other words, what is the social and institutional context that confers the right to judge?

These initial questions are hardly insignificant: the devising of criteria and the assessment of worth are already functions of institutional and cultural authority. At the same time, the assessment of quilting raises other questions, ones that cannot be answered by constructing a system of criteria or even determining who is a legitimate judge. Quilting is a female, rural, working-class tradition. Amongst African Americans, it is associated with family memory and the beauty of the everyday; among Latin Americans it is associated with political resistance and social change.[14] Thus, its formal evaluation cannot be separated from larger questions of value and reward; it depends on the valuing of handicraft as opposed to mass production industry, of women's craft and knowledge, of non-European folk traditions and political struggles, of home- and community-based skills. Moreover, a given quilt is often the product of collective design and activity. Its assessment requires recognition of communal skills and artistry, in which the expertise of individuals cannot always be differentiated.

Any assessment policy must begin with the acknowledgement that RPL can never be neutral. It is a material practice through which specific knowledge – and, therefore, specific knowers – are publicly and institutionally valued, and in which questions of epistemological authority explicitly confront questions of social inequality. As instruments for recognizing knowledge, methodologies for measuring experiential learning will reflect the power relationships of the society within which they function. At bottom, the values reflected in assessment criteria will be political and social, not epistemological; or, rather, they will be located at the site where knowledge and power collide.

It is for this reason that RPL is so significant in the current South African context. RPL policies here confront a history in which political oppression was rationalized, in part, by perceived differentials in cultural value and in which European traditions of individualized skill and mastery opposed indigenous traditions of communal knowledge and dialogic artistry.[15] Further, contemporary schemes to measure knowledge and skill cannot be separated from a history of proscribed education and outlawed communication, in which the withholding of knowledge and information was an explicit repressive tool. Even more pivotal is RPL's placement within the current debate about the relationship of national economic development to social equity. In large part, of course, these realities are shared by other countries with a colonialist past, including mine. But the historical matrix is publicly acknowledged here and policies are taking shape at a time in which their invariably political nature is still visible. South Africa thus provides us with the opportunity to revisit the political and social context within which experiential learning is always recognized.

The rhetoric concerning RPL in South Africa is consistent with that of the English-speaking world: it posits RPL as a win–win situation in which 'consensus' rules and all 'stakeholders' gain, and in which a variety of social and economic objectives can be served simultaneously. The objectives of the National Qualifications Framework (NQF), of which RPL is an important feature, are to:

> a) create an integrated national framework for learning achievements; b) facilitate access to, and mobility and progression within education, training, and career paths; c) enhance quality; d) accelerate the redress of past unfair discrimination in education, training and employment opportunities; and thereby e) contribute to the full personal development of each learner and the social and economic development of the nation at large.[16]

For obvious historical reasons, the 'redress of past unfair discrimination' is a major theme in South African discussions of RPL. It is widely acknowledged that 'formal qualifications have a special importance in the South African context [because] apartheid policies and practices denied qualifications to many South Africans and functioned as an exclusionary mechanism'.[17] RPL is seen as one of the 'new education and training policies to address the legacies of underdevelopment and inequitable development', specifically by enabling the NQF to 'open doors of opportunity for people whose academic or career paths have been needlessly blocked because their prior learning (acquired informally or by work experience) has not been assessed and certified'.[18]

Thus, RPL carries with it an explicit expectation: that it will aid in overcoming historical inequities and, in the process, help to create a more democratic and fluid workplace. Here, as elsewhere, the goal of greater social justice appears merged with the goal of economic development:

> Successful modern economies and societies require the elimination of artificial hierarchies, in social organization, in the organization and management of work and in the way in which learning is organized and certified. They require citizens with a strong foundation of general education, the desire and ability to continue to learn, to adapt to and develop new knowledge, skills, and technologies, to move flexibly between occupations, to take responsibility for personal performance, to set and achieve high standards, and to work co-operatively.[19]

Within certain parameters, RPL can indeed support the goal of social mobility. Yet it does not do so automatically, and many factors can militate against achieving that goal. The remainder of this chapter examines the relationship of RPL to the redress of racial and gender discrimination and the transformation of the South African workplace in the direction of greater democracy. In so doing, it argues that, rhetoric aside, RPL

policies will, of necessity, reflect specific social and economic interests
and further some goals at the direct expense of others. Whose interests
and which goals will be best served will depend on the vision of the
'new' South Africa within which RPL policies are designed.

To begin to examine how this might work in practice, let us consider
the issue of language, specifically the relationship of language skills to
skilled and professional employment and decision-making authority. On
one level the obvious question is: Which language will be required? Will
all levels of skills assessment be carried out in the eleven official languages, or will RPL structure the hierarchy of languages into the hierarchy of knowledge and skill? Even within unilingual models, the criteria
through which candidates are assessed have raised difficult issues in regard to language, literacy and/or proficiency requirements that are not
demanded by the skills themselves; or else the criteria are phrased in
language that disadvantages working-class candidates.[20]

It is important, then, to consider how this might play out in South
Africa. Clearly, the question of language policy is not specific to RPL; but
how South Africa heals from a painful and contested linguistic legacy –
and how that legacy will influence norms – is a question that assessment
schemes will have to consider. Whether multilingualism is a social and
economic liability or whether, rather, multilingualism will be considered
a social and economic advantage, will be concretely reflected in RPL
policies. RPL is therefore a site for intervention, perhaps a critical one.

Language aside, however, RPL policies run the risk of implicit Eurocentric and sexist bias, even when the principle of equity informs policy.
Yet Nancy Mills speaks for many, in New Zealand and elsewhere, in
fearing

> that RPL will work well for those who can afford it, but not for those who ...
> have been disadvantaged in terms of access to education and training in the
> past: rural folks, the indigenous Maori, women, disabled ... It is hoped that
> RPL will open new pathways to education, training and qualification, and not
> just advantage the already advantaged.[21]

Advantaging the 'already advantaged' can take numerous forms, many
of them related to cultural expectations that naturalize Eurocentric and
male-normed ways of knowing and individualized theories of cognition.
In academic assessment, for example, the equation is often made between experiential learning and what education theorists call critical self-
reflection;[22] for knowledge to be recognized as such, it must have the
quality of self-conscious individualism that is the mark – some would say
the curse – of the masculinist, imperialist West. This not only disadvantages specific groups of people, many women and non-Europeans among
them, but devalues traditions in which group memory and collective
activity are seen as points of origin for both knowledge and practical

skills. Again, South Africa provides the occasion for revisiting these issues. What does it mean to treat knowledge as an internalized individual achievement in the face of a culture that has historically used the shared ownership of knowledge both as a form of political resistance and as a survival strategy? What, moreover, does 'critical self-reflection' mean: the ability to learn from experience as a function of one's own internalized cognitive development, or the ability to locate one's experience of the world within social history?[23]

One specific problem in this regard is that assessable skills are articulated according to mainstream organizations of knowledge. Because specific standards and criteria must be met, and because these tend to be formalized in academic and vocational settings, RPL is not always suited to meeting the needs of disadvantaged racial groups or the needs of women. A tension exists between the highly structured organization of knowledge within which RPL typically functions and the legacy of race and gender bias. New Zealand educator Jeanie Harre Hindemarch poses the question of

> how to recognize appropriately and to legitimate knowledge and skills of women and of ethnic minority groups – many of which are not recognized in courses in patriarchal/Western dominated institutions. If women's and minority groups' knowledge and skills are not in the outcome statement, they cannot be in RPL.... Some knowledges and skills women bring to study are more in line with unspecified credit than credit specifiable to vocational outcomes: for example organizational, interpersonal and time management skills. Thus if RPL ... concentrates on ... specified credit, those who have been out of the workforce are automatically disadvantaged.[24]

To ensure that RPL standards and criteria do not simply serve the already advantaged, British scholars Cecilia McKelvey and Helen Peters have recommended specific practices for avoiding sexism and ethnocentricity in RPL. Some of these recommendations focus on categories of qualifications: assessable skills should include those based both on unpaid work and on a full range of ethnically specific competencies, not only French cuisine, for example, but 'Indian vegetarian cookery, Chinese cookery, Hallal (Muslim ritual) butchery'.[25] Clearly, such policies could be written into the RPL framework in South Africa.

And yet, there is a larger issue here than is answered by McKelvey and Peters' recommendations. South Africa contains two disparate legacies of 'prior learning', the first of which both justified and sustained apartheid and the second of which provided the insurgent skills and knowledge that led to its overthrow. Viewed most broadly, the issue at stake here is the definition of socially useful knowledge. What vision of society will be written into that definition? Whose interests will that definition serve?

Let me again use specific examples to make the point. What kind of expertise should be required for decision-making authority over labour law: a degree in comparative legal systems or experience of life as a migrant worker? What competencies will be listed under a skill called 'Leadership': the ability to take appropriate action 'when a budget shortfall is likely to occur', as British standards maintain,[26] or the ability to sustain a community in the face of the direst poverty? The answers depend on and will importantly reflect fundamental social dynamics: definitions of law and of leadership, the function of collective memory, the explicit and implicit uses of power, the meaning of democracy.

The value system built into assessment is not simply concerned with knowledge and skill; RPL will inscribe, not only certain kinds of workers, but certain kinds of workplaces and therefore certain kinds of social relations, both at the workplace and beyond. In effect, the introduction of RPL provides the occasion for re-examining the relationship between knowledge and authority. A democratic workplace is not simply a function of mobility among job descriptions, but resides in the organization of life and work and in the nature of social relations within the job descriptions themselves.

Two contrary examples from Britain make this point. Both the construction and mining industries have written interpersonal skills into performance criteria. The criteria for mine-workers require that 'overall behaviour and attitude is consistent with the organization's practices; essential information is passed on to appropriate person(s) accurately; ... [and] lines of communication and reporting are maintained'. That this communication is structured within rigid lines of authority is pointed up by an additional criterion that essentially requires employees to spy on their fellow workers: 'factors which lead to conflict or cause operations to be disrupted are noted and reported to the appropriate persons'.[27] The comparable criteria for wood occupations in construction both mandate and enable a far more democratic workplace in which workers' knowledge is valued even if it is not shared by management: 'time is taken, within operational constraints, to establish productive relationships; opportunities provided to discuss work-related matters are readily exploited; conflicts of interest are dealt with in ways which minimise offence and maintain mutual respect; colleagues are encouraged to offer views'.[28] The differences between these two cannot be reduced to differences in specific skills; these two sets of criteria produce different workplaces and, indeed, different visions of civil society.

Which vision of society is written into South African policies for RPL will depend on many factors, not the least of which will be the venue in which they are written. Who will be empowered to set standards? Who will compose the assessment criteria? Who will be among the 'stakeholders' whose concurrence must be gained? As has already been remarked on, there is an over-representation of corporate interests in the designing of many national assessment grids, which reflect the values and needs of management. The active participation of working-class institutions such as trade unions is crucial to addressing that problem. On the other hand, substituting a workerist for a corporatist agenda can still lead to the denigration of non-industrial knowledge, including that of women and of men in some communities.

Second, once the criteria are written, who will be authorized to perform assessments? Assessments are acts of communication; they are carried out by human beings whose own experiences inform their values – about competence, appropriate performance, cultural conformity, mutual respect. In a number of places, assessment policies have been explicitly negotiated in a way that involves local and indigenous communities; in New Zealand, for example, the Maori have both struggled to have their traditional crafts made part of the national assessment scheme and been given the right to carry out individual assessments within the local community. In others, expectations of non-racist and non-sexist behaviour have been written into the actual standards and criteria; performance criteria for British health-care workers include 'promotes equality for all individuals' and require that 'the worker's behaviour in the work setting demonstrates recognized good anti-discriminatory practices and is not exploitive or abusive'.[29] It may be important to identify comparable venues in South Africa for both the mandating of non-biased behaviours and shared epistemological authority.

RPL policies have direct economic implications, both at the level of the diversion of labour on the ground and in the kinds of economic and social democracy a given society entertains. Specific features of the grid of standards and criteria will invariably advance or impede specific social agendas. They will further or hamper the access of specific groups of people to skilled employment and decision-making authority.

But whether the issue is the national economic development or the promotion of social justice, not only economic power is at stake. Also at stake are the kinds of knowledge we value and who we tell ourselves we are. Is it enough to use assessment schemes to allow some women, some non-whites, some workers into the enchanted authoritative circle, or must we challenge the criteria through which some knowledge and not other knowledge is legitimated, as feminist and anti-racist theory has tried to do, and value knowledge that is not necessarily available from the position of institutionalized authority? As philosopher Elizabeth Minnich has put it,

> to help liberate humankind from past prejudices and beliefs that derived from and justified the assignment of physical and daily maintenance work to lower-caste people, we need to know much more about all that truly makes life possible and humane, from mothering, to community-building, to surviving with imagination and dignity intact in deprivation and poverty, to working with our hands with art and integrity.[30]

Seen in slightly other terms, experience is another word for history: whose counts, whose is remembered, whose attains the status of exemplary. RPL is about the stories a society chooses to tell about itself. It is a way of negotiating the politics of memory, which are always more about the future than the past. New York City poet Langston Hughes carried with him a deep sense of the relationship between our memories and our choices: 'So we stand here,' he wrote,

> at the edge of hell
> in Harlem
> And look out at the world
> And wonder
> What we're gonna do
> In the face of
> What we remember.

Notes

1. Weil and McGill 1989; McKelvey and Peters 1993; Sheckley, Lamdin and Keeton 1993.
2. Sheckley, Lamdin, and Keeton 1993: 137–8.
3. Zakos 1993: 3–4.
4. McKelvey and Peters 1993.
5. McKelvey and Peters 1993: 29.
6. Minnich 1990: 45.
7. Nkomo 1991: 309.
8. Nkomo 1991: 309.
9. External Student Program 1995: 7.
10. Evans and Bailleux 1993: xii.
11. Mills, quoted in Cohen and Whitaker 1994: 41.
12. McKelvey and Peters 1993: 16.
13. Weil and McGill 1989: 13.
14. Aptheker 1989: 73; Collins 1991: 89; Minnich 1990: 105.
15. McClintock 1995: 308.
16. RSA 1995.
17. Human Sciences Research Council 1995: 13.
18. Department of Education 1995: 3 clause 16; 2 clause 7.
19. Department of Education 1995: 5 clause 2.
20. McKelvey and Peters 1993: 79–81.
21. McKelvey and Peters 1993: 79–81.
22. Mezirow 1990: xvi.
23. Kemmis 1985: 142–3.
24. Cohen and Whitaker 1994: 46–7.
25. McKelvey and Peters 1993: 16.
26. McKelvey and Peters 1993: 163.
27. McKelvey and Peters 1993: 163.
28. National Council on Vocational Qualifications: Wood Occupations, Level 2.
29. National Council on Vocational Qualifications: Care, all levels.
30. Minnich 1990: 118.

References

Aptheker, B. (1989) *Tapestries of Life: Women's Work, Women's Consciousness, and the Meaning of Daily Experience,* University of Massachusetts Press, Amherst.

Cohen, R. and Whitaker, U. (1994) 'Assessing Learning from Experience', in Keeton, M.T. (ed.), *Perspectives on Experiential Learning: Prelude to a Global Conversation about Learning,* Council on Adult and Experiential Learning, Chicago.

Collins, P. H. (1991) *Black Feminist Thought: Knowledge, Consciousness, and the Politics of Empowerment,* Routledge, New York.

Department of Education (1995) *A National Adult Basic Education and Training Framework: Interim Guidelines,* Department of Education, Pretoria.

Evans, N. and Bailleux, M. (1993) 'Forward to the Series', in McKelvey, C. and Peters, H. (ed.) *APL: Equal Opportunities for All?,* Routledge, London.

External Student Program (1995) Ohio University Printing Office, Ohio University, Athens, OH.

Human Sciences Research Council (HSRC) (1995) *Ways of Seeing the National Qualifications Framework,* HSRC, Pretoria.

Kemmis, S. (1985) 'Action Research and the Politics of Reflection', in Boud, D, Keogh, R. and Walker, D. (eds), *Reflection: Turning Experience into Learning,* Kogan Page, London.

McClintock, A. (1995) *Imperial Leather: Race, Gender, and Sexuality in the Colonial Contest,* Routledge, New York.

McKelvey, C. and Peters, H. (1993) *APL: Equal Opportunity For All?,* Routledge, London.

Mezirow, J. (1990) Preface in J. Mezirow and Associates, *Fostering Critical Reflection in Adulthood: A Guide to Transformative and Emancipatory Learning,* Jossey-Bass, San Francisco.

Minnich, E.K. (1990) *Transforming Knowledge,* Temple University Press, Philadelphia.

Nkomo, M. (1991) 'Epistemological and Disciplinary Transformations in a Post-apartheid South Africa', in Jansen, J.D. (ed.), *Knowledge and Power in South Africa: Critical Perspectives across the Disciplines,* Skotaville, Johannesburg.

Sheckley, B., Lamdin, L. and Keeton, M. (1993) *Employability in a High-Performance Economy,* Council for Adult and Experiential Learning, Chicago.

Weil, S.W. and McGill, I. (eds) (1989) Introduction to *Making Sense of Experiential Learning: Diversity in Theory and Practice,* Milton Keynes: Society into Research in Higher Education, Open University Press.

Zakos, P. (1993) Unpublished paper presented at the Conference of the Council for Adult and Experiential Learning, New Orleans.

15

Workplace Training and Enskilling

Jonathan and Ruth Winterton

The restructuring of Western industries and the transition of Eastern European economies raise issues which are paralleled by reconstruction in South Africa. Notwithstanding the enormity of the social problems associated with restructuring, transition and reconstruction, these changes present an opportunity to design work organization to improve the quality of working life. The changes have been accompanied by the development of new human resource strategies, which claim to offer new approaches to the management of employee relations more appropriate to emerging forms of work.

In the context of the United Kingdom, the attempts to reform industrial relations in the 1960s and 1970s gave way to widespread deconstruction of collective bargaining during the 1980s, especially in the public sector.[1] The predominant government strategies, which have accompanied massive restructuring, have involved a combination of macho management and modern paternalism. During the 1990s, an integrative alternative has begun to emerge at lead sites, and is more durable since it is not predicated upon the assumption that management power will remain uncontested. The collaborative relations necessary to develop an integrative strategy must be underpinned by empowerment and enskilling.

Empowerment is implicit to the institutional arrangements developed to accommodate the conflicting interests of management and workers. Traditional arrangements (participation and collective bargaining) involve relatively little power-sharing. The empowerment necessary to develop an integrative strategy must involve co-determination at the superstructure level and forms of autonomous work organization in the substructure.

Co-determination arrangements have operated effectively in Sweden and Germany for many years and are being generalized throughout the European Union under the Social Chapter. Autonomous work groups are well established in Scandinavia, such as the Kalmar motor vehicle plant opened by Volvo in 1974, which was designed from the outset around team-working, rather than a rigid machine-paced line for final assembly. Although the Kalmar plant is now closed, it demonstrated the extent to which job autonomy is conducive to improved quality, efficiency and job satisfaction.

Enskilling entails increasing both the breadth and depth of skills required to undertake functions, and therefore the competences acquired by individuals to perform those functions. The traditional specializations created shallow, narrow, Taylorized,[2] unskilled work, and deep, but equally narrow, craft work. Recent innovations have promoted a broadening of both Taylorist work, multi-tasking through job rotation and job enlargement, and of craft work, through multiskilling. The adaptive training which has facilitated this enskilling has imposed new demands on continuing vocational education and training.

This chapter explores the implications for training and adult education strategies of an integrative human resource strategy built upon empowerment and enskilling. From an analysis of attempts to introduce multiskilling in four workplaces, the necessary conditions for an anthropocentric form of work organization are identified, and characterized as autonomous work groups of multiskilled employees.

Training strategies

Restructuring, transition and reconstruction impose new demands in relation to adult education and training, especially in relation to Continuing Vocational Education and Training. In the past decade, as UK industry has restructured, there has been growing evidence that the workforce is inadequately trained in comparison with major industrial competitors. In 1985, for example, 35,000 individuals qualified at craft level in engineering and technology in the UK; the comparable figures for France and Germany were, respectively, 92,000 and 120,000.[3] Similarly, while 24 per cent of top managers in the UK are graduates, in France and Germany the percentage is more than twice that and in Japan and the USA, 85 per cent of top managers have degree-level qualifications. As a result, organizations such as the Institute for Personnel and Development and the Institute of Management have argued the need for a new national training and development strategy.[4]

Recognizing that the level of training was insufficient to meet the demand for skilled workers during the 1990s, the government emphasized in a series of White Papers the important role which vocational education and training for workers and managers plays in promoting international competitiveness.[5] At the same time, the system of vocational education and training in the UK was radically overhauled. First, training organizations at sector level have been deregulated, so the statutory Industry Training Boards have (in all but two cases) been replaced by employer-led Industry Training Organizations. Second, a unified system of work-based qualifications is being developed following the establishment in 1986 of the National Council for Vocational Qualifications. In this chapter we focus on workplace training and enskilling.

Workplace training and enskilling

If the unions have made limited progress in negotiating training agreements, one possible explanation is that despite training often being regarded as consensual within industrial relations, the interests of the different parties are not entirely congruent. In the abstract, employers and employers' associations, along with employees and trade unions, will pronounce themselves in favour of training, but their motives invariably encompass more than an attachment to a highly educated workforce. Employers want a workforce with the competences to perform in accordance with business objectives. For employees, training and the validation of that training represents a means of having their skills and competences acknowledged, which in turn should provide a route to higher earnings, improved job satisfaction and security, and increased labour market mobility. The representative bodies, employers' associations and trade unions, may also have a wider agenda. The employers' associations may see training as a mechanism to support job restructuring through promoting multiskilling and functional flexibility. The trade unions may regard training as a route to increasing autonomy and control over the job, as well as maintaining pay rates. While all parties have modified their views considerably in recent years, there is still potential for conflictual objectives over training.

Skill is a contentious area because it forms a link between the apparently consensual issue of training and the inevitably conflictual question of pay. Skills and competences are at the centre of training arrangements but also feature on the industrial relations agenda as a question of appropriate remuneration for the skills required to perform the job. The problems stem from a confusion between the two processes. Rainbird[6] for example, claims that 'up-grading and de-skilling are social relationships rather than empirically measurable phenomena'. This approach conflates two separate dimensions of skill: the genuine foundation, which is related only to the competences required to undertake the tasks, and the socially constructed skill labels manifest in the grading structure, which reflect also, and on occasions primarily, the power relations and social values of the parties to negotiation. Genuine skill is clearly the province of training, while grading is a matter for the bargaining system. The questions of upskilling and deskilling (changes in the genuine skill foundation) are analytically distinct from those of up-grading and down-grading (socially constructed skill labels).

Despite the unions' limited progress in establishing Workplace Training Committees, seven enterprise case studies undertaken for the European Commission revealed a high degree of concordance between a highly skilled workforce, significant job restructuring underpinned by employer attitudes conducive to responsible autonomy, and the involvement of trade unions in training.[7] Two of these enterprises were included, with two others, in a further study of the relationship between multiskilling, training and new forms of work organization.

Multi-skilling, training and work organization

In all four enterprises studied, management emphasized the role of training to promote multiskilling and support job restructuring. The study sought to determine in each case whether multiskilling represented the acquisition of significant new skills or whether it was a social construct designed to promote flexibility and mask deskilling. The research aimed to identify whether significant multiskilling existed in practice beyond management rhetoric, and the costs and benefits to management and workforce. Finally, factors explaining the different experiences of multi-skilling were considered.

Coal mining

The colliery studied is in Selby, the most technologically advanced mine complex in the world, which comprises five mines linked by underground roadways to two 12 kilometre-long drifts through which over ten million tonnes of coal per annum are raised. A 'quality circle' approach had been attempted to reduce production delays by training miners in 'problem-solving' techniques to become 'analytical troubleshooters', constantly on the look-out for potential production problems and tracing faults back to originating causes to prevent a repetition.[8]

The motives for seeking multiskilling were particularly acute at Selby because of its technological infrastructure: the need for a higher return on capital investment through fuller utilization of assets, coupled with reducing manpower and intensifying work in order to increase profitability. While the development of new technologies was acknowledged as a factor facilitating multiskilling, the defeat of the 1984–85 miners' strike was seen as equally important.[9]

Multiskilling included fitters doing welding, and electro-mechanical craftsmen replacing electricians and fitters; loco drivers undertaking methane boring, and surface workers deployed generally to a whole range of tasks. At the coalface, craft workers were involved in driving the shearer, 'chocking' (moving the face supports) and 'putting packs on' (building timber supports at the gate ends), while face workers undertook nuisance breakdown repairs: 'every miner now carries a spanner'.[10]

Job restructuring was associated with very little increase in task complexity for most workers. For fitters, 'the work tends to involve module replacement', although task complexity was thought to have increased for electricians. By contrast task variety has increased significantly: 'most people now have more jobs to do'. The process of job restructuring began in 1992, when union resistance diminished after geological problems led to the abandonment of several faces and the closure of the mine was threatened.

For the most part, the greater task flexibility apparent in the colliery has not involved the acquisition of additional operational skills. Only a proportion of electricians had been required to acquire new conceptual skills in order to understand, for example, remote control and monitoring equipment, although new switchgear demanded more conceptual skills from most electricians. In most cases, individuals were not being equipped with any additional skills, but were being called upon to use those in which they were already trained.

Individuals who were using a wider range of competencies, and those who were acquiring additional competencies (such as the electro-mechanical craft workers), received no additional remuneration. Multiskilling contributed to the dramatic increase in productivity achieved in recent years, although it is difficult to establish the additionality of multiskilling given the range of factors contributing to productivity growth.[11] The only advantages of job restructuring cited by management were the opportunity to work more overtime and the greater job security from making the colliery competitive. Union respondents characterized the changes in terms of work intensification, 'even where there is a broadening of skills, these are not transferable'.

In general, multiskilling was more concerned with increasing task flexibility than with the acquisition of additional skills, apart from a minority of electricians. Task flexibility was extensive and there was evidence of substantial job restructuring. The attraction of the job restructuring to management was in terms of reducing manpower and therefore total labour costs, and increasing machine utilization. The benefits to individual workers were minimal because the new skills were largely non-transferable, there was no additional remuneration for increased task flexibility, and work was intensified.

Clothing

The enterprise, part of a larger clothing group described as a principal contract supplier, supplies ladies' trousers to a dominant high-street chain store. In the workforce of 250 at the site studied, all the machinists were female and approximately half were under 18 years of age. The company had difficulties in attracting and retaining labour; labour turnover had exceeded 90 per cent.

Teamworking was part of a strategy to improve labour retention, and this necessitated multiskilling. Traditionally clothing is manufactured using a progressive bundle system, where machines are arranged in the order that operations are carried out for a particular garment. Bundles of garments are passed from one machine to another, machinists become specialized in one operation, and this changes little even with the introduction of a new style.[12]

Under teamworking, each team of eight workers was assigned a U-shaped bank of stand-up sewing machines covering the full range of operations, from overlocking to buttonholing. The machinery and most of the tasks were unaltered, but the system required machinists to be able to do a wider range of tasks. Initially all machinists were to be trained to perform 50 per cent of the 12 to 14 tasks required for an individual style, but most machinists were able to perform three operations, and tended to concentrate on one.

The progressive bundle system presented classic assembly-line balancing problems, and these remained under teamworking, but machinists could move to perform operations where the need was greatest to keep the line running smoothly. In the best teams, workers were able to cover for up to three missing members without any management involvement. Task variety increased for all machinists and the work was less predictable. Task complexity also increased, first, because it took an individual longer to learn several operations, and second, because line balancing involved all team members in understanding the whole process.

The operational (or manual) skills have not changed significantly, but the conceptual skills have increased considerably. On the traditional system a machinist 'did not have to think at all, but just undertake the same simple task or operation repeatedly'; bundles of garments were brought to the machine and passed on to the next machine. In the new system, by making teams responsible for their own line balancing, machinists need to employ a much higher level of conceptual skills.

There was no change in grading or the skill labels attached to operatives as a result of teamworking. Machining was always considered unskilled, so the processes of social construction continued to work to the detriment of skill definition for sewing machinists, even though the skill level increased. For management the new working arrangements had contributed to reducing labour turnover from 90 per cent to 26 per cent, and absenteeism from 10 per cent to 6 per cent. For operatives, teamworking offered less work tedium and higher earnings, although this is a result of increased productivity under payment by results. All of the machinists interviewed said that they preferred the new system because it was less boring than the traditional lines; although they had to work harder, none wanted to return to the traditional work organization.

Chemicals

The company is the fine chemicals division of a transnational chemicals group, with a total divisional workforce, excluding contractors, of 830: 57 per cent blue-collar, 32 per cent white-collar and 10 per cent managerial. Contractors are used extensively to increase flexibility and reduce overheads. Labour turnover is low, probably under 2.5 per cent, and the average length of service is thought to be about 15 years.

The company recognized a direct link between training and performance improvement to enhance profitability. Training is viewed in developmental terms and objectives are formulated clearly in relation to corporate objectives. In 1989 the main trade union brought forward a draft flexibility agreement for discussion, and this resulted in a framework 'to harmonize the conditions of employment of all employees and improve the profitability and competitiveness of the company, by changing the working practices and skills of employees'.[13] The agreement was also designed to improve the quality of working life through job enhancement and increased autonomy.

Multiskilling was central to the flexibility agreement. Craft multiskilling was designed to broaden skills; all craft workers could gain an additional area of competence outside their major specialism. For example, a fitter might learn how to disconnect a pump without needing to involve an electrician. Craft workers were also able to deepen existing skills: for example, a general welder could acquire competence in coded welding. The union representatives viewed flexibility in terms of adding on competences to those already possessed, the most significant being process workers undertaking maintenance work.

Multiskilling altered work organization through increasing task variety, especially for process workers, although this was attributed largely to new technology, which required the shop-floor operative to have more knowledge of the process. Task variety was reduced for craft workers because technological changes demanded greater specialization. Flexibility and multiskilling were associated with the acquisition of significant new operational skills for all workers.

The new skills were acquired through in-house structured training programmes, in line with the training philosophy of the flexibility agreement: enhancing skills and requiring employees to accept flexibility and mobility within their normal jobs. Employees undertake all duties for which they are trained: 'There will be no demarcation other than natural ability and the requirements of safe working. Regular training will support innovation, new technology and working methods, service and quality.'

The flexibility agreement also explicitly contained provision for additional remuneration: 'Those who reach new standards of skill will be rewarded accordingly.'

The main benefit of multiskilling for management is in reduced plant down-time, and the 'removal of demarcation mentality'. Union representatives thought workers had gained higher earnings, increased job satisfaction and more control over their immediate work environment. Multiskilling in this case appeared to represent the acquisition of significant new skills for both operators and craft workers. Operators developed analytical (conceptual) skills as well as maintenance (operational) skills. Craft workers broadened and deepened skills (lateral and vertical multiskilling). The multiskilling and flexibility was acknowledged in a revised grading structure, giving the workforce increased remuneration as well as job satisfaction and control. At the same time, managerial objectives of reduced plant down-time were attained.

Engineering

The company is a specialist manufacturer of aeroplane components. The total workforce of 320 at the company's single factory comprises 160 direct workers (involved in manufacturing activities), all of whom are skilled to varying degrees, and 160 support workers (research, design, managerial, white-collar and ancillary activities). Multiskilling and teamworking at this site arose out of cellular manufacture, which was facilitated by the make-up of the company's products. The strategic objectives of multiskilling were described in terms of improving labour retention and product quality.

Training is seen as a way of promoting attitudinal or cultural change in the enterprise, and is designed 'to support strategic directions of the business, such as moving into new technologies of manufacture including new product materials and process innovations'. At the centre of the multiskilling initiative in this company is a 'Four Star Plan' developed in 1990 to introduce cellular manufacture and to reward people for the acquisition of lateral skills. This major initiative was designed to support modular manufacture by introducing multiskilling, whereby direct workers acquire lateral skills within their work cells. To a degree, it was also designed to facilitate movement between work cells. All maintenance workers are multiskilled electro-mechanics, and in addition many have specialist skills associated with the company's particular requirements. As part of Total Productive Maintenance, production workers undertake certain routine repairs. The next stage will involve integrating personnel of the works engineering department into the work cells and devolving responsibility for maintenance totally.

The job restructuring which these initiatives have entailed have not generally increased task complexity, since the tasks to be completed have remained constant as a function of the range of products. The programme has, however, substantially increased task variety, which is a function of the authority of the individual (in terms of their star rating). A related initiative described as 'Delegated Authority' entailed removing inspectors over a four-year period and making workers responsible for their own quality assurance. In general broader operational skills have been developed within the work cells, but not particularly higher skills. Delegated Authority, however, has increased the conceptual skills substantially: 'individuals need to be able to identify whether something is right when inspecting their own work'.

The Four Star Plan and Delegated Authority together earned the company a National Training Award in 1990. The impact of these initiatives on profitability and productivity is difficult to measure, especially given other changes as a result of economic recession. There is anecdotal evidence of improved quality, and absenteeism has fallen from 6 per cent to 2.7 per cent, which may demonstrate increased employee commitment. The direct workers appear to have gained most from multiskilling, in terms of increased task variety and responsibility as well as the opportunity to deploy more conceptual skills.

In this case, multiskilling entails the acquisition of significant new (lateral) operational skills, and, in conjunction with Delegated Authority, the introduction of higher conceptual skills. Increased task flexibility is a key objective of the changes. There are evident benefits to the workforce both in terms of additional remuneration and increased job satisfaction deriving from the task variety and responsible autonomy built into the jobs, as well as obvious benefits which accrue to management.

Conclusions

The case studies reveal fundamental differences in the nature of multiskilling at the four sites. The engineering and chemicals cases each involved the acquisition of significant skills, both lateral (mainly operational) and vertical (mainly conceptual). In the clothing case, both task complexity and task variety increased, the first demanding new conceptual skills but the second not requiring significant lateral skills. In the coal case, the emphasis was on task flexibility and the fuller utilization of existing skills, rather than the acquisition of new skills.

The engineering and chemicals cases required substantial additional on-the-job training to equip individuals with the necessary skills to cope with the demands of increased task variety and task complexity. Training in the clothing case was less extensive, while in coal there was no additional training, with the exception of those craft workers involved in maintaining the remote control and monitoring systems.

The four cases also show significant variation in the extent to which workers share the benefits of multiskilling and increased task flexibility. The engineering case showed the clearest linking of remuneration to the acquisition of new competences, although the additional remuneration was more significant in absolute terms in the chemicals case, and in relative terms in the clothing case. All three cases also showed increased job satisfaction and autonomy. By contrast, in the coal case, there was no additional remuneration for multiskilling or functional flexibility, and no reported improvements in job satisfaction.

The benefits to management emphasized in the four cases show most variation. In engineering, the issues are quality and labour flexibility, which are functions of the specialized, small-batch product base of the company. In chemicals, higher capital utilization is the main benefit. In the clothing industry, labour productivity is the key factor. In coal, both higher capital utilization and increased labour productivity are stressed. All four examples may be interpreted as attempts to reduce the 'porosity of the working day', but the extent to which this is manifested as work intensification varies from chemicals at one extreme to coal at the other.

Overall, the different experience of multiskilling in these four cases appears to be related to the balance of power between the forces of production within the enterprises. The strategic power of the workforce in chemicals, arising from the high organic composition of capital, coupled with a history of generally harmonious industrial relations, led to the multiskilling initiative being initiated by the union, and resulted in more benefits accruing to the workers. In the engineering case, the labour force was already highly skilled and workplace union organization was sufficiently powerful for management to involve the union in the multi-skilling initiative, again resulting in significant benefits to the workers involved. In clothing, the union posed no challenge to management plans to introduce teamworking and multiskilling, but this was a response to labour retention problems which could only be resolved by improvements to remuneration and working conditions. While the local labour market was conducive to these clothing workers obtaining a share of the benefits, they nevertheless experienced work intensification. In the coal case, the defeat of the union nationally in 1985 and the weakening of branch organization at colliery level in 1991, removed worker resistance and allowed management to introduce functional flexibility and work intensification without sharing the benefits of improved asset utilization, either in the form of additional remuneration, improved job satisfaction or reduced working time.

Notes

1. Pendleton and Winterton (eds) 1993.
2. Named after F.W. Taylor, who propagated the system of Scientific Management which underpinned highly specialized assembly lines.
3. Confederation of British Industry 1989.
4. Institute of Personnel Management 1992.
5. Winterton and Winterton 1996.
6. Rainbird 1990.
7. Winterton and Winterton 1994a.
8. Winterton 1991.
9. Winterton and Winterton 1989.
10. Leman and Winterton 1991.
11. Winterton and Winterton 1994b.
12. Barlow and Winterton 1996.
13. Winterton and Winterton 1994a: 34–5.

References

Barlow, A. and Winterton, J. (1996) 'Restructuring Production and Work Organization', in Taplin, I. and Winterton, J. (eds), *Restructuring within a Labour Intensive Industry*, Aldershot, Avebury, pp. 176–98.

Leman, S. and Winterton, J. (1991) 'New Technology and the Restructuring of Pit-Level Industrial Relations in the British Coal Industry', *New Technology, Work and Employment*, Vol. 6, No. 1, pp. 54–64.

Pendleton, A. and Winterton, J. (eds) (1993) *Public Enterprise in Transition: Industrial Relations in State and Privatized Corporations*, Routledge, London.

Rainbird, H. (1990) *Training Matters: Union Perspectives on Industrial Restructuring and Training*, Blackwell, Oxford.

Winterton, J. and Winterton, R. (1989) *Coal, Crisis and Conflict: The 1984–85 Miners' Strike in Yorkshire*, Manchester University Press, Manchester.

Winterton, J. (1991) 'Flexibility, New Technology and British Coal', in Blyton, P. And Morris, J. (eds), *A Flexible Future?*, De Gruyter, Berlin, pp. 275–94.

Winterton, J. and Winterton, R. (1994a) *Collective Bargaining and Consultation over Continuing Vocational Training*, RM. 7, Employment Department, Sheffield.

Winterton, J. and Winterton, R. (1994b) *Productivity and its Impact on Employment and Labour Relations in the Coal Mining Industry in the United Kingdom*, International Labour Office, Geneva.

Winterton, J. and Winterton, R. (1996) *The Business Benefits of Competence Based Management Development*, Department for Education and Training, HMSO, London.

Part III

Participation:
Problems and Possibilities

This section presents descriptions and analyses of local, engaged practices of adult educators and trainers as they work with the majority of people who are poor, working-class, women and children, living in urban and rural areas. The chapters are illustrative of issues and concerns in different sites of practice, including primary health-care, local politics, indigenous education, and civil society organizations.

The concept of participation in adult education and training is critiqued either explicitly or implicitly. Simplistic deficit models of learners make way for complex, nuanced arguments as to why particular target populations may not participate fully in adult education and training programmes. Shefer, Samuels and Sardien assess a course for adult educators which aims to train practitioners to understand and work with race, gender, culture and class as it constructs relationships among learners, and between practitioners and learners. They argue for more sophisticated theoretical approaches than are often used in workshop models. In turn, Gustavsson and Osman critique multicultural and anti-racist approaches, and begin to theorize a 'third way' which affirms agency in the learners to overcome barriers to their participation. They argue that the way to the universal is through recognition and knowledge of the other, the foreign and radically different.

Holt, Christie and Fry describe the struggle of Aboriginal people in Australia for indigenous education that affirms indigenous knowledge and processes, part of a global movement of indigenous people who are fighting back to have their histories and their understandings of the world recognized. They argue that colonial and imperialist attitudes continue to deny the value of indigenous knowledge; much of the adult education and training that is delivered in Australia is therefore inappropriate to Aborigines.

The question as to why more illiterate adults in South Africa do not campaign for better adult education facilities underpins the research described in the chapter by Breier. She presents a complex picture of the realities of unschooled adults who have multiple literacies acquired in informal ways, for example through modelling and informal apprenticeships. By implication the simplistic policies and practices pursued by many authorities, such as those described by Amutabi to 'eradicate illiteracy' in Kenya, are roundly criticized. Amutabi describes the contradictory history of adult education in Kenya, which resonates with histories elsewhere, where rhetorical support is not matched with adequate resources. Problems of achieving the goal of real participation within poor working-class communities are given texture in the descriptions of South African case studies by Matiwana, and Venter-Hildebrand and Houston.

16

Race, Class, Gender and Culture: A Possible Programme

Tammy Shefer, Joe Samuels and Tony Sardien

Adult educators challenging inequity in South Africa have focused on two key concerns: (1) developing tools with groups of adults to challenge oppression directly through, for example, anti-racism programmes and gender awareness training; and (2) creating awareness among adult educators of power relations and oppression in their own classrooms so they may detect and challenge these.

Much of the anti-oppression work has focused on the development of educational packages, often borrowed from European and American contexts, and their implementation within corporate, industrial and educational environments. The demand for work-based training has emerged from the context of affirmative action policy implementation and the consequent conflicts and difficulties this has raised at shop-floor level.[1] The demand for education and school-based training seems to be related to racism that has emerged from the process of integrating schools. Here the search has been for an inclusive curriculum (termed 'multiculturalism' or 'interculturalism') and methods to challenge discrimination in the classroom. Valuable work has been done at the level of early childhood by training preschool teachers.[2]

While it is not the task of this chapter to provide a rigorous critique of popular programmes,[3] their limitations or failings need to be discussed briefly as background to the present intervention.

The problem

First, many of the popular programmes attempt to provide a ready-made model. There is little space for critical discussion of theory in relation to oppression or critical evaluation of the model presented and other models in use. As they are presented as universal and able to fit any context, these abstract models lend themselves to unsophisticated application and ignore the complexities of different environments. The issue is not with the use of the models as educational tools, but with the uncritical way in which they are presented to trainees.

A second problem is that most current programmes focus on challenging single forms of oppression, such as racism or gender. They may make reference to other forms of oppression but do not attempt to provide an integrative theory of the interplay of different forms.

The failure to conceptualize the articulation of different forms of power may distort any analysis of or challenge to a particular oppression. In speaking of the oppression of women, for example, it has been pointed out by black[4] and other feminists[5] that black, working-class women experience gender oppression very differently from white, middle-class women. Early attempts by feminists to lump women into a homogeneous category with common experiences, interests and struggle have been overturned. It is now widely acknowledged that race, class, gender and other differences interact in ways that construct very different lived experiences of the different forms of oppression.[6]

There has been much criticism of early approaches such as the additive approach, which sees the different oppressions as acting together in a simplistic add-on way, as in the notion of triple oppression which has had much currency in South Africa, and the reductionist approach which sees one of the oppressions as determining all others, as in early Marxism.[7]

In grappling with the same issue, new perspectives are being developed in black feminism, socialist/Marxist feminism and post-structuralist/post-colonial feminist work. From these discourses emerged the notion of a complex intersection of oppression and subject positions, in which different oppressions overlap, interconnect, are involved in the construction of each other and may contradict each other in certain instances.[8]

A common thread within these perspectives is that it is imperative to acknowledge the differences in experiences of oppression and how different forms of oppression interact and act upon each other. Thus, a black woman is not simply doubly oppressed as a black person and a woman, but her oppression as a black woman is of a totally different nature from that of a white woman and a black man. An intervention which, for example, is not sensitive to the differences between men and women in the experience of racism may inhibit change by missing what is going on for half of the grouping.

Third, a further problem in much of the anti-racist and some of the gender work is that theory and conceptual frameworks rarely appear to be engaged with. The ready-made model includes and is informed by an uncontested theoretical framework. Concepts are used without question and may in themselves unintentionally perpetuate racism. An example is the commonly used phrase 'education for tolerance'. The ethnocentrism and racism inherent in the use of the word tolerance appears to escape question when used within a broader context apparently challenging these very things. Concepts such as culture and the apartheid categories of identity such as coloured, black, African, Indian and white are often used uncritically.

Race, class, gender and culture: a possible programme

A five-week module was presented as part of the Advanced Diploma for Educators of Adults course at the University of the Western Cape. It attempted to address the problems that have been highlighted. Thirty-five adult educators working within NGOs participated. They were men and women of diverse cultural backgrounds and predominantly black (i.e. formerly disenfranchised). The major aims of the module were:

- to explore participants' awareness of the impact of race, class, gender and culture on their own lives, including their work, their home and their organizations;
- to deepen participants' understanding of some of the theoretical perspectives on race, gender, class and culture with emphasis on the interaction of various forms of oppression; and
- to enable participants to explore critically the implications for their own and others' educational practices.

The module was theoretical; policy and practice were dealt with only in the drawing out of guidelines for these areas. Practical methods and techniques were to be picked up within a later section of the course on facilitation skills and educational methods.

Participatory methods, with a lot of group work, were used together with lecture inputs, which formed a key part of the input. Lectures were complemented by frequent use of audio-visual aids such as videos, charts and theoretical maps.

Experiential exercises helped clarify and concretize theoretically complex topics, particularly issues around the articulation of oppression. Here role-plays, visual displays and maps proved useful, while one of the most powerful techniques proved to be that of group drawing which stimulated many valuable and rich contributions from participants.

Participants were supplied with a course reader when the module commenced and were required to do an assignment at the end of the course.

Impact on participants

A written and oral evaluation of the module was undertaken. It should be remembered that participants constituted a diverse group from different organizational and occupational settings. This created different needs and their evaluations need to be viewed in this light.

Value of the course for adult educators' work

Some participants felt the theoretical input should have been more closely linked to the field of adult education and that they needed exposure to strategies to address the areas of power, inequality and oppression raised in the course. One student wrote: 'I was looking for more. Now that we have dealt with each factor, I wanted to see the knowledge linked to adult education.' While the module was not intended to deal with methods and techniques on the practical level, it was clearly a frustration for students that a movement to this level was not the logical conclusion. Perhaps the course also failed to address how power relations emerge in adult educational settings.

By contrast, some participants felt the theoretical insights gained could impact positively. One admitted: 'I became aware of differences in social structure, which I [usually] take for granted.' The discussion of culture as a potential source of both oppression and liberation motivated a number of participants to 'find out more about the other cultural groups' interests and ways of living'. The students appeared to have gained both through the theory and in observing the methods used by facilitators. One student pointed out: 'I will immediately change my method of assessment for groups/workshops and include various methods/theories that I have learnt.'

While the theoretical discourse may have been valuable, it was also overwhelming for some participants. 'There were a few sessions where there seemed to be an enormous amount of theory and I felt really drained and confused,' was one comment. The facilitators intended the module to provide rigorous exposure to theory which would elicit equally vigorous debate, but there are lessons to be learned from participants' experiences of overload and a sense of not bridging the gap between theory and practice.

Raising consciousness and sensitivity to issues of oppression

Participants drew important political conclusions about the historical nature of oppressions and the ways in which socio-historical transformations are partial processes. Said one: 'The course created an awareness that if a political struggle is over it does not mean that the other struggles are finished as well.... The struggles for [the] liberation of women [have] only started.'

While participants may already have been aware of the workings of power relations and oppression, the course stimulated a heightened awareness of these. One participant pointed out that the course facilitated a greater sensitivity to 'where the other person is coming from' and appreciation of how daily life is affected by these complex power relations.

Increased understanding

'I have a new understanding of our situation in South Africa and I am now in a position to analyse critically and objectively. The multidisciplinary approach to issues and topics creates awareness of the many different ways of looking at an issue.' These words reflected a general expression of having gained in understanding through exposure to critical theory. Another participant spoke of having always viewed racism as synonymous with apartheid but now having a 'dimensional view of race and racism from different contexts'.

Gaining skills/methods for dealing with the issues

While some may have found the theoretical focus of the course frustrating, they gained from observing the methods used in the delivery of the module; gained tools to deal with discriminatory attitudes in the workplace, and their educational work, and built elements of a framework for effecting and maintaining equitable working conditions.

Salient themes

A number of different themes emerged from delivery of the module which themselves reflect current areas of debate and contest in the larger South African context.

Critical questioning of categories

The sessions yielded much debate as to what constitutes the different social categories on which oppression and inequality are based. This was not surprising; during the post-election period particularly, social identities have been questioned in the light of political changes and the realignment of power provincially and nationally.

In the Western Cape, particularly among coloured people, there has been intense discussion concerning identity, given the ongoing radicalization politics of the main contending political parties.[9] In the course, discussions around what constitutes coloured identity, coloured culture and whether there is a coloured community or communities, reflected broader debates in the country.[10] The views expressed by participants ranged from ethnic nationalism to complete denial of any significant difference.

Personal tales highlighted the fluidity of socially constructed race differences. Examples were given of family relations who were white enough to pass for white, while other members of the same family were classified coloured. Similarly, notions of static, never-changing culture were deconstructed. One of the participants, classified African in old South

Africa, highlighted the contradictions between old and new cultures with which many people live. She sat with a blanket on her knees to keep her warm and spoke of how she received the blanket from her in-laws when marrying her husband. When she visits in the rural home of her husband's family, the blanket becomes a symbol of her married, mature woman status and she wears it over her body. The blanket is a symbolic way of putting on and taking off culture and the traditions that go with it.

Another example was a discussion on the shifting context of the tradition of circumcision: rather than the traditional 'going to the bush',[11] some African men are having a hospital operation. This was further evidence of the changing nature of culture and helped demonstrate for participants that culture was non-static and historically contextualized.

Not all participants agreed with notions that culture is in constant flux. These participants tended to be proponents of multiculturalism and argued that whether or not certain cultures like 'the coloured culture' have been created by apartheid, they now exist and constitute a shared body of experience and ways of being in the world, and must therefore be acknowledged as real cultures. While few of those disagreeing would disavow the existence of a real 'coloured culture', they questioned the assumption that this is something static and homogeneous. Those questioning the multicultural approach were concerned about the emergence of racism in the new guise of culture.

The question of culture raised debates on how to deal with it in an educational setting. It became clear that multicultural education has different meanings for different participants which reflects major debates in the educational and political arena. Two major discourses emerged in this respect which broadly fall into the categories outlined by Basil Moore[12] who identifies two groups of people, the 'realists' and the 'constructionists' in the anti-apartheid camp's views on culture. Realists argue that culture is a concept that exists materially and therefore cannot be discarded but should be separated from its apartheid origins. Constructionists argue that the notion of culture itself must be questioned and used strategically to build society.

Naming difference

> What are the people of the new South Africa going to be called? Will the crazy apartheid nomenclature for the different races be retained or will we all be Africans?... Now, of course, we've all been here in our home on the southern tip long enough to know what is meant by these terms [apartheid terminology], some of which predate the disastrous scholarship of Dr Verwoerd. But are they the terms we want to take with us into the new society?[13]

The question raised in terms of the social construction of difference and inequality was how to speak of difference without perpetuating old South

African notions of difference and inequality. The experience was one of not having words to speak of difference in a way which is not racist, sexist or classist. Our categories are full of a history of oppression; using them may be seen as an acceptance and perpetuation of this. It was clear that using a certain term to describe a perceived difference continues to have political significance, for example, the designating of African people in different coloured or African camps continues to divide the Western Cape electorate.

Another salient point to emerge in debates on naming difference is that at different times in history it becomes more popular to use different ways of naming – which might just be new words for old power. Thus speaking of different cultures rather than different races has become popular in the new racism described by theorists internationally.[14] Similar processes are clearly taking place in the South African context as well.[15]

Skutnabb-Kangas puts it this way:

> But racism has not died with the death of biological races. It is still needed for the unequal division of power and resources (there are other reasons, too, less functionalistic). Present-day racism has changed shape in order to seem more plausible.... Biologically-based racism has in most European and Europeanized countries been replaced by more sophisticated forms of racism, ethnicism and linguicism. These use the ethnicities, cultures and languages of different groups as defining criteria and as a basis for hierarchization.[16]

Participants' opinions ranged from the view that different identities exist and should be named as such, no matter what the origins of the names, to those who questioned altogether the current nomenclature and argued for a more critical process of naming difference.

Debates on national unity

'Difference has been well and openly marked in South Africa; the South African problem now is how to find some kind of common denominator for all groups, that is, how to forge some kind of common nationality out of a perceived entrenched diversity without segregating groups.'[17]

Much debate centred on the process of overcoming the historical divides of the old South Africa. What was emphasized was that this has to be carried out in a way that does not ignore the disadvantages that remain and will continue. Class inequality, for example, has not even begun to be addressed. Thus, while the state apparatuses have removed legalized racism, class inequalities forged historically on racial lines remain. Gender inequality is still firmly entrenched and racism is still present.

Differing views emerged on how South Africans should achieve a nation reflecting contemporary political debate. The primary tension was between the multicultural approach and those critical of the approach.

Those who embraced the multicultural approach felt that clear differences exist and need to be acknowledged.

Others felt that this acceptance of categories is too simplistic and ignores the differences within groupings, for example the way gender and class cut across cultural and ethnic groupings. Holding to old categories in this view was seen as dangerous in its maintaining of divides which lead to racism, ethnocentrism and unequal power relations. These participants agreed with Neville Alexander's[18] comment that 'if the nation does not become the primary identity of the people of South Africa, they will willy-nilly imbibe all manner of ethnic and racial allegiances or sub-identities as their ideological life-blood'.

Sharing life stories and experiences of difference

The sharing of biographies was a powerful aspect of the course and facilitated an appreciation of difference and the variety of experiences. It forced students to acknowledge differences within common categories, for example the different experiences of black people and class and gender differences that cut across the grouping. Participants spoke of how powerful the categorization was and how one was sanctioned for not fitting a stereotype.

Articulating articulation

A central objective of the course was to deal with the different forms of oppression in an integrated way through addressing each area separately in the first few sessions and then to spend the last few developing a theory of articulation. The design was exploratory and some difficulties did emerge.

We attempted to construct a theory based on participants' experience and the theoretical framework for articulation between various oppressions became much clearer to the facilitators towards the end of the module. Particularly instructive was the fifth session where the discourse on articulation was pulled together. Some key points emerged regarding the nature of articulation which are similar to some of the major points made in the literature.

More time should have been spent exploring how articulation occurs in the lived experience of people in order to materialize the theoretical framework. Participants' assignments showed they were able to integrate a framework of articulation effectively because many were able to explore in writing experiences where more than one oppression was involved.

One of the difficulties was that gender was ignored during the integration discussions. It seemed more difficult to acknowledge gender's role in the sessions on race, class and culture than it was to acknowledge and highlight the role of race, class and culture in the section on gender.

This might be related to the special salience given to race, ethnicity and culture and to the fact that the struggle for non-sexism has historically been marginalized in South African resistance politics.

Real issues in people's lives

The course dealt with real issues for people that impacted on all aspects of their daily lives, whether political, social, economic, interpersonal or personal. The material was thus neither abstract nor academic, and participants felt it had real implications for their personal lives.

Facilitation factors

A key difficulty was to what extent facilitators should guide and direct the thinking of participants. Popular education is traditionally non-directive and the presenters wanted participants to emerge with their own conclusions and therefore held back on their own views. In this context, this form of facilitation does not feel comfortable given the political import of the issues. In reflection we felt that facilitators have a right and responsibility to be more transparent as regards their own position and challenge what they see as problematic contributions.

Another problem related to the team work and issues of gender. The two male facilitators were mainly responsible for the facilitation and this was challenged in the first session by the group. Further, the gender session was facilitated by the female facilitator while the race, class and culture sessions were facilitated by the two male facilitators. While this reflected our areas of expertise, it may have reinforced the feeling that gender was being marginalized as only a women's issue. The group did, however, play an active role in challenging moments of gender marginalization as they emerged. It is therefore recommended that facilitators represent as far as possible a range of different group identities (including racial, gender and cultural) in the South African context.

Conclusion

The main lessons learnt in evaluating the module can be outlined as follows:

- *Theory moving into practice.* It is important in an academic setting to develop participants' critical abilities but equally important to provide space for thinking about the practical implications of theory for adult education practice.
- *An integrated account of oppression/inequality.* In any training/educational process dealing with oppression the articulation of oppression needs to occupy a central position.

- *The presentation of various debates and schools of thought.* This does not mean one should present a value-free face, but that one should present a range of theoretical frameworks for critical appraisal. In the very manner of presenting the course the potential of bias exists which needs to be spelled out rather than disguised. For example, the decision to place articulation centre stage illustrated a rejection of additive or reductionist approaches.
- *The questioning of assumed divisions, groupings and identities.* This involves critical discussion of existing notions of culture, race, ethnicity and gender. In summing up the position of a group of South African educators, Moore states: 'Students need to be able to deconstruct the concept of culture both intellectually and, more importantly, emotionally if they are going to find new ways of understanding who they are and what they can become.'[19]

The course makes two major contributions to the developing area of education challenging inequality and oppression: first, in the use of articulation as the central theoretical construct; and second, in presenting a range of theoretical perspectives, including those questioning the notion of fixed social identity, rather than a single module for consumption. Finally, to present any single model of intervention uncritically as a total solution will do adult educators an injustice and compromise the struggle for genuine equality and recognition of diversity in South Africa.

Notes

1. This point is based on personal communication by Tammy Shefer with trainers in the Post Office Services and Spoornet.
2. Notably the work done by the Early Learning Resource Unit (ELRU) based in Cape Town.
3. The critical comments made are not based on a rigorous evaluation of the arena but rather on impressions gained through a review of different organizations and individuals involved in the area of anti-racist and gender awareness training, including work done by CACE, Centre for Anti-Racism and Anti-Sexism Trust (CARAS), Centre for Cognitive Development, former Open School Association, Early Learning Resource Unit (ELRU), various consultancies, etc. The comments made are also generalized and we should remember that not all programmes in currency fall prey to all of the problems raised above.
4. We believe that these categories are all socially constructed. An African culture or European culture is no more real than a coloured culture. We assume that all social identity and all social categorization whether based on biological differences (as in sex differences) or not are socially constructed. Group identity, and the sense of shared history, norms and tradition are undeniably real, but does not remove the fact that they are socially constructed and shift and change through history and contexts.
5. See for example Anthias and Yuval-Davis 1992; Bottomly, De Lepervanche, and Martin 1991; Collins 1991; hooks 1981; hooks 1984; hooks 1988; King 1990;

and in South Africa, Barret *et al.* 1985; Cock 1980; Hendriks and Lewis 1994; Meer *et al.* n.d.; Walker 1990.

6. Barrett and Phillips 1992; Lennon and Whitford 1994; Anthias and Yuval-Davis 1992.

7. Barrett 1980; King 1990; Anthias and Yuval-Davis 1992.

8. Anthias and Yuval-Davis 1992; Bottomley, De Lepervanche and Martin 1991; Collins 1991; King 1990; Rajan 1993; Rajan 1994.

9. Samuels 1994.

10. Rasool 1995; Simone 1994.

11. This refers to the traditional practice of young males retreating from the community in order to undergo circumcision rites, administered by older men, and obviously without the use of Western medical techniques like anaesthetics and antibiotics, such as one might find in a hospital situation.

12. Moore 1994.

13. Johnson 1994.

14. Miles 1989; Skutnabb-Kangas 1990.

15. Mkwanazi and Carrim 1992.

16. Skutnabb-Kangas 1990.

17. Ribiero 1993.

18. Alexander 1995: 1.

19. Moore 1994: 261.

References

Alexander, N. (1995) 'The Great Gariep: Metaphors of National Unity in the New South Africa', Paper presented at the Institute for Democracy in South Africa Conference on National Unity and the Politics of Diversity: The Case of the Western Cape, Cape Town, 18–20 August.

Anthias, F. and Yuval-Davis, N. (1992) *Racialised Boundries: Race, Nation, Gender, Colour and Class and the Anti-Racist Struggles*, Routledge, London.

Barret, J., Dawber, A., Klugman, B., Obery, I., Shindler, J. and Yawitch, J. (1985) *Vukani Makhosikazi: South African Women Speak*, CIIR/Sigma Press, London.

Barrett, M. (1980) *Women's Oppression Today: Problems in Marxist Feminist Analysis*, Verso, London.

Barrett, M. and Phillips, A. (eds) (1992) *Destabilizing Theory*, Polity, Cambridge.

Bottomley, G., De Lepervanche, M. and Martin, J. (1991) *Intersexions: Gender, Class, Culture, Ethnicity*, Allen & Unwin, Sydney.

Cock, J. (1980) *Maids and Madams: A Study in the Politics of Exploitation*, Ravan Press, Johannesburg.

Collins, P.H. (1991) *Black Feminist Thought: Knowledge, Consciousness, and the Politics of Empowerment*, Chapman & Hall, New York.

Hendricks, C. and Lewis, D. (1994) 'Voices from the Margins', *Agenda*, Vol. 20, pp. 61–75.

hooks, b. (1981) *Ain't I a Woman: Black Women and Feminism*, South End Press, Boston.

hooks, b. (1984) *Feminist Theory: From Margin to Center*, South End Press, Boston.

hooks, b. (1988) *Talking Back: Thinking Feminist, Thinking Black*, Between the Lines, Toronto.

Johnson, S. (1994) 'Whats-In-A-Name Game', *The Saturday Argus*, 26 February.

King, D. (1990) 'Multiple Jeopardy, Multiple Consciousness: The Context of a

Black Feminist Ideology', in Malson, M., Mudimbe-Boyi, E., O'Barr, J. and Wyer, M. (eds), *Black Women in America: Social Science Perspectives*, University of Chicago Press, Chicago.

Lennon, K. and Whitford, M. (1994) *Knowing The Difference: Feminist Perspectives in Epistemology*, Routledge, London and New York.

Meer, F. *et al.* (n.d.) *Black Woman Worker: A Study in Patriarchy and Women Production Workers in South Africa*, Madiba Publications for IBR, Durban.

Miles, R. (1989) *Racism*, Routledge, London.

Mkwanazi, Z. and Carrim, N. (1992) 'From Apartheid to Modern Racism: The Case of Open Schools in South Africa', paper presented at Kenton Conference, Broederstroom 30 October–2 November.

Moore, B. (1994) 'Multicultural Education in South Africa: Some Theoretical and Political Issues', *Perspectives in Education*, Vol. 15, No. 2.

Rajan, R.S. (1993) *Real and Imagined Women: Gender, Culture and Postcolonialism*, Routledge, London.

Rajan, R.S. (1994) 'Ameena: Gender, Crisis and National Identity', *Oxford Literary Review*, Vol. 16, No. 1–2, pp. 147–76.

Rasool, E. (1995) 'Identity Questions in the Coloured Community: Unveiling the Heart of the Fear', paper presented at the Institute for Democracy in South Africa Conference on National Unity and the Politics of Diversity: The Case of the Western Cape, Cape Town, 18–20 August 1995.

Ribiero, R.F. (1993) 'Race and Nationality in Brazil and South Arica: Towards a Comparative Perspective', paper presented at the African Seminar, Centre for African Studies, University of Cape Town, 2 March.

Samuels, J. (1994) '"You People Liked Kriel So Much, That You Voted For Him": Categorization in the New South Africa and Implications for Adult Education', paper presented at Kenton 21 Conference, Gordon's Bay, 28–31 October 1994.

Simone, A.M. (1994) 'In the Mix: Remaking Coloured Identities', *Africa Insight*, Vol. 24, No. 3, pp. 161–73.

Skutnabb-Kangas, T. (1990) 'Legitimating or Delegitimating New Forms of Racism – The Role of Researchers', *Journal of Multilingual and Multicultural Development*, Vol. 11, No. 1–2.

Walker, C. (ed.) (1990) *Women and Gender in Southern Africa to 1945*, David Philip, Cape Town.

17

Multicultural Education and Life-long Learning

Berndt Gustavsson and Ali Osman

The recently revised curriculum in Sweden defines comprehensive and upper secondary education as 'Western' and 'Christian'. However, the nature of Swedish society and the policy espoused above are contradictory. Swedish society, with its large element of foreign cultures, is no longer a homogeneous one. These contradictions have created difficulties for the school system in handling cultural differences.

The educational system in Sweden today is facing issues and conflicts similar to those with which many multicultural and multiracial countries have wrestled, and continue to wrestle. For instance, when Muslim parents prevent their children from taking part in certain activities, such as gymnastics or eating certain foods, school leaders react often negatively by pointing out that it is in breach of the Swedish Education Act. It is also sometimes emphasized that as they now live in Sweden, they have to conform to the rules and regulations of the educational system in the country. An attitude like this towards other cultures follows a pattern which says that people who immigrate to Sweden must be assimilated or integrated into Swedish society. They have to become 'Swedes'. Integration, in this case, means that there is a mutual pattern codified in laws and decrees, or customs and ethnic rules, which everyone must follow. At the same time it is said that cultural differences should be maintained, but in educational politics and education this is never practised. This kind of immigration politics is based on the principle of similarity. It focuses on similarity as society encourages people to adapt to a common norm. Quite often this is done using the concept of equality, by reducing a complex concept such as multicultural understanding to that of a homogeneous melting-pot.

Different countries find themselves in different phases of multiculturalism. This influences their approach to social interaction, including society's attitude to education. If South Africa or Canada, which have been multicultural societies for a long time, are compared to the Nordic countries, then Scandinavia has many lessons to learn.

Multicultural education in a learning perspective

The debate in multicultural education and the different views on which it focuses emphasizes either external sociological factors or cultural factors. Such factors are no doubt important in understanding the issues and are a starting-point in understanding what is possible in a learning situation. A macro-level analysis of education has to be complemented by a micro-analysis of educational institutions. Such an approach is capable of providing insights into the experiences of the major actors in the system, the process that arises in complex organization and the social construction of knowledge.

Life-long learning is conceptualized as integrative. This view claims that people learn, though in different ways,[1] no matter where or when. An important consequence of such a view is that the learning which takes place in everyday life, whether it is at work, in the club, or through the media, should be integrated in the formal learning which takes place in different forms of education. Another consequence is that a community which encourages life-long learning also puts money into adult education. However, the implementation of these ideas in a multicultural situation raises complex issues: it involves taking into account the different experiences and histories of the various social groups in that society which have shaped their present realities and experiences.

A common starting-point for learning within the field of adult education, including popular education and learning in the workplace, is that learning must start with what is usually referred to as 'personal experience'.[2] Personal experience can be either practical and connected with working with the hands, or it can be theoretical and thus connected with the mind. When expressed in this way, learning new things is often interpreted as something one has encountered, and has been a part of, or experienced in such a tangible way that it has made imprints in, the adult student's conception of the world.

We, however, want to widen the concept of experience as it concerns the vantage point of adult learning to what, in the widest sense, is included in the expression 'everyday life'. 'Everyday' means everything around us that seems familiar, that is close and perceived as self-evident and unquestionable – in other words, the immediate interpretations we make of the world around us. It is evidently not a question of proceeding from 'the empirically observable', as one would phrase it with an empiricist view of knowledge. Nor is it a question of proceeding from 'practice', as is often said in a pragmatic understanding of knowledge.

Such inherited views on knowledge do not consider the cultural and philological frame of reference that is part and parcel of our perception of the world and interpretation. To start from the familiar means to start from what we have in our minds and in our bodies. This perspective is related to phenomenology, but goes beyond the view of Husserl.[3]

Expressions like 'learning has its starting point in everyday life' are saying that learning refers to the already known. Thus, all learning could be reduced to the dialectics between the known and the unknown. But what then is the unknown?[4] In order to clarify this, let us go back to Rousseau, with whom this whole discussion appears to have begun. According to Charles Taylor, Rousseau was the first to clarify the thought of acknowledgement. Rousseau constitutes the beginning of the progressivist tradition in education. He has also been used, first to demonstrate how women are excluded, and then how cultures other than the Western are excluded from learning and knowledge.

Rousseau's *Émile*, for instance, says that knowledge begins with the senses and the self-made experiences. Then follows the description of *sensus communis*, the sense which unites and synthesizes that knowledge which has its origin in the five senses. It is through this description that the Copernican shift takes place in the view of knowledge as being a product of a person's self-activity and creative power rather than a passive reflection of the outer world through sensory perceptions.

What is less well known is that in Rousseau's writings there is also a first trace of the dialectics of learning, saying that people change their views of everyday life by encountering what is strange and different. Suddenly, the stranger is standing here among us, a fact that may change our view both of ourselves and of our everyday life – we have encountered the unknown.[5]

When Charles Taylor discusses the possibilities of gaining knowledge in the meeting between different cultures, he refers to Gadamer's concept of horizon:

> What must happen is what Gadamer has called 'a coalescence of horizons'. We learn how to move within a wider horizon, where what we earlier took for granted as a background to our values can be attached as a possibility to the different background in a formerly unfamiliar culture.[6]

When Gadamer formulates this view in *Wahrheit und Methode*, he starts out from Hegel's thought about man's self-alienation. Already in their practical work people leave themselves by objectifying themselves in the object of work. They do it in another way by reflecting theoretically on the world. When an individual has thus restored and incorporated the work or the reflection with himself, he has also reinterpreted the world and at the same time become someone else. In that way the hermeneutic circle goes round and round: we constantly incorporate new horizons with ourselves and with our conception of the world. This view of the growth of knowledge and learning has been named the hermeneutics of reconciliation.[7] In the dialogue between cultures it is possible to reconcile differences and build up understanding between them.

We intend here to formulate a different view on learning, without disregarding the suspicion and the critical eye which must be added to the acquisition of knowledge, and which put a conflict perspective on the antagonisms that are built into the relationship between different culture groups.

Hereby, in the spirit of Ricoeur, we put stress on out-distancing ourselves from what is mundane, familiar and nearby. To out-distance oneself means something much more problematic and extensive than what Gadamer and Taylor include in the ability to meet what is foreign and different. It includes a concept of interpretation which stipulates that learning does not occur only, or even primarily, when consciousness meets consciousness in an eternal dialogue where the horizons of understanding widen organically and in circles, but is something that happens when an individual meets unfamiliar perspectives and surprising aspects of existence. And that is precisely what happens when perspectives from separate cultures meet.[8]

The different perspectives represented by, for example, different religions and languages have great difficulties in meeting, and even greater difficulties in achieving immediate understanding of one another. In an ordinary adult school-class in South Africa, for instance, four different languages and as many religions might be represented by black, coloured, Asian and white people. Yet English is the dominant language and Christianity the dominant religion. The mere fact that people from these groups have come together in the same classroom is an exception in a country which has systematically kept the ethnic groups apart. We know ourselves how difficult it is to understand, for instance, a Muslim way of thinking, and for Muslims to understand a Christian way of thinking.

What we want to say by these examples is that it is not an easy thing to widen the horizons of understanding in real life. Understanding must pass through a deep comprehension of one's own identity. Therefore, all learning begins with self-identification, which belongs to what we call everyday life. But, as so many in modern psychology and sociology have pointed out, we have no immediate access to our own self. Many do not even believe that we have an authentic personality to refer to. We do not deny this, but even so, we think it is a difficult point.[9]

The first difficulty lies in the question of what the core of our personal identity really consists of. Some would say individuality, others would put it down to ethnic group or gender. We would say that we are humans primarily by virtue of our all belonging to one and the same race, namely the human race. Every one of us represents the broadly humane and we do so by virtue of our differences and dissimilarities, as well as our similarities.[10]

What is discussed in the flood of recently published literature concerning relations between cultures is the recognition of dissimilarities. This means a relativization of Western culture which, in its claim to represent the broadly humane, has, for centuries, oppressed, dominated and almost destroyed large parts of the populations of the earth and trampled down its diversity of cultures. This fact is easily forgotten by all essentialists who in Western cultural inheritance only see the good, the right and the beautiful. The dominating, oppressive and destructive side of Western culture is concealed in such a perspective. Authors and scientists with their roots in the Third World are now cognizant of this.

In a more truly humanist perspective which does not count the broadly humane as belonging solely to the West, but to the great variety of all mankind, a truer human face may emerge. Here, variety would be seen as a wealth and an asset, and not as a threat. This would require the members in every cultural group to leave their habitual patterns in order to approach the unknown and foreign.

A traditional humanist departure point considers the perspective that human beings transcend themselves: that in order to learn something new one has to unlearn entrenched perspectives. The fundamental metaphors which represent such a view can be found in the Bible, but also in the Greek tradition. A closely related humanistic device says that 'nothing human is foreign to me'. The first idea means that humans learn about themselves through the unknown. The other means that nothing is so foreign to me that I am afraid to meet the truly human.[11] Not even the dark, destructive and aggressive sides, which have always been a part of human life, are excluded. Ricoeur claims that people learn about themselves through the traces and marks they have made in the history of their own culture. We think this is also a step, but only a first step, in a universal educational process. It is only in meetings with the other, which to us represents a foreign culture, that we can learn about our own culture. The road towards the universal goes through recognition and knowledge about the other, the foreign and the radically different.[12]

Multicultural and anti-racist education

Research and debate on education in culturally diverse communities has been polarized in the same manner as the debate and research in educational sociology between those who defend multicultural education, and those who defend anti-racist education. The purpose and aim of multicultural education according to Banks is 'to remodel schools and other educational institutions so as to make it possible for students belonging to different classes or racial or ethnic groups to experience success and social mobility'.[13] There have been a variety of approaches that have been developed for this purpose. Some focus on the content of the curricula with the intention of including experiences from formerly excluded groups, those having been subject to the 'blindness of specific features'. Other approaches focus on goals and strategies which could improve the academic performance of students from lower social classes or other disadvantaged groups. Banks has identified five such different dimensions and practices in multicultural education which can be viewed as distinct but also as interrelated:

- Integration of content, which aims to incorporate the experiences, the struggle and the culture of minorities into the curricula.
- Construction of knowledge, which focuses on what methods scientists use to construct knowledge.
- Reduction of prejudice.
- Equality pedagogy.
- Strengthening of school culture.

Unlike Banks however, Grinter contends that the two approaches are different and cannot be reconciled. First and foremost, he points out that those working with multicultural education regard social structures as wrong, and that they can be reformed by incorporating separate parts of cultures in one and the same social value system. By projecting a positive picture of different cultures in society they think that all groups might be favoured – 'underachievement is seen in terms of cultural interference'.[14] An anti-racist view of education is based on the idea that unequal distribution of power and resources in society is the fundamental issue or problem, not culture. Conflict is, consequently, seen as an important element in the social system. The community is not regarded as a neutral area for common values, but 'as an arena in which dominating values change themselves into cultures which are not seen as equal in power and value'.

Second, educational policy does not play a central role in anti-racist education as it does in multicultural education. The purpose of policy in multicultural education is to convince individuals to change their attitude towards other cultures and to prevent the fragmentation of society; as a result, reforms play a central role in multicultural education. Race is primarily defined in cultural terms and thus de-politicized. In anti-racist education, racism is seen as 'the organized principle of the social and political structure, closely related to class and other forms of discrimination which deny human rights – an artificial construction created to underpin inequality'.[15] The system of discrimination can only be confronted by examining the power distribution in a society, which makes some groups powerless. The purpose must, in such a perspective, be to improve the life chances of minorities, rather than to understand and inform the majority group about the lifestyles or cultures of minority groups.

Third, both views work for greater justice. Multicultural education does this in the form of values, while anti-racist education does it by giving equal possibilities of success to the members of all racial groups. For a long time, students from working-class and cultural minorities have been subjected to special measures, because they were considered to have poorer qualifications and requirements for studies, compared to the majority of students.[16] These deficiencies were explained in cultural terms, hence victimizing the victim, and avoiding the analysis of the power structures in the society and the role of education in maintaining and reproducing these structures.

Many countries have, as a consequence, accepted a policy that accentuates assimilation and emphasizes 'incorporation into the dominating culture and language, which is seen as the means to eradicate these differences'.[17] Implicit in this view is a notion of common values, structural functionalism, universalism and individualism in a Western cultural conception. Yet this policy of assimilation has not improved opportunities or academic performance for minorities in multicultural societies. Nor has it improved the socio-cultural position of students from minority groups. This policy has thus turned into one which emphasizes integration. Such a liberal-democratic concept is based on equal opportunities for education. Rhetorically it has had an accepting attitude towards minority cultures, but underneath there is an implicit assumption of cultural inequality.

The Swedish debate has swung between these two perspectives, assimilation and integration. Culture and language have all the time been said to be the explanatory variables for failure in studies. The most significant fact in Sweden is that the educational system has been defined as Swedish and Eurocentric, despite all the talk about our living in a multicultural society. Neither the assimilationist nor integrationist perspectives have hitherto succeeded in showing any improved opportunities or results as regards educational opportunities for minority groups.

The point of conflict between the two views is what is meant by the concept of culture. The culture-concept as it is used in the discussion of multicultural education has been criticized chiefly by those who speak in favour of anti-racist education. Here one points out that 'multicultural education is based on the belief that racism is founded on misunderstanding and ignorance which leaves the individuals open to a racist misinterpretation of non-white roads in life and value systems'.[18]

Contrary to this is the view by anti-racist educators 'that racism is an ideology based on an acquired (learned) attitude of white superiority towards human groups that Europe and North America have exploited throughout history'. Inequality of power and distribution of resources between different cultural groups, and the acceptance of this as a natural state of affairs, are consequences of this attitude. The structural factors which have caused this have not been questioned. Multicultural education, whose philosophy is understanding the cultures of minority groups, thus cannot eradicate racism, because racism is neither rooted in cultural misunderstanding nor in negative images of black cultures. Positive images are always exposed to the erosive effect from competition for resources and opportunities of social and economic conditions.[19]

The controversy between the two approaches – multiculturalism and anti-racist education – resembles, in many ways, the controversy which characterizes the sociological debate on education. Anti-racism focuses on power and structural imbalance, whereas multiculturalism, as practised today, emphasizes cultural understanding, tolerance and universal value systems as instruments of integration, with the aim of maintaining unity in diversity.

Both views, however, in Europe and North America regard minorities and immigrants as victims of circumstances, who lack cultural resources to survive in their new environment, or as members of an ethnic group and therefore victims of discrimination and racism. Both approaches are simple images of a complex problem. First, they assume that all immigrants have similar problems in their new countries, independent of background. Second, both approaches deny the existence of a free will and creativity and the ability of individuals to change their situations.

Notes

1. Dave 1972.
2. Börlin *et al.* 1990.
3. A phenomenological view of knowledge in the widest sense is included in broad and influential perspectives like hermeneutics, from Gadamer to Ricoeur.
4. Rousseau, in Gallagher 1992.
5. Gallagher 1992: 124.
6. Gutman and Taylor 1992: 69.
7. Weinsheimer 1985.
8. Valdés 1991.
9. Ricoeur thinks that we have access to our own self via man's objectifications. This could be a possible view to develop, in connection with learning between cultures. It implies that there is no need to be imprisoned in one's own context.
10. Garcia 1983: 113f.
11. This thought is represented in a broad humanistic tradition from Montaigne onwards.
12. Aho 1994.
13. Banks 1993.
14. Grinter 1992.
15. Grinter 1992.
16. May 1994: 32.
17. Grinter 1992.

18. Grinter 1992.
19. Grinter 1992.

References

Aho, J. (1994) *This Thing of Darkness, A Sociology of the Enemy*, Washington DC.
Banks, J.A. (1993) 'Multicultural Education: Historical Developments, Dimensions, and Practice', in Hammond, L.D. (ed.), *Review of Research in Education*, American Educational Research Association, Washington DC.
Börlin *et al.* (1990) *Att utbilda vuxna*, Stockholm.
Dave, R.H. (1972) *Foundations of Lifelong Education*, Pergamon Press, New York.
Gallagher, S. (1992) *Hermeneutics and Education*, State University of New York Press, New York.
Garcia, R. (1983) 'Cultural Diversity and Minority Rights: A Consummation Devoutly to Be Demurred', in Lynch, J. and Mogdil, C. (eds), *Human Rights, Education and Global Responsibilities*, Falmer Press, London.
Grinter, R. (1992) 'Multicultural or Antiracist Education? The Need to Choose', in *Education for Cultural Diversity: Convergence and Divergence*, Vol. 1, Falmer Press, London.
Gutman, A. and Taylor, C. (1992) *Multiculturalism and 'The Politics of Recognition': An Essay by Charles Taylor*, Princeton University Press, Princeton, NJ.
May, S. (1994) *Making Multicultural Education Work*, Ontario Institute for Studies in Education, Toronto.
Valdés, M.J. (1991) *A Ricoeur Reader: Reflection and Imagination*, Harvester Wheatsheaf, Toronto.
Weinsheimer, J. (1985) *Gadamer's Hermeneutics, A Reading of Truth and Method*, London.

18

Aboriginal Education: A Case for Self-determination

Lillian Holt, Michael F. Christie and Norman Fry

There is an Aboriginal[1] dot painting on the cover of the summary and recommendations volume of the 1994 *National Review of Education for Aboriginal and Torres Strait Islander Peoples*. The painting is the work of four Walungurru (Kintore) artists, and its symbolic shapes and colours express a message about Aboriginal education. Put simply, in the words of the artists, the message is: 'At Walungurru the yanangu people now know about schools – they are going to control their own school ... if the walypala [whites] remain solely in charge, our children will not learn properly at all.' In the report that message is repeated again and again. Aboriginal involvement and self-determination in the education process is vital, it says, and a major goal of any future policy is to increase such participation at all levels.[2]

This sentiment resonates with the feelings of indigenous peoples around the world. In 1993 it was the United Nations Year of the Indigenous People. During this period indigenous education and the prevalent denial of special provisions in form and content of education for indigenous populations were widely discussed. The struggle of Aboriginal people in Australia for indigenous education which affirms indigenous knowledge and processes is part of the global movement of indigenous people for their rights and values.

The 1994 report, which was chaired by Mandawuy Yunupingu, referred back to an earlier Aboriginal education policy task force that had been set up in 1988. The aim of this group had been to address the fact that after two hundred years of white occupation 'Aborigines remain the most severely educationally disadvantaged people in Australia'. The task force recommended a national policy (hereafter the Joint Policy) that was endorsed by all governments in Australia and came into effect on 1 January 1990. There were 21 long-term goals set out under four headings: involvement, access, participation and outcomes. A recurring theme is that despite the expenditure of large sums of money and a long history of government initiatives, Aborigines still lag behind other Australians in all four areas.

The two documents are well intentioned. The prominence given to graphs and figures from the Australian Bureau of Statistics, however, emphasizes the importance given to quantifiable rather than qualitative data. Figures are important and we have no objection to data that puts beyond dispute the fact that Aborigines, particularly Aboriginal males, do not participate in formal education to the same extent as other Australians. Our objection is that the particular figures used in the reports force us to focus on current models of mainstream education. There are no figures showing how many Aborigines participate in Aboriginal education. The figures imply that all learning occurs in formal educational settings when we know that a great deal of education takes place in informal settings – in community development employment projects for example, or in the store or the art outlet. Perhaps the most damaging assumption implicit in the figures is that more is better. So what if more Aboriginal children stay on longer at school if that school experience is demoralizing, if it is a negative rather than a positive personal experience. Statistics show nevertheless that Aborigines have a smaller slice of the education pie.

The 1994 review obviously anticipated the sort of objections raised when it recommended that 'education provided for Aboriginal peoples and Torres Strait Islanders must be culturally appropriate'. But even here we detect a certain intransigence. Perhaps it is only a case of poor phrasing but the words 'provided for' imply that Aborigines will continue to be recipients, a group provided for by others rather than serviced by themselves. The saving grace of this report is that Aborigines were included on the panels, in the consultations and among the submissions that were received. More importantly it insists that local Aboriginal control be an essential ingredient in any future Aboriginal educational policy.

It also notes the 1990 Joint Policy's 'silence about supporting alternative and community controlled education initiatives' and acknowledges that its language and recommendations could be construed as assimilationist. It is a pity, given this perspicacity, that the 1994 report continued to focus for the most part on mainstream white education and did not recommend more appropriate models of education, particularly in the area of adult education. Many Aboriginal adults feel rejected by mainstream education. The competitive nature of Western primary and lower secondary education, with its emphasis on grades and comparative performance, has often proved a stumbling block for them.

The problem is that there are so few non-threatening pathways back to formal study for those Aborigines who wish to have a second go at it. Bridging courses exist but they are usually located on Technical and Further Education (TAFE) or university campuses, and aim to prepare students for academic courses rather than simply revivifying a love of learning. In such a situation the emphasis is once again on academic or vocational skills rather than on life skills, on immediate rather than long-term learning goals. Our argument is that the current TAFE and university system may work well for particular types of learners but that low enrolment and high drop-out figures among Aboriginal students could point to the need for alternative models of adult education.

One exception is Tauondi in Port Adelaide, South Australia. The word 'Tauondi' is a local Kaurna word (the tribe which originally inhabited the Adelaide plains) and means 'breakthrough'. The name was changed last year after having been known for many years as the Aboriginal Community College. A name change was needed as the college was often mixed up with other local mainstream educational institutions such as the local TAFE college. Tauondi is an autonomous entity, funded approximately half and half by the Commonwealth and state governments.

Tauondi has been in existence since 1973. It came about partly as a result of Aboriginal activism and the success of the 1967 referendum which allowed for Aboriginal people to be counted in the census, and which gave responsibility for the welfare of Aboriginal people to the Commonwealth government. Over 90 per cent of Australians voted 'yes' to the referendum, and politicians, keen to be part of the more positive climate in Aboriginal affairs, made money available for the establishment of Tauondi.

In a nutshell, Tauondi is for Aboriginal people over 18 years of age. There are no prerequisite or entry exams. The college has based its programmes on a holistic philosophy of education which includes the physical, mental and spiritual dimensions. Crucial to providing the right environment for learning are a sense of ownership, Aboriginality and autonomy. Aboriginal people have decision-making powers over their own affairs and Aboriginal culture is acknowledged and affirmed. This fosters self-esteem and pride in Aboriginal identity. Tauondi is a type of 'community college' and offers personal, work and community-related programmes.[3]

Why the need for a separate college for adult Aboriginal people, we may well ask? The historical legacies of dislocation, dispersion, denigration – a form of cultural genocide – had been thoroughly entrenched by the early sixties, not only in the psyche of Aboriginal people but also in the minds of non-Aboriginals. It was a case of 'them and us'. Australia certainly had its own form of homelands. From the earliest years of white invasion, Aborigines were gathered (at times by force) on settlements that were scattered in out-of-the way locations and controlled by missionaries or Boards for the Protection of Aborigines. Lillian Holt's grandfather was sent, in 1919, to one of these settlements, Cherbourg in Queensland, which was originally set up in 1908 for so-called 'disadvantaged or difficult Aborigines'.

Such punishment in the form of banishment meant that cultural castration took place and language, kinship and country were lost or adulterated to a great extent. Incarceration and separation took their toll. However, out of it all came survival and now revival. Australia's treatment of Aboriginal people has a long and murky history which is only just being unravelled and revealed. It parallels the treatment of other indigenous people around the world. There are many painful similarities and in terms of education many lessons to be shared.

In Scandinavia, for instance, the indigenous Sami, whose contact history and current circumstances have some parallels with those of Aboriginal people, have their own 'folk high schools'. They are independent and focused specifically on the promotion of Sami language and culture. In terms of their aims and operation there are some interesting comparisons to be made with Tauondi.

When people ask, 'Why the need for an Aboriginal-only institution?' the answers can be found in the forced eviction of Aborigines from their own land, the theft of that land, forced assimilation, the introduction of alcohol, and the imposition of foreign religion and education systems.

Policies prevailed over people and by the 1930s it was thought that Aborigines would somehow just 'die out'. By the 1960s, however, Aboriginal people, whilst down, were definitely not out. Aboriginal people and their supporters did not sit idly by and allow such indignities to be thrust upon them. Part of their response was to establish Aboriginal organizations and schools as a cultural bulwark against the invasive and often addictive nature of Western mores.

Indigenous Australia has always been the shadow side of non-indigenous Australia and by the early 1970s – following the referendum of 1967 – money started to be pumped in to do something about the so-called 'Aboriginal problem'. It was thought that education, health and employment could and should be improved, thereby allowing Aboriginal people to make it into the mainstream. Grand programmes accompanied by grand slogans such as 'self-determination' were set up.

Places such as Tauondi were started with the aim of addressing the over-riding and often overwhelming concerns of their clientele. These included the issues of racism, economic disadvantage, health and education – the concomitants of colonialism. Things grew slowly but surely, and it would be churlish to understate the progress that has been made. Numbers of Aboriginal people have gone on to higher education and are working in many areas of the workforce, where black faces were never seen before.

New and deeper issues, however, are arising. These issues are more internal than external and this is where discussion of such issues can become fuzzy, because often one is misinterpreted or dismissed as speaking in a philosophical sense rather than a fundamental one. It is not that these issues have not always been there, but with the emergence of the generation of so-called 'educated' Aborigines they are beginning to be articulated, and demand to be addressed. They are spiritual questions and go to the core of identity of indigenous people. Questions such as 'Education for what, by whom and for whom?' Questions such as 'How does one combat inherent institutional racism, which one encounters whether one is educated or not?' Such questions need to be examined in the context of: 'What is education?' What is on offer? Is it just about mere schooling and qualifications, rather than life-long and life-affirming education which encompasses learning from one another through cultural diversity and integrity? Is it about assimilation and acceptability, that is 'putting spit and polish' on blacks, or is it about dignity and discovery?

In the clamour for qualifications, Aboriginal Australians have had to work twice as hard at 'getting educated' whilst at the same time having to cope with the everyday issues of racism. This is in addition to educating non-Aboriginal people as to the true history and blueprint of the country. It is a somewhat burdensome task given that the population of Australia at the last census was approximately 17 million and the population of Aboriginal people was only 265,458 – just over a quarter of a million. Small stakes and status in the overall big picture! But big spiritual costs in a one-way process called the education of Aboriginal people.

Given the strides of the last quarter century and the fact that education for and by Aborigines is much more acceptable today, there is now a feeling among indigenous people that as more needs are addressed, more questions also arise. In a place like Tauondi, the concern has always been about the sort of person we wish to turn out. A clever person or a wise person? A merely qualified person or a dignified person? It has been an enormous struggle to keep our agenda upfront, and not fall into the danger of turning out 'skilled barbarians', as a report on higher education warned some years back.

Education thus means different things for different people and should not just be about perpetuating the status quo and the paraphernalia of power, property, prestige and possessions. Aboriginal people are beginning to highlight the deficits of education whereby identity loss has come at the cost of accreditation. The white education pie is not necessarily wholesome. Aboriginal people are questioning more and more aspects of success which conspire against their identity. Having been adulterated and assimilated, more and more are returning to their roots and rejecting the outside labels – both negative and positive.

We do not believe that mindless pursuit of material success and status, where the externals are more important than the internals and where one is judged to be a decent human merely by the benefit of such status, is the way to go. This is not readily accepted by indigenous people, and it is natural that more and more questions are being asked about this education process. It is the marginalized and the excluded who will point out the inadequacies of the processes.

As we enter the twenty-first century, indigenous education is in a unique position to point the way, not just for indigenous people but for Westerners as well. It can point to the need for wholeness, based on a holistic approach to education, the physical, mental and spiritual. It can point to the need for atmosphere in learning environments as opposed to the hugely monolithic and often impersonal and daunting structures of learning institutions. It can point to the need for humour which, as Edward De Bono, the lateral thinker, says is the most underutilized factor in Western intellectual education. It can point to the need to address where people come from and where they are at, and not just assume that access equals equality. It also includes the need to honour intuition, passion and one's own spirituality within it all.

'Indigenous education can point the way for ALL – not just indigenous people – to acknowledge the pain of the past and confront the pain of the present'.[4] This can confront the reality of racism and uproot cultural arrogance.

Cultural arrogance, as practised overtly or covertly through deficit curriculum, is narrow, single-minded and arrogant when it fails to incorporate another world view. White Australia has been left severely diminished and bereft through its lack of inclusion of the Aboriginal world view and its accompanying history. Australia has a black history (no pun intended!) which extends some forty thousand years prior to European arrival. This is something which non-Aboriginal Australian eyes are now beginning to behold not only with awe and wonder but with pain and guilt. Nevertheless, the latter may be a necessary requirement of their own exorcism.

There is an old Russian proverb which says, 'Dwell on the past and you lose one eye, forget the past and you lose two.' The past informs the present. It is a process of rectifying rather than regretting. And the past need only be as recent as twenty years. New lessons have to be learned, and old pains confronted. It is about discovering, recovering and uncovering. Given that indigenous education has mainly been about a more benign process of assimilation and integration, it is now time to heed the call of the inherent issues of our own humanity within the process of education.

Too often the virtues of education are propounded without questioning some of the processes involved. In Australia, the juggernaut of economic rationalism is driving the education agenda. This means that education is mostly seen in terms of accreditation, skills and qualifications. This is a myopic view because although these are badly needed in a highly complex and technological society, they need to be augmented with more human qualities.

We need to think more laterally and holistically about what the term education means. Who benefits? Education for what, for whom, and why? In doing so we may have to incorporate new language and imagery. Perhaps it will mean that we need to go deeper, and ponder the question of a new vision of work. These are serious spiritual questions, born of a yearning that comes from working within and with indigenous institutions for many years where we have learned far more than we could ever possibly teach. They are questions which will drive the agenda of indigenous education in Australia into the twenty-first century and, hopefully, inform and impact on the agenda of non-indigenous Australia.

This is already happening to a degree in Australia, what with an official policy of reconciliation with its indigenous people through the Federal Government and its Council for Aboriginal Reconciliation, where questions at all levels are beginning to be announced and addressed. In that sense, non-Aboriginal people are being educated freely and wholly through an inclusive history. Perhaps, as a result, it will mean the rediscovery of Australia's authentic as opposed to Eurocentric cultural identity. Such a discovery could mean an acceptable cultural identity for all – Aborigines as well as the waves of migrants who have arrived here since 1788. It will mean dignity and wisdom, inclusion rather than exclusion, connectedness rather than disconnectedness, and reconciling with rather than recoiling from the issues.

Writers like Stephen Harris, Jackie Wolfe and Michael J. Christie have contrasted Western knowledge systems with those of Aboriginal people. Western education tends to be reductionist, objective and positivist whereas Aboriginal education has traditionally been holistic, subjective and experiential.[5] Western schools separate learning and life, reduce knowledge into subjects and segments, and teach according to set curricula via blocks of time and graduated classes. Traditional Aboriginal education takes place at any time and is grounded in interaction rather than presentation. Essential elements of the Aboriginal world are not subject to scientific inquiry or proof. Because Aboriginal survival has depended on reciprocity, learning has always been characterized by co-operation rather than competition. In formal Western adult education the gap between Aboriginal and Western styles has widened recently with the emphasis on competency-based training (CBT) and assessment. CBT reduces knowledge to component parts which can be learned and tested according to set levels of competence. Such a system tends to diminish interaction among learners and between learners and their teachers.

Tauondi aspires to an holistic approach where learning is carried out in a context that values personal experiences, emotions and the mind. The objective is the concern with the improvement of an individual's specific skills and knowledge and with the development of the whole person.

Affirmation of Aboriginal education in Australia can be seen as part of a global movement 'from below' to affirm the value of indigenous knowledge everywhere. A holistic, people-centred approach to adult learning which acknowledges learning in the family, in the community, in inter-personal interactions at the workplace, is critical as a counter-balance to a reductionist human capital view. Knowledge is not owned by formal education institutions. It also resides in people, in their oral histories, stories, riddles, ballads, legends, song cycles, poems, legends and folk tales.

Notes

1. 'Aboriginal' is used in this article to denote both Aboriginal and Torres Strait Islander peoples.
2. *National Review of Education for Aboriginal and Torres Strait Islander Peoples. Summary and Recommendations* 1994: 6.
3. Gray, M. (ed.) 1993.
4. Howard 1991.
5. Wolf *et al.* 1991; Christie 1985; Harris 1990.

References

Christie, M.J. (1985) *Aboriginal Perspectives on Experience and Learning: The Role of Language in Aboriginal Education*, Deakin University Press, Geelong.
Gray, M. (ed.) (1993) *Tauondi: A Record of the Aboriginal Community College's First 20 Years*, Aboriginal Community College, Adelaide.
Howard, G. (1991) *A White American*, Reach Centre for Multicultural and Global Education, Seattle, Washington.
Harris, S. (1990) *Culture and Learning: Tradition and Education in North East Arnhem Land*, NT Education Department, Darwin.
National Review of Education for Aboriginal and Torres Strait Islander Peoples. Summary and Recommendations (1994), AGPS, Canberra.
Wolfe, J. *et al.* (1991) *Indigenous and Western Knowledge and Resource Management Systems*, University of Guelph, Guelph.

19

The Plight of Adult Education in Kenya

Maurice Amutabi

In traditional Kenyan societies, education was an all-round, continuous process. It was based on a common understanding of relevance, compromise, universality, generality and continuity. It was both practical and theoretical. In a sense, it was also experimental and conditioned by the need for understanding and appreciating the intrinsic and complex socio-political and natural environment. Because of its universality, it excluded nobody. Indeed, all members of society participated as teacher and learner according to their rank, calling and gender in what was a holistic educational framework.

At the end of the nineteenth century, the advent of schools and formal education disrupted the egalitarian basis of knowledge acquisition. Kenya was colonized in 1895. A plethora of Christian mission stations completely overshadowed almost 1,000 years of Islamic presence. Reading and writing soon became the most sought-after 'magic'. Although society's poor could not afford the cost of education, for many the newly introduced, selective and segregative school system became the norm. This created rifts not only between the people and the environment, but also between literate and illiterate persons. By giving supremacy to book knowledge and time-framed learning, the education system created by the Christian missionaries and the colonial government marginalized indigenous knowledge. It led to large and ever-increasing numbers of 'illiterate' people.

In 1948 the Universal Declaration of Human Rights addressed the concerns of this disadvantaged sector by proclaiming basic education for all as a fundamental right. In the light of this declaration and partly due to other social, economic and political forces, the colonial government developed centres to train adults with the aim of improving the capacity of the colonial machinery. At independence the Kenyan government appeared set to improve upon the colonial record in this sector. The major drive came in 1966, three years after independence, with the launching of the National Literacy Campaign by President Jomo Kenyatta.

Before independence in 1963, Kenya did not have a development plan for adult education because the colonial government was more concerned with basic primary education for children: this provided the government with low-level functionaries for the bureaucracy. The majority of the pupils became unskilled labourers on white farms and in industries. At the time, adult education and training was also concentrated in the military where recruits were trained for military duty.

At the time of independence, the Kenyan government set out to improve the education sector. At that time about 90 per cent of Kenyans were illiterate. As a direct result of the National Literacy Campaign the rate was reduced to 80 per cent by 1970. During the 1970s the Kenyan government addressed the issue of adult education, culminating in the enactment of the Adult Education Act of 1979. The dynamism, however, started to wane in the 1980s with the implementation of Kenya's Structural Adjustment Programme (SAP). This was imposed by the World Bank and International Monetary Fund as part of the conditions for receiving their loans. It implied restrictions on the expenditure of education and social services. Adult education – already marginalized – found itself even further on the periphery, while school education was emphasized.

The Kenyan African National Union, the political party that won the elections at independence, had the eradication of illiteracy, poverty and disease as one of its main aims. The fact that illiteracy was identified by the party as one of the obstacles to development was remarkable but one would have expected the zeal to go beyond mere pamphleteering. It was not until sixteen years later that adult education was inaugurated under an Act of Parliament, and a Department of Adult Education was created with a Director in the Ministry of Culture and Social Services. It has remained there ever since.

The present level of Kenya's literacy stands at approximately 65 per cent according to the government statistical data released in mid-1996. (This has been criticized subsequently as inaccurate.) While the total enrolment in adult literacy classes recovered from a negative growth rate of 2 per cent in 1993 to a positive growth rate of 6.5 per cent in 1994, the numbers still show a decline in comparison with earlier years. Illiteracy remains high in many areas. In the predominantly Islamic Coast Province (except Taita Tavetta), among pastoral communities of the Eastern Rift Valley and North Eastern provinces, about 60 to 70 per cent of the population cannot read or write. Many adult education centres in these areas are without teachers.

The role and purpose of adult education and training

The role of adult education and training in Kenya is multifaceted. In the colonial period, it was used to improve literacy skills amongst workers to enhance the operations of the colonial machinery. At independence, the Kenyan government looked upon adult education as an instrument of redress. It saw adult education as an opportunity to train those who had missed out during colonial rule, in order to prepare them for participation in national development and to take over positions formerly occupied by white expatriates. Many Kenyans were registered in the few adult centres and training institutions and did eventually become literate and find their way into leading positions.[1]

Adult education and training has played an important role in the acquisition of literacy skills and modern farming methods, and in the promotion of health and nutrition. But some of the bureaucrats have argued that adult education has an even wider role to play, and that it should:

- enhance citizens' participation in social, political and cultural processes;
- promote the use of Kiswahili as Kenya's national language as a unifying factor in nation-building;
- stimulate the creation of additional learning opportunities in order to enhance participation in new technologies, adoption of new methods and sharing in co-operative organization;
- promote the culture of life-long learning and its significance in the spheres of community, society and the economy.

While colonialism ensured that the majority of citizens received a very low level of education, the current situation is not much better. There is a major focus on the school system while the bulk of the adult population remains educationally impoverished. It also seems as if the state pays mere lip-service to the concept of life-long learning. Of course, this focus is in line with the emphasis imposed as part of the SAPs.

Challenges

In an editorial in the *Daily Nation* (8 July 1996), the headline stated, 'We are losing the illiteracy fight'. The editor pointed out that the 'national adult literacy programme is dying a gradual and painful death'. In 1978 the government pledged to make every Kenyan literate within five years. The Adult Education Department was reinforced and many teachers recruited. The 1979 Adult Education Act was the first formal recognition of the adult education sector. But there has been a steady decline since that landmark event when literacy attendance peaked. The euphoria waned and frustration set in as programmes did not get off the ground, and policies were not implemented due to the lack of financial resources.

This trend continues today and is partly responsible for the morass in which the sector finds itself.

Another challenge facing adult education concerns teachers. Only 1,200 of the required 4,000 full-time teaching posts are filled. This is insufficient – especially bearing in mind that officially, one out of three primary schools is supposed to be a centre for adult learning, and there are 16,000 primary schools. Most of the adult literacy programmes, in fact, rely mainly on part-time educators and volunteers.[2]

Compounding the problem is the phenomenon of unqualified teachers. Only 25 per cent of adult education teachers in Kenya are trained, according to the Director of Adult Education.[3] There are only five adult education teacher-training centres in the country, situated at Ahero, Kakamega, Kitui, Isenya and Muratha Ngari, and their capacity is limited to approximately 250 instructors annually. But a major issue is the low remuneration packages for literacy teachers, who receive a paltry 300 Kenyan shillings (about US$6) as a salary. Those joining the Department do so as a last resort having been rejected by primary and pre-primary education. This is an indication of the low status of the sector.

A recent drive to attract people into the industrial sector has placed much emphasis on technical education at primary and secondary school level. This has further lowered the financial allocation for adult education as well as for tertiary institutions.[4] There exists the danger that adult education will suffer further marginalization. While the government is advocating economic growth for reducing poverty and employment, it does not place much emphasis on human resources development and education. The questions remain: How can the economy grow, how can poverty be reduced and how can employment opportunities be increased if education and training are disregarded? The government policy-makers ignore the lessons of the benefits of education and training to countries such as Sweden, Denmark, South Korea, Japan, Singapore and Mauritius.

While infrastructure is an important aspect of sectoral development, the adult education sector in Kenya does not boast a single building it can call its own. It has depended on other ministries for infrastructural support since independence. For example, adult literacy classes are held in primary school classes after school hours, which means activities cannot occur during normal working hours.

Adult learners now have to pay more to attend classes. Previously the government provided textbooks, chalk, stationery and other support structures. Today students have to buy their own educational material, while the state provides teachers and classrooms. The Kenyan people have not accepted this: in a society where widespread poverty prevails, education is seen as a basic human right – the responsibility of the state. This is one reason for the decline in class attendance.

Because of increasing poverty and escalating costs, adult learners –

like many other Kenyans – have started income-generating groups to supplement their income. Many are now engaged in farming activities and this has resulted in poor attendance of adult education classes.[5]

In 1988 a presidential working party on education and manpower training produced the Kamunge Report which emphasized the strategic importance of the Board of Adult Education in the harmonization of all adult education programmes. It suggested that the Board be strengthened with more human and material resources to enhance and intensify its role and responsibilities. It stated that the Board should be given the opportunity to establish training colleges for adult education instructors and the recruitment of personnel should be according to merit. They argued that a level of prestige needs to be given to the occupation so that respect and confidence in adult education can be cultivated. It is evident that the recommendations of the Kamunge Report were not taken seriously and the report did not influence Kenyan education policies.

Conclusion

In Kenya there is a need for a change of outlook towards and perception of adult education. The current focus on primary education and technical education is not entirely negative but the government needs to realize that development requires a holistic approach which also takes the global context into account. No aspect of education can be ignored. The full participation of the majority of the Kenyan people in the development of the country is critical. They need educational support to enhance their prospects for greater success in the economic, political and social spheres. While adult education is regarded in such a marginal way by the international agencies like the World Bank and the IMF, who in turn pressurize governments to abandon commitments to adult education and other social services, the situation will remain bleak.

The future of adult education in Kenya is intimately tied into the future social, cultural, economic and political development strategies of Africa. Ultimately, it cannot be discussed in isolation from other international and national developments.

Notes

1. Bogonko 1992; Sifuna 1974.
2. *Daily Nation*, 8 July 1996: 16.
3. *Daily Nation*, 10 August 1996: 16.
4. *Daily Nation*, 20 July 1996: 15, 16.
5. *Daily Nation*, 10 August 1996: 16.

References

Bogonko, S.N. (1992) *History of Education in Kenya*, EALB, Nairobi.
Sifuna, D.N. (1974) *Vocational Education and Training*, Nairobi.

20

Literacy Strategies among Unschooled Workers

Mignonne Breier

This chapter[1] reflects on a research project that explored the uses of literacy in a range of work sites, among people who could be considered targets for adult literacy provision schemes. The project focused on the micro-details of practices involving reading, writing and written texts, at a time when large-scale literacy campaigns were being proposed at macro-policy level. The findings present a powerful challenge to a dominant literacy discourse that associates economic development with workers' literacy levels and places the blame for poor productivity on individual skill deficits.

The Social Uses of Literacy (SoUL) research project[2] arose out of concern about a paradox in the adult basic education field in South Africa. Policy proposals were being formulated for mass-scale provision of adult basic education and training, but practitioners in the field were experiencing low enrolment and high drop-out rates that raised questions about the assumed demand for literacy provision. The SoUL project attempted to throw light on the issue by following a tradition of literacy research that has come to be known as 'the new literacy studies'.

The project undertook to turn the focus of attention away from the discourses and practices of literacy providers and explore the uses of literacy among people who are traditionally the targets of adult literacy provision schemes. The University of Cape Town research team concentrated on the uses of literacy in geographically defined communities in the Western and Eastern Cape. University of the Western Cape (UWC) researchers explored the uses of literacy in a range of work sites: among workers at a Cape Town school, on farms in the Western Cape, in a Brackenfell factory and in the minibus taxi industry in the Western Cape and Gauteng.

The following is essentially an overview of various papers and reports produced by the UWC Centre for Adult and Continuing Education

(CACE) research team and will not attempt to provide the kind of detail that is contained in these other sources.[3] The chapter begins with a discussion of the theoretical and methodological framework of the research before discussing four main themes that emerged in the work and considering the implications of these themes for adult educators.

The research suggests that adult educators can be advised to:

- pay attention to the internal dynamics of industries or work sectors and the way in which literacy is used and valued within those contexts;
- research and build on local knowledges and literacy strategies and informal education procedures (apprenticeship learning and mediation processes in particular), while recognizing the limitations of these strategies and the need, in certain circumstances, to introduce adults to other more efficient, marketable or transferable procedures;
- discard the 'deficit' model of workers and adult learners or, as Hull[4] puts it, 'cast workers in a different light, one that gives their expertise its due';
- make use of the written texts that are already part of learners' valued life experiences and realize that for some unschooled adults, literacy classes are not a worthwhile option.

The theoretical and methodological framework

Like other researchers within the 'new literacy studies' tradition, SoUL researchers took the term 'literacy' beyond its traditional meaning in which it is conceptualized in individual, technical terms as simply the ability to read and write. The following became key terms in their research:

- literacies, in the plural, as opposed to 'literacy' in the singular, to indicate the existence of multiple forms of literacy even if our society has tended to privilege only one, namely schooled literacy;[5]
- literacy events, defined by Heath as 'occasions in which written language is integral to the nature of participants' interactions and their interpretative processes and strategies';[6]
- literacy practices, defined by Street as a 'broader concept (than that of literacy event) pitched at a higher level of abstraction and referring to both behaviour and conceptualisations related to the use of reading and/or writing';[7]
- communicative practices:[8] literacy practices were seen as types of communicative practice as defined by Grillo[9] and, accordingly, needed to be analysed in terms of the social activities, institutional settings and social processes in which they are embedded as well as the organization of the practices themselves, their labelling, the ideologies accompanying them and the texts that are their outcome;

- numeracy practice: this term was arrived at by extending Street's concept of literacy practice and linking it to definitions of 'numeracy'[10] to refer to both behaviour and conceptualizations related to the use of arithmetic in daily life;
- discourse, understood in the Foucauldian sense to mean unities of statements whose conditions of existence can be defined. This approach to discourse also assumes that there are subtle, unwritten, often unconscious, rules, which make it possible for certain statements and not others to occur at particular times, places and institutional locations;[11]
- discourse as defined by Gee as 'a socially accepted association among ways of using language, of thinking, feeling, believing, valuing and of acting that can be used to identify oneself as a member of a socially meaningful group or "social network" or to signal (that one is playing) a socially meaningful role';[12]
- primary discourse, defined by Gee as 'the discourse one acquires "free" in communication with family and intimates';[13]
- secondary discourses, defined by Gee as the discourses which we acquire in our interaction with people with whom we are not intimate or where one is being 'formal'.

Theoretical tools like these provided researchers with a particular lens with which to approach their fieldwork. They encouraged and enabled researchers to look for:

- the social practices accompanying reading and writing;
- discourses about literacy and schooling and the construction of 'literacy' and 'illiteracy' through language;
- the relationship between literacy and discourse.

Researchers used mainly ethnographic techniques: participant observation, unstructured, open-ended interviews and life-history interviews. At CACE we also made use of secondary sources and various other techniques suggested by Hammersley[14] to extend the applicability of our findings.

Some key themes

1. Unschooled adults are not a homogeneous group of people with identical interests and capabilities. The kind of literacy that is associated with schooling is not uniformly beneficial in the workplace.

Traditional approaches to literacy have tended to construct the 'illiterate' adult as a dependent, disadvantaged, unskilled individual, both socially and economically. This image has been challenged in research elsewhere, particularly the work of Fingeret,[15] O'Connor, Hull and Gowen.[16] These writers urge one to look beyond traditional representations of adult 'illiterates', both by the mass media and by academic writers, and encounter the complexities of actual lives.

Locally, the traditional approach was encapsulated at the time of our research in the following extract from a major current policy document:

> The lack of access to basic education, including literacy and numeracy, has consigned millions of our people to silence and marginalization from effective and meaningful participation in social and economic development. This has a particular impact on women who comprise a large proportion of the illiterate.[17]

In contrast to the deficit model of the unschooled adult presented here, the research provided images of people who were not only *not* silenced or marginalized but played a powerful role in the social and economic development of the country. We were not able to say what proportion they formed of the vast mass of unschooled adults but we could say that they were a force to be reckoned with. In fact they made it impossible to talk of unschooled adults in terms of a homogeneous mass with similar needs and interests. Some of the highest paid workers on the farms which Gibson studied, for example, were unschooled men who performed complicated tasks like the laying of irrigation systems and the building of wagons.[18] Breier, Taetsane and Sait[19] found that the minibus taxi industry, a multi-million-rand industry that straddles the formal and informal sectors of the economy, and is the major form of worker transport in this country, had become a source of employment for people – specifically men – with little or no schooling.[20]

At the same time the research showed that schooling was not necessarily valued and utilized in the workplace. On the farms that Gibson studied, women had more education than the men and, contrary to the gist of the ANC policy statement quoted above, this held no advantage for them in the workplace. They performed less skilled work and earned lower wages than unschooled men. In Watters'[21] study of the service staff in a Western Cape school, most of the workers had a basic education yet were seldom required to use their literacy skills.

2. Some unschooled adults have developed ingenious strategies to cope with the literacy and numeracy demands of their daily lives. However, these strategies have their limitations and are dependent on context.

The SoUL project at UWC attempted to document, in micro-detail, the literacy and numeracy strategies of unschooled workers encountered in its studies.

Breier, Taetsane and Sait[22] described various ways in which unschooled taxi drivers cope with the literacy demands of their work. These included:

• getting help from traffic officials who believed that unschooled drivers were safer and had 'a better attitude' than their more educated counterparts, and therefore offered oral tests for unschooled drivers and were prepared to complete forms on their behalf;

- operating illegally;
- use of support systems, including family, colleagues and passengers, to help them complete forms, or read signs;
- informal education by colleagues, family and friends. Unschooled drivers often got family members or colleagues to help them learn traffic rules by rote. At the ranks there were various procedures to introduce newcomers to the unwritten rules of the business;
- learning by observation or apprenticeship. We encountered drivers who had learned the meaning of traffic signs by watching traffic behaviour. Some had learned to drive by watching the manoeuvres of experienced drivers.

Gibson paid attention to the procedures used by unschooled male workers to perform complex and highly valued tasks on a farm, and gave a detailed account of the way in which one unschooled worker, Migiel Hendriks, made wagons. She said Hendriks's competencies confirmed O'Connor's[23] argument that workers who regularly performed various complex physical and cognitive tasks could not be described as unskilled or lacking knowledge.

Hendriks's competencies also gave support to Scribner's[24] notion of 'working intelligence'. Gibson compared Migiel's strategies with the 'non-literal strategies' documented by Scribner in her study of dairy workers, in which she found that the non-literal ways in which they conceptualized and organized their work were more effective than the school-mathematics kind of approach which high-school students brought to the same task. (Scribner compared the dairy workers' ways of working direct from the 'visual display' with those of master chess players who develop vocabularies of perceptual units or configurations of pieces which enable them to 'see' possibilities rapidly and without recourse to verbal analysis.)

Hendriks ascribed his competencies to 'common sense' but his description showed an understanding of concepts such as leverage and two and three dimensional constructions, and also indicated that he could think spatially. According to Gee's[25] definition of literacy, he could even be called 'literate' in that he had mastered a secondary discourse which involved 'a great many of the same skills, behaviours and ways of thinking that we associate with literacy' — even though he is not able to read and write.

Muller also credited Hendriks with a kind of literacy. Drawing on the concepts and terminology of Bernstein, he says that Hendriks 'displays elements of a primitive (in the sense of under-elaborated) faculty of verticality. This takes the form of a germinal horizontal knowledge structure, admittedly with a highly simple grammar.'[26] Drawing on Durkheim, Muller referred to Hendriks's 'rather sacred form of common sense'.

At this point, one needs to draw on the school education debate about everyday knowledges and their significance for school curricula. A strong argument has been put forward for not including everyday knowledge in curricula. Dowling[27] argued that the constructivist approach, as it is called in these debates, can serve to disadvantage already disadvantaged students even further. He concluded that the mathematical texts used by 'lower ability' students in the UK, which incorporate numerous examples intended to model everyday situations, succeed only in further excluding their readers from the esoteric discourse. 'Higher ability' students, on the other hand, were inducted directly into 'esoteric mathematics'.

Muller and Taylor summarized Dowling's argument as follows:[28]

> The recontextualisation of public domain (what we would call the field of everyday life) material into the curriculum for disadvantaged learners involves a two-fold deformation. Firstly, it does violence to its public domain setting in that the material in which the learner is supposed to recognize him/herself parades as real life, but is recontextualized according to the curricular needs of the mathematics it purports to exemplify. The result is neither 'real' maths nor recognisably 'real life'. Secondly, it does violence to the student in inculcating a view of mathematics as a series of specialized solutions to particular problems, rather than as a connected set of axioms and theorems; in substituting procedure for discourse, constructivism obscures the esoteric or sacred nature of school mathematics and precludes the induction of the student into the discipline of mathematics because the 'localising strategy' of indigenous examples induces the student to mistake 'algorithmic' solutions for generalisable principles, and thus to mistake the nature of mathematical practices. For higher ability students, by contrast, the discursive elaboration of generalisable principles is foregrounded; they must learn to 'speak mathematics'...

This debate raises two questions around research such as ours which sought to explore and document everyday knowledges, namely:

- Of what value is such research and the information it produces to adult literacy and basic education teachers?
- Would recontextualisations of everyday knowledges into adult education curricula disadvantage adult learners in the same way that school mathematics pupils could be disadvantaged?

Behind these questions is a more general one about the relationship between the debate which Muller and Taylor describe, which is related to mathematics education, and other disciplines, particularly the social studies disciplines such as history and geography which have less clearly defined boundaries.

In the adult education field, the debate would seem to have particular relevance for 'second chance' schooling where adults are required to master the same kinds of esoteric domains as schoolchildren in order to gain formal school-equivalent qualifications. The Dowling argument could apply here although further research, of the kind which led to Dowling's conclusions with regard to school mathematics education, is needed before a definite connection can be asserted.

In the meantime one could argue that educators (in conventional schooling as well as adult learning centres) need information about learners' everyday knowledge and practices to facilitate communication in the classroom situation.

Research by Scollon and Scollon[29] has shown the importance of an understanding of local discourse systems in cross cultural (inter-ethnic) classroom situations. An understanding of the esoteric domain of learners' local knowledges (this may include literacy and numeracy practices, but not necessarily so) will help educators to design appropriate starting points. This does not mean that such strategies have to be recontextualized into the curriculum at every stage or that the learner has to be confined to the type of knowledge with which he/she came to the class situation.

The challenge for future research, as Muller has identified, is to find out how Hendriks (and others like him) came to develop their peculiar cognitive skills. Such information can make an important contribution to the new literacy studies theories of acquisition and pave the way for more focused and effective linkages between school and everyday knowledges.

3. In the workplace, the written word is used as a means of control as well as communication. There is also a connection between the way in which work is organized and the nature and frequency of literacy practices.

In interviews conducted within two companies in this project, the personnel managers said they were hoping that literacy education would help to facilitate communication between management and worker and thereby prevent industrial relations disputes.

At the same time our research showed that a major purpose of written materials in the various workplaces which we researched was not communication but control. This added a new dimension to the seven uses of literacy listed by Heath.[30] Taxi drivers were controlled by licences, summonses, permits, all expressed in formal, legal language. Workers in the school were subject to letters of appointment which enforced conditions of work but also protected the interests of the employer. Factory workers with little or no schooling were obliged to conform to rules that were put up on a notice board. While often translated into Xhosa, they remained in formal legal language. We found few examples of management or official texts that made a genuine attempt to communicate with workers, and where they did do so, they tended to be on topics that showed little or no appreciation or understanding of workers' discourses. In this way, for example, the factory management put out a newsletter which listed workers' birthdays along with news of achievement awards and lessons on quality control. The research showed that the only information which interested the workers was news about the deaths of fellow workers and advertisements for jobs.

A safety representative system, with the ostensible purpose of facilitating communication between worker and management on health issues, also appeared on close examination to have the effect of controlling rather than facilitating workers' complaints. In terms of this procedure elected workers' safety representatives were required to fill in blank forms each month prior to a meeting with management at a monthly safety committee.

On the one hand, the format of the forms reminded workers of aspects of the factory that needed to be checked and provided neat spaces in which they could place their answers. On the other hand, by simply providing a list of their own for the workers to follow, they limited the range of probable answers and made it difficult for workers to raise new categories or sites for inspection. Although workers' conversations were suffused with narratives about pain and suffering in relation to the asbestos with which they worked, the various categories mentioned for inspection did not mention the word. There was only one category where it might have been appropriate and this was entitled 'pollution'.

In the school where Watters did her research, workers were found to use literacy practices as a form of control. The laundry workers at the school, unlike other service staff, were not visibly supervised and worked fairly independently. They were involved in handling lists which they had created, as well as lists created by their clients, the school pupils. These lists became a powerful form of control for these workers – controlling quantities as well as controlling the pupils. Value was placed on being able to accurately check linen leaving and returning to the boarding house. By the time Watters did her research, the lists had become very complicated for the function they served. The lists were described to Watters several times before she was able to grasp the basic elements. She was assured by the workers, however, that the system was simple once one was used to it.

Here literacy was being used to construct a form of permanent record that could be used in situations of contestation. The laundry staff were also maintaining a form of subtle control for as long as they are the only ones who understood how 'it' works, then they could not be checked. However, they were able to interpret the information to prove they had not lost items. Watters said this was the only example which she found of service workers using a form of literacy for control. She believed it was only possible because of the difference in the way the work of the laundry is organized. There was a tolerant first-line supervisor in the boarding house and workers were allowed to work fairly independently.

In the process they made their own use of literacy for control. Elsewhere the service staff of the school operated in 'low skill' mode with the work of the various service departments fragmented and reduced to small repetitive pieces of work, usually without significant involvement of reading and writing. Where workers were involved in literacy practices in the course of their work, they were usually about recording and transporting information.

Watters came to the conclusion that if companies wanted to develop literacy capacity, they would also need to create opportunities for literacy practices to occur. This could mean shifting the overall modes of communication in the workplace and attention to the way in which work was organized. Her work indicated, for example, that literacy practices were more likely to occur in situations where the work was less closely supervised and fragmented, and where workers were given space to introduce their own forms of control over the work process.

4. Unschooled workers might not be able to read and write but their lives are permeated with texts which they use and value.

In an adult literacy class at the factory, workers were drilled week after week with words like 'brand' and 'Omo' and 'Surf'. The programme had attempted to make use of everyday texts in the course of its curriculum but the nature of the texts selected indicated the commercial interests of the sponsors of the programme rather than a deep understanding of the discourses and practices of the learners.

One learner in that class had been attending for months and before that had been to another Freirean-type literacy class. The experience had not helped him to decipher a scrap of paper which he brought to work to show a researcher. He believed it confirmed that he had asbestosis badly enough to warrant early retirement. In fact it was an appendix to a letter sent by union medical representatives to the Workmen's Compensation recommending that he be declared ill enough to warrant compensation. The request was denied and the scrap of paper had no value to this learner except to indicate that he was once thought to have been ill enough to warrant compensation. Although this text dominated this learner's conversations with the researcher, he had not produced it for deciphering in the literacy class he attended week after week. Nor, as far as we could establish, had the literacy teacher engaged him in the kind of conversation which might have led to his producing it.

Elsewhere in the research we encountered other texts that played important roles in the lives of workers whom we interviewed, including some unschooled people. Most prominent of these was probably the Bible and the various hymn and prayer books used in the churches frequented by workers. The texts produced by employers were frequently ignored by workers, but some managed to meet workers' concerns and interests and were read, by those who could read, and the information was passed on to those who couldn't. Such texts included:

• death notices and job advertisements on the notice board of the factory we researched;

• the various books of traffic rules and signs which learner drivers are required to read and learn to pass the learner's licence test;

• the letters of appointment issued to service workers at the school and the contracts signed by the workers on the farms.

The challenge to adult educators is to make use of texts such as these that are already part of learners' valued life experiences. In the process they might need to develop new understandings of the role of literacy in the lives of unschooled people. They might find that some adults have developed such ingenious ways of coping without literacy, as it is conventionally understood, that they have little need for literacy classes. And they are sure to find that 'deficit' notions of 'illiterate' adults are entirely inappropriate.

Notes

1. Based on research by Mignonne Breier, Kathy Watters, Diana Gibson, Matsepela Taetsane and Lynette Sait.
2. The Social Uses of Literacy (SoUL) Research Project was a joint initiative involving the Centre for Adult and Continuing Education at the University of the Western Cape and the Department of Adult Education at the University of Cape Town.
3. For a full list of forthcoming publications on the research project, see the reference list at the end of this paper, under the following names: Prinsloo and Breier; Breier, Taetsane and Sait; Watters; Gibson.
4. Hull 1994: 52.
5. Gee 1990; Street and Street 1991.
6. Heath 1982.
7. Street 1993.
8. Street 1993.
9. Grillo 1989.
10. Mathews 1990; Baker 1993; Castle 1994.
11. Foucault 1972; Fairclough 1992.
12. Gee 1990: 43.
13. Gee 1990: 151.
14. Hammersley 1992: 89–90.
15. Fingeret 1984.
16. O'Connor, Hull and Gowen, all in O'Connor 1994a.
17. ANC 1994: 87.
18. Gibson 1996a; Gibson 1996b.
19. Breier *et al.* 1996.
20. See also Kell 1996.

21. Watters 1996.
22. Breier *et al.* 1996.
23. O'Connor 1994a: 278.
24. Scribner 1984.
25. Gee 1990: 153.
26. Muller 1995.
27. Dowling 1993.
28. Muller and Taylor 1995.
29. Scollon and SBK 1981.
30. Heath 1986.

References

African National Congress Education Department (1994) *A Policy Framework for Education and Training*, draft discussion document.

Breier, M., Taetsane, M. and Sait, L. (1996) 'Taking Literacy for a Ride: Reading and Writing in the Taxi Industry', in Prinsloo, M. and Breier, M. (eds), *The Social Uses of Literacy*, Sached Books, Cape Town and John Benjamin Publishers, Amsterdam and Pennsylvania.

Castle, J. (1994) 'Adult Numeracy Education: More than the Third "R"', in Hutton, B. (ed.), *Adult Education in South Africa*, Oxford University Press, Cape Town.

Dowling, P. (1993) 'Mathematics, Theoretical "Totems": A Sociological Language for Educational Practice', in Julie, C., Angelis, D. and Davis, Z. (eds), *Proceedings of Political Dimensions of Mathematics Education, Second International Conference*, Johannesburg.

Fairclough, N. (1992) *Discourse and Social Change*, Polity Press, Cambridge.

Fingeret, A. (1984) 'Social Network: A New Perspective on Independence and Illiterate Adults', *Adult Education Quarterly*, Vol. 33, No. 3.

Foucault, M. (1972) *The Archaeology of Knowledge*, Routledge, London.

Gee, J. (1990) *Social Linguistics and Literacies: Ideology in Discourses*, The Falmer Press, Basingstoke.

Gibson, D. (1996a) *Farmworkers, Literacy and Literacy Practices in the Breeriver Valley*, CACE, UWC and UCT.

Gibson, D. (1996b) 'Literacy, Knowledge, Gender and Power in the Workplace on Three Farms in the Western Cape', in Prinsloo, M. and Breier, M. (eds), *The Social Uses of Literacy*, Sached Books, Cape Town and John Benjamin Publishers, Amsterdam and Philadelphia.

Grillo, R.D. (1989) *Dominant Languages*, Cambridge University Press, New York.

Gowen, S. (1994) '"I'm No Fool": Reconsidering American Workers and Their Literacies', in O'Connor, P. (ed.), *Thinking Work 1: Theoretical Perspectives on Workers' Literacies*, ALBSAC, Sydney.

Hammersley, M. (1992) *What's Wrong with Ethnography?*, Routledge, London.

Heath, S.B. (1982) 'What No Bedtime Story Means: Narrative Skills at Home and School', *Language and Society*, Vol. 11, pp. 4–76.

Heath, S.B. (1986) 'The Functions and Uses of Literacy', in De Castell, S., Luke, A., Egan, K. (eds), *Literacy, Society and Schooling: A Reader*, Cambridge University Press, Cambridge.

Hull, G. (1994) 'Hearing Other Voices: A Critical Assessment of Popular Views on Literacy and Work', in O'Connor, P. (ed.), *Thinking Work 1: Theoretical Perspectives on Workers' Literacies*, ALBSAC, Sydney, Australia.

Kell, C. (1996) 'Literacy Practices in an Informal Settlement', in Prinsloo, M. and Breier, M. (eds), *The Social Uses of Literacy*, Sached Books, Cape Town and John Benjamin Publishers, Amsterdam and Philadelphia.

Mathews, D. (1990) 'The Role of Number in Working and Training', in Harris, M. (ed.), *Schools, Mathematics and Work*, The Falmer Press, Basingstoke.

Muller, J. and Taylor, N. (1995) 'Schooling and Everyday Life: Knowledges Sacred and Profane', paper presented at a seminar in the Faculty of Education, University of Cape Town and University of the Western Cape.

Muller, J. (1995) 'Intimations of Boundlessness: Literacy, Verticality and the Sacred', paper presented to the Second Theory, Culture and Society Conference on Culture and Identity, Berlin.

O'Connor, P. (ed.) (1994a) *Thinking Work 1: Theoretical Perspectives on Workers' Literacies*, ALBSAC, Sydney, Australia.

O'Connor, P. (ed.) (1994b) 'Contexts, Conundrums and Constructing Possibilities in Workers Literacy', in O'Connor, P. (ed.), *Thinking Work 1: Theoretical Perspectives on Workers' Literacies*, ALBSAC, Sydney, Australia.

O'Connor, P (ed.) (1994c) 'Workplaces as Sites of Learning', in O'Connor, P. (ed.), *Thinking Work 1: Theoretical Perspectives on Workers' Literacies*, ALBSAC, Sydney, Australia.

Prinsloo, M. and Breier, M. (eds) (1996), *The Social Uses of Literacy*, Sached Books, Cape Town and John Benjamin Publishers, Amsterdam and Pennsylvania.

Scollon, R. and SBK (1981) *Narrative, Literacy and Face in Inter-ethnic Communication*, Ablex Publishing Company, New Jersey.

Scribner, S. (1984) 'Studying Working Intelligence', in Rogoff, B. and Lave, J. (eds), *Everyday Cognition: Its Development in Social Context*, Harvard University Press, Cambridge, MA.

Street, B.V. and Street, J. (1991) 'The Schooling of Literacy', in Barton, D. and Ivanic, R. (eds), *Writing in the Community*, Sage, London.

Street, B.V. (1993) *Cross-Cultural Approaches to Literacy*, Cambridge University Press, New York.

Watters, K. (1996) 'Communicative Practices of the Service Staff of a School in the Western Cape', in Prinsloo, M. and Breier, M. (eds), *The Social Uses of Literacy*, Sached Books, Cape Town and John Benjamin Publishers, Amsterdam and Philadelphia.

21

Dynamics and Process in the Training of Health Committees

Mizana Matiwana

The National Progressive Primary Health Care Network

The National Progressive Primary Health Care Network (NPPHCN) is a South African, national, non-governmental health advocacy network. The network comprises health and development projects and individual role-players. Its mission is to promote primary health care through collaboration with other sectors, to encourage participatory research and policy formulation, to direct appropriate training programmes and to support organizational development. The network affirms values and approaches which recognize universal human rights and which support the promotion of comprehensive, equitable and accessible provision of health services. The NPPHCN has, since its inception, encouraged health workers in groups or as individuals to develop skills and experience in community organization and in primary health care.

The network supports health programmes in under-resourced communities. It believes that fundamental to the success of the NPPHCN are well-trained health committee members who will support health workers and health programmes in their local communities. It further believes that it is crucial to facilitate health committees to make decisions about health at a local level. The network considers community participation in decision-making processes about health to be a crucial component in the process of restructuring the health system.

This chapter briefly describes the NPPHCN and discusses the process of training community health committee members. It also highlights the problems and possibilities for grassroots participation.

Functions

The network originated in April 1987. Some health workers saw the need to promote primary health care and to develop a national primary health-care strategy for South Africa. The legacy of apartheid has created a society of enormous inequalities in wealth, opportunity and access to health care. Added to this is the uncontrolled violence, severe economic hardship, poverty and rampant unemployment. This reality has pushed South African health services into a severe crisis which the NPPHCN has attempted to address by building the capacity of existing health programmes.

Operations

As a national network it has a national office in Johannesburg, Gauteng. A National Council consisting of two representatives from each of South Africa's nine provinces meets twice a year. Each province has a provincial executive committee and a provincial office which is staffed by a provincial co-ordinator and in most cases a provincial administrator. The provincial staff ensure programme implementation and the day-to-day running of the network.

The network is dependent on its members to assist staff to implement the programmes. There are limitations as to what network members can do, however, since they are primarily accountable to and responsible for their own projects which in most cases are also constrained by inadequate resources.

Training the community health committee

NPPHCN conceptualizes the training process as consisting of three stages. The first stage consists of building a partnership which is the task of the service developer. The second stage consists of implementing the negotiated training programme which is the responsibility of the trainer. The third stage includes follow-up support for the newly-trained community health committee, the task of the service developer.

Stage 1: Building partnerships

Fundamental to the success of primary health care is active community participation. NPPHCN has worked in under-resourced communities and one of the valuable lessons of this experience is the building of a relationship and partnership with the community. This process is not easy and takes time. However, the NPPHCN has identified this partnership-building process as a crucial step prior to the implementation of the training programme for the health committee.

Community needs are taken into account during the process and they become an integral part of the community development process. Their efforts to take responsibility for health are supported by the NPPHCN.

In addition, the partnership includes back-up after the completion of the training programme. For example, when the community health committee applies for funding to support a health programme, funding organizations may not be willing to give support without being reassured that the money will be used for what is requested. Funding organizations often request that a legal trust is formed to safeguard the use of funds and supervise the implementation of programmes. It is at this point that the health committee approaches NPPHCN to facilitate the formation of such a trust. What is important about the partnership is that it is based on the principle of co-operation in which NPPHCN motivates and supports and does not impose. This is the task of the 'service developer'.

Starting a dialogue – the role of service developer

The service developer is the first person in the NPPHCN training unit with whom community representatives would consult. In this consultation the service developer discusses the need to train health committees with the community representatives. This consultative process may take up to three months or more depending on what groundwork has been done and how available community members are for meetings. It is necessary to note that often, when community representatives approach NPPHCN for training, they are not clear what the request entails. At the best of times it is a request that comes about because they have seen other health committees trained by NPPHCN. Dialogue between those who desire the training and those who have the capacity and experience is essential to ensure that training matches health committee members' needs.

This marks the beginning of a relationship which will help identify the health needs and the resources within the specific community. During this process the service developer learns to understand how the community views the process of identifying the community representatives who often become the community health committee and who will approach NPPHCN for health training. It is necessary to check their credentials and the process in which these representatives are elected so that NPPHCN does not fall victim to self-interest groups.

Setting the framework for the training programme

The consultations pave the way for the service developer to ascertain the parameters of the mandate as well as information such as:

1. Who asked the group to approach the training organization?
2. How was the group elected?
3. Was a community meeting called by the civic structure?

These questions are key to understanding community structures and their powers.

At the end of a series of consultations the service developer should be satisfied that the community health committee was elected at a meeting called by the civic structure and that the community was involved in the process.

Health worker vs health committee member

Another important issue that is clarified during these consultations is the difference between the health committee and the community health workers. Many community members who are elected as health committee members often understand the training process as preparing them to be health workers. It is the task of the service developer to explain the different roles of the health workers and the health committee. Health workers generally provide a 24-hour service to the community, while health committee members, on the other hand, support the health workers by securing funds to sustain the work done by them.

Health workers are employed and get paid while the health committee members work voluntarily. When this distinction becomes clear some committee members lose interest because they would rather be paid workers than volunteers. What is important however is that those committee members who do continue, understand clearly that their commitment is voluntary. While explaining the constraints and demands of the two different positions is important, it does not always appease the health committee members who are expected to perform duties as volunteers. This is a particularly difficult situation, as many volunteer members also need payment for their services. However, by explaining the resource constraints and the division of roles, training is not lost on people that may drop out as a result of being misinformed. At this point the service developer is ready to hand the process over to the trainers who will provide the appropriate skills and knowledge.

Stage 2: The training programme

The principles that govern the relationship between the service developer and the health committee are reflected in the training programme. In terms of the training programme, committee members may have different interpretations of what it means to support and promote health workers and health programmes. It is the responsibility of the trainers to develop the committee's understanding and commitment to providing support. It then becomes important to develop a sense of trust and consensus between the committee members, particularly in new communities and in informal settlements.

The emphasis of the training programme is to build the capacity of the health committee members. The range of skills developed should be as broad as possible so that committee members can use them anywhere and can become effective participants in the community in which they choose to settle. The training programme includes the following foci: Life Skills, Understanding Primary Health Care, Consulting with the Community, Goal Setting and Planning, Developing a Funding Proposal, and Evaluation.

Life skills

At this point the work started by the service developer is reinforced. In an effort to build trust among the committee members they are taught the following skills: decision-making, listening, giving and receiving feedback, and conflict management. This prepares them to grapple with the understanding and practice of democratic participation. It should be noted that many of the participants come from a culture of intolerance of opposing ideas. In this process they have become very poor listeners and are also timid participants lest they say something unacceptable. It becomes a challenge to the trainer to model these underlying values and strategies of tolerance during the training. Very often the trainer comes from the same culture of intolerance and may find this process of demonstrating tolerance difficult.

Understanding primary health care

The second focus of the NPPHCN is to develop knowledge of health with an emphasis on primary health care. It is important for committee members to understand the basic principles of primary health care which include accessibility, affordability, acceptability and sustainability. It is equally important to understand that primary health care is not just the provision of health services but also includes involving community members in making decisions about health. This understanding helps committees to start appreciating a concept of health which moves away from the idea of curing disease and instead focuses on the promotion of the well-being of the individual in a healthy society.

Health is linked to larger social issues like social justice, access to clean water and toilets, adequate food production and education. It means breaking down the barriers between different sectors of development like agriculture, town planning, education and health. Ultimately, it means working together in a holistic manner with all the factors that impact positively and negatively on health.

Community consultation

The key to primary health care is community participation and the community's involvement in the decision-making processes. To ensure that the community becomes actively involved in decisions about health requires that health workers listen to the community they serve. Here the emphasis is on accountability and transparency.

The running of and planning for meetings becomes as important as most of the work that will be conducted through the meetings. As advocates for proper health services, the committee needs to know about the important structures of power, how to access them so that their health issues are placed on the agendas of the decision makers, and the roles and responsibilities of community structures and committees.

Planning and fund-raising

An efficient and effective health committee is one that has a clear vision of health in its community. The committee has to learn how to plan and set clear goals and objectives. Committees are taught the skills of health planning through structuring their own activities such as fund raising and community consultations. In the process of advocating for services, they also need to know how to take financial responsibility for what is needed in their communities. Controlling and looking after finances becomes another area of skill. Community health committees are taught basic accounting and also how to write financial and progress reports.

Challenges

Selection criteria

The selection of members of a health committee is not primarily determined by their educational background. Members are selected on the basis of their commitment and active involvement in community initiatives. The selection criteria at times seem to be based on individual interest, recognized potential and popularity in a community. The community seldom places emphasis on the literacy levels of participants. It is a challenge to the trainer to design the training programme in such a way that all members of the committee can participate in training activities. This necessitates that training is done in the language of the participants. However, some committee members need to have some level of writing skills since they will be required to record important information that can be used after the training.

Choice of training methods

The challenge for the trainer is that she or he has to be innovative in terms of training methods that can be used in order to involve all the members. As the training is normally done in the language of the participants, it is important that the trainer understands the cultural richness carried by language. This understanding helps in the selection of training methods that do not clash with or impact negatively on committee members' views about certain matters. Trainers often use their own experiences to focus on during discussion sessions and then write in short clear sentences what emerged from the deliberations. This ensures that important lessons and relevant points in the work are recorded and remembered.

Mandates

Communities consist of ordinary human beings with strengths and weaknesses. Given human fallibility, people can be corrupted when the opportunity arises. When communities approach a training organization it is important for these communities to have mechanisms in place that make their mandate a collective community effort, rather than one to promote individual interests. While individual self-interest is normal, it is not acceptable in a community development set-up. It is thus important to take the mandate back for consultation with the community so that they can verify it. It is important for a trainer not to get involved in community squabbles or disputes since his or her role is to guide and help facilitate so that communities themselves can find solutions to their problems.

Support for trainer

Training programmes normally take place at a time suitable for participants. In most cases this would be after work in the evenings because often the trainer and participants have been working during the day. This raises questions about the quality of the trainer's input since non-governmental training organizations have limited resources and the capacity of trainers is often taxed to the limit. The irony is that trainers also need support but this is often not available, with the result that many trainers suffer burn-out.

Reward for work

A sensitive and very important issue facing communities is the fact that, on the one hand, most of the health committees members are unemployed people while, on the other hand, their task is to select and employ community health workers. This creates tensions since they feel that they could and should be employed to do the work. This has always been a cause for conflict and disintegration of the health committee. However, in the process of consultation with the service developer this issue is clearly spelt out, so that those who do remain in the health committee continue to give their services voluntarily.

Conclusion

The Reconstruction and Development Programme (RDP) is aimed at rebuilding and developing the country through meeting basic needs – one of which is health care. The current emphasis of NPPHCN is to complement statutory government health services by strengthening community participation and encouraging collaboration across government and non-government sectors which impact on primary health care.

The key to a holistic development process is the involvement and commitment of people to take responsibility for their own growth and to contribute to the development of their communities. For people to be able to take responsibility, they need to feel that they are in control of their lives so as to change the conditions that affect, amongst other issues, health in their communities. Community participation, however, is a complex concept and may be viewed as slowing down development when quick answers are needed for massive problems.

Community participation, as part of the democratic process, is complex because of the lack of human capacity, organizational and infrastructural development, and the low level of education in the communities.

To realize the NPPHCN's view of development as optimally people-centred and participatory, it is important that the education and training of adults concerned with the implementation and execution of healthcare programmes is structured to involve them in every step of the planning. Given the severe poverty and backlogs in South African communities, it is encouraging that people want to participate actively in the broader development processes.

We have to consider, however, the critical issue of the extent to which we can expect unemployed community members to make unrewarded contributions to restructuring and these broader development processes. The reality is that some people commit themselves with the hope that at some point there will be employment opportunities. This does not often happen, as the non-governmental sector in South Africa suffers severe financial constraints and has very limited resources to offer, whether in the form of employment or support.

22

Is Consensus Possible?

Minnie Venter-Hildebrand
and Charlene Houston

This chapter explores the obstacles to consensus-building in South Africa's process of transformation, the factors impacting on the community consensus-building processes and the notion that community consensus-building is linked to the enhancement of people's capacity.

Development, as used here, encompasses the education and empowerment of individuals, by creating a sense of authority over their lives through the acquisition of knowledge and skills in order to be in control of decision-making processes. It further entails the strengthening of community organizations to operate on democratic principles with legitimate representatives and to make decisions collectively. Another component of community development is the creation of a conducive environment in which building of capacity and consensus can occur. State policies, mechanisms to implement the policies and individual capacity to embrace or oppose the policies in a democratic manner are other important components.

The first assumption is that consensus about community needs, development, education and training approaches and goals is needed for development to take place. Second, it is assumed that development processes are sequential. As consensus impacts on the root of development, the different components function in tandem: if individuals are empowered, community organizations stand a better chance of functioning well. When community organizations function effectively, with strong, legitimate and representative leadership, communities benefit through increased cohesion, and the potential for consensus is enhanced through effective communication.

South Africa's development processes

The development processes in a post-apartheid South Africa have to encompass the whole spectrum of society in a holistic and people-centred manner. The obvious concentration of effort has to be within the country's disadvantaged and poor communities, which consist of predominantly black people in the sprawling urban townships and the vast rural communities. Two different programmes and campaigns have been adopted by the new South African government to address development in general and economic growth specifically. The Reconstruction and Development Plan (RDP) is the government's holistic socio-economic policy framework, while the Masakhane Campaign is an all-inclusive awareness campaign to encourage South Africa's people to contribute to the country's socio-economic upliftment by supporting and paying for housing and infrastructural services.[1] The two programmes are mutually dependent on one another.

Obstacles to consensus-building

Development goals vs political interests

While there is no ideological conflict between the state's national policies and development, the interactive *processes* between these two concepts are inherently adversarial and ill-designed to facilitate accountability, achieve consensus and resolve conflicts. Where conflicts exist and are fuelled in communities, consensus-building will be hampered.

In a recent research impact study[2] on the effect of adult education and training on communities it was found that rifts inside community organizations are developing between political parties and civic organizations, and between these organizations and the technocrats in local authorities. South Africa's political history is at the root of this: the transition from a highly politicized frame of mind which focused on the eradication of apartheid to one which focuses on socio-economic growth and development is not easy. The rallying point during the previous era was that of the common enemy with promises of a better world for all. The majority consensus around this was shown by the 1994 election results.

One hundred per cent of research interviews revealed that party political interference in development plans was derailing or stalling the process and hampering consensus in communities. The reasons for interference seem simple: aid organizations move into the communities, relying on the existing level of community leadership; they channel their education and training through these leaders and rely on them to disseminate the information to the rest of their communities. In principle there is nothing wrong with this approach because it is probably the only feasible way in which to go about informing and contacting South Africa's disadvantaged people.

Leadership vacuum

Taking the country's political past into consideration, it is easy to understand the fuzzy line between political and civics[3] leaders – during the liberation struggle they used to be the same people. But in a multi-party democracy, roles become more defined and the divisive nature of politics necessarily determine that politicians vie for constituencies. In this same process, development workers and adult educators and trainers are trying to move the same constituencies in a cohesive manner towards consensus around development and economic growth issues. While certain people, then, are dividing communities along party political lines, the same people are trying to bring the same communities together along development lines. This does not work.

Another reason for the current discord between the civic organizations and the politicians is that since 1990 leaders (mainly political) have been given leadership training and education concerning organizational roles and responsibilities and development processes. At the time it seemed fine because of the thin line between political and development interests. However, national, provincial and local government elections separated the politicians from the development and civic workers. Many of the first-tier leadership moved on to their political homes in the different levels of democratic government, leaving behind community organizations with no or insufficiently trained second-tier leaders. At this point then, it seemed easy for political organizations to usurp civic structures and other community organizations for political gain.

Operationalization of national programmes

The RDP is the Government of National Unity's flagship and main policy framework for pulling South Africa out of the lopsided and unequal social, educational and economic disaster. After 1994, the RDP had a specific Ministry, based in the Office of the President, to follow through the setting up of provincial and local RDP offices and fora, funding from the Treasury, from donor agencies and bilateral funding. Two years down the line, the national and provincial RDP offices closed, ostensibly as 'an administrative measure, designed to bring about greater efficiency in the delivery of social services',[4] but according to a non-governmental organization spokesperson it was

> a slap in the face [for NGOs] … the way it happened – first the political announcement, then the task team to work out the details – suggests that the government was in a hurry for political reasons to get rid of the RDP without thinking through the implications. The chaos that has ensued since the closure of the RDP office has thrown into question the government's commitment to the ideals of the RDP.[5]

A potentially powerful mechanism and sensible, humane policy framework, which is embraced by all political parties, development organs and commercial stakeholders, was manipulated without consulting the communities and organizations involved with RDP programmes. This has made the division between the politicians and the local RDP fora and development workers even wider than before, because it has left many with the impression that nothing much will happen from now on. Instead of Masakhane being a goal-oriented programme of consensus and the RDP being the socio-economic policy to be implemented by community structures, these two potential consensus-building blocks have become political tools.

Since both the RDP and the Masakhane campaign implementation mechanisms are designed to work through local government structures, the closure of the national RDP office and concomitant absence of firm channels through which to work will be problematic. But this is only part of the problem, as the obstacles to creating consensus include questions about how to use the RDP resources, what to use them for, and who gets how much and for what type of programmes. In addition, the different roles of politicians and development workers inside communities extend beyond these questions into the arena where the role of the local policy-makers (local government politicians) and the implementors of the policies (community organizations) are muddled. This still relates partly to leadership vacuums, but includes the age-old conflict between available resources over which the state has jurisdiction as contrasted with the community's expectations. While the disbursement of resources is in the hands of the politicians and technocrats – some from the previous regime – the realities show that political interests are often the main determinants for these disbursements rather than the needs of the communities.

The RDP was to be operationalized in local communities through the establishment of RDP fora. Where RDP fora had underdeveloped civic structures, they were to be assisted by the provincial and national RDP offices. A description of obstacles to consensus-building in the following case study of the Greater Grassy Park RDP forum in the Western Cape will illustrate some of the challenges.[6] In communities where there are no RDP fora, the civic association, in line with the Masakhane campaign principles, has embarked on the formation of development fora and legal trusts which fulfil similar tasks to the RDP fora.

The Greater Grassy Park RDP forum – a case study

The Greater Grassy Park RDP forum consists of about eighty organizations: schools, religious groupings, political parties, welfare bodies, community organizations and sports clubs. While the purpose of the forum is to unite community efforts and to find the resources to meet development needs, the diversity of the member organizations, each representing different interests, reflects very different perceptions of what they consider to be basic needs. Because it is the task of the forum to address all those needs and not just the needs of any one organization, it involves a high level of conflict management between the different interest groups.

Of the five key RDP programmes,[7] the communities seem to be interested in the first one only, namely 'Meeting Basic Needs'. At a local level the forum is challenged to sustain the involvement of all groups through participation and through linking the two processes of consensus-building and education.

The forum has the task of developing networks. This includes building relationships between the local authority, business and member organizations, because each of these has a particular role to play in the implementation of the development goals. The forum has to ensure that those who take responsibility actually deliver.

The national and provincial RDP offices[8] have not equipped local RDP fora with offices, equipment, paid staff and funds to enable them to facilitate implementation. The relationship between the provincial RDP office and local RDP fora is weak with very little assistance in, for instance, establishing fora and preparing funding proposals. Many leaders in local fora have full-time jobs and, as volunteers, can spend limited time on RDP activities. In many cases discord exists between current civics leaders still active in the communities and former civics leaders who have assumed political posts after the 1994 national and provincial elections and the 1996 local elections.

These problems are exacerbated by the fact that government funding for the RDP is channelled through local authority. Local fora do not have statutory powers which thus make them dependent on a co-operative relationship with these local authorities. This is often very difficult, because not all councillors and officials are committed to the ideals of the RDP, and some have political vested interests. In cases where the local authority is sympathetic, budgetary constraints make it impossible to fund all the reconstruction and development needs identified by a community. What people expect from the RDP forum and what it can realistically deliver in the light of the mentioned constraints put enormous pressure on the community workers and forum members to make programme implementation possible.

Added to these constraints, issues of conflict resolution, consensus-building and maintaining unity as well as working with very few resources constantly undermine the processes.

These constraints also exacerbate the planning and development processes. Invitations for project proposals from the local authorities often arrive at the local fora too late for them to consult with their communities or do needs assessments. On the one hand, it will be difficult to convince the community that it was correct to let this opportunity for funding pass because the proper planning had not been done; on the other hand, the communities are in dire need of development programmes.

This results in programmes being initiated *ad hoc* so as not to lose the opportunity to get funding. The forum finds itself having to manage tensions between the planning process and scarce resources. In addition, competition for scarce resources between member organizations creates further divisions.

The closure of the national RDP office sent shockwaves through the development community and has led people to ask about the seriousness of the government's commitment to RDP ideals. The government in turn defends its actions by saying RDP funding is now channelled through line departments which will help integrate development more firmly in the mainstream functioning of government. For the likes of the Grassy Park forum it has caused confusion and despondency. It has weakened the possibility that the RDP might provide the social cohesion that is needed to achieve consensus in local communities.

Approaches to adult education and training

From the Grassy Park case study it is clear that the current community development processes are flawed. Lack of resources (human and economic), lack of training for proper planning and leadership, lack of understanding of the development process and insufficient knowledge leaving gaps for abuse of power influence the implementation and sustainability of development programmes. At the root of this lies the lack of training, the lack of capacity in the communities and the concomitant lack of consensus.

In terms of training alone, problems emerge in the manner in which programmes are designed for community education, such as the RDP, Masakhane and development programmes funded by international donors. A number of important components are neglected in the training designs. For example, trainers and facilitators often go into communities with education and training designs developed in urban offices or university campuses, with little regard for the needs of the communities for which these designs are meant. In all ten communities surveyed in the Community and Urban Support Project (CUSSP), the recipients complained that they were being taught issues that they neither see the relevance of, nor understand. In the programme designing process, community training, needs assessments, skills audits and human resource surveys seem to be thought of as appendices of benchmarks and number crunching.

While capacity-building training in fields such as organizational development and leadership training is crucial for the implementation and understanding of Masakhane and the RDP, the link between this and technical and skills training and job creation seems to be missing. And sadly, this link is the foundation for building consensus in the communities.

In communities where the adult education accent was on technical training (covering areas such as how to use the government's housing subsidy, build a house, make bricks or access finance) the civic organizations, with the leadership problems described before, were not strong enough to disseminate the information or to organize the community in such a way that they could move forward as a cohesive unit. In other communities, where no technical or skills training took place, and where the accent was on capacity-building interventions such as organizational development and information dissemination, communities became impatient and wondered why they were not being educated in issues that will bring about change in their lives or help them to build houses.

Lessons for adult education and training

It is clear that capacity-building (leadership training, for example) and technical skills education and training (computer skills, how to build a house, financial and accounting skills) have to run parallel to one another to link the goals of policy (RDP) and service delivery (Masakhane), depending on which developmental level the community finds itself at. From the research it became clear that a starting-point from which educators and trainers as well as community development workers could work may be:

- programmes to manage or resolve community conflict (conflict was present in eight out of nine communities);
- the identification of community needs;
- structuring education and training programmes around identified needs;
- structuring the capacity-building education and training around organizational development and strong leadership training;
- consolidating and strengthening organizations to disseminate development information to their communities;
- at the same time and after the needs assessments and skills audits have been done, proceeding with technical and skills training (using community members as resource persons where possible);
- after the consolidation of organizations and structures, forming a legal community entity to take charge of the financial disbursements and development plans.

The above is a simplistic sequence of activities that hinges on the assumption that educators and planners have taken cognizance of the following aspects:

Community participation: It is important that communities are involved in the training design and implementation to ensure a participatory approach. It is equally important that evaluations are done to monitor community understanding of the subjects and to react to feedback.

Community insights: The educator or trainer should be familiar with the community itself otherwise the training may not be appropriate. In this regard it is important to take note of the advice of community and field workers.

Language: When training and materials are not presented in the vernacular, misunderstanding and resentment occur.

Materials: Community-specific materials should be developed and should be available for distribution and re-use in the communities.

Level: The training provided should be geared to the specific community needs, for instance, levels of literacy and numeracy.

Objectives: If the purpose of the training is unclear or misunderstood and objectives are not attainable or cannot be measured, impact cannot be demonstrated and community members may be frustrated and see the training as irrelevant.

Delivery: The physical location where training takes place is important and has an effect on the cost and accessibility to the community. While training delivery in a more formal setting is seen as respectable and professional, conducting it inside the community is considered as more hands-on and relevant.

Only when a structured training approach, which takes the community's level of development and their needs into account, is adopted throughout the country, can real progress be made in terms of both Masakhane and RDP implementation.

In conclusion

Given the complexities of extraneous influences in South Africa's communities, the inbuilt potential for dissent, the scarcity of resources, existing training design deficiencies and delivery obstacles, the question remains: What then can be done to foster community consensus? In the light of the bleak picture painted, is community consensus possible?

A good start may be to structure the training and delivery approaches so that they take into account the effect on the desired long-term educational impact and the concomitant decrease in the effect of political and other extraneous factors. However, to build total consensus is a pipe-dream because communities are not homogeneous and people do not have the same aspirations. The best that one can do is to look at the largest number of commonalities, and use a structured and focused training design approach so as to appeal to different sectoral interests on different levels at the same time. Masakhane or educating people in the principles of Masakhane cannot possibly have the same effect on both the employed person with available money and the unemployed with no hope or desire to pay for services.

The current Masakhane campaign budget of R30 million has had little effect on communities with a history of rent and services boycotts, high unemployment, abject poverty and very little infrastructural amenities to entice them to pay for their housing services. The answer obviously does not lie in the mobilization or sensitization of civil responsibilities, but rather in the economic development and growth components of upliftment.

Consensus will be easier if it is aimed at policy implementation (the RDP) and delivery. It will stand at least a modicum of a chance if the development role-players (policy-makers, implementors, educators and adult learners) are all simultaneously mobilized around a non-party-political approach to the development process.

Community structures, such as the RDP fora, development fora and legal development trusts should include all the development role-players, irrespective of their political or civil stance. They need the policy-makers who have the political power, the local government structures who have the land and resources, and the civic organizations who hold the key to community development. These structures should usurp the delivery promises made by the politicians and hold them to their word. But this can only happen if the capacity exists inside these structures to do so. And only education and training can fulfil this role.

Finally, how can consensus be built while a low-level scarcity war is being fought throughout South Africa's disadvantaged communities? Again, education is the key in teaching people leadership skills, about the development processes, the delivery time of these processes and the limitations of state resources. Once this understanding has taken root, much of the conflict around scarce resources will become more manageable and communities may start to move as cohesive units towards common development goals. Consensus may be a pipe-dream in the short term, but it is a possibility to work towards as a long-term goal.

Notes

1. Turok 1995.
2. For the Community and Urban Support Project (CUSSP), a USAID-funded housing development initiative, the author (Venter-Hildebrand) interviewed 152 adult recipients, trainers and community development workers for an average of three hours each on a one-to-one basis by using open-ended qualitative question-naires. The projects were concerned with greenfield sites, integrated development, consolidation and squatter areas, township and hostel upgrading and divestiture in the following disadvantaged communities: Bo-Kaap, Franschhoek, Knysna and New Rest in the Western Cape; Duncan Village in the Eastern Cape; KwaDinabakubo, Lamontville and Wiggins Fast Track in KwaZulu-Natal; and Tshikota in Gauteng.

3. The term 'civic' or 'civics' is used in the South African context to denote a civic organization, a non-official body in local government.

4. Senior ANC source in 'Reconstruct' 1996.

5. Rams Ramashia of the NGO Coalition in 'Reconstruct' 1996.

6. This case study is based on the submission from Charlene Houston, the assistant co-ordinator of the Greater Grassy Park RDP forum.

7. The five key programmes of the RDP are: Meeting Basic Needs, Developing Human Resources, Building the Economy, Democratizing the State and Society, Implementing the RDP.

8. This case study was compiled before the RDP offices closed down.

References

'Reconstruct' (1996), supplement to the *Mail and Guardian*, 20 July.

Turok, B. (1995) 'Reconstruction and Development in South Africa', paper presented at Conference on the Role of Adult Education in Reconstruction and Development: Lessons from North and South, Cape Town.

Part IV

Life-long Learning Reconsidered

The chapters below begin to redefine and reconceptualize adult education and training in a way that challenges the human-capital approach. The dominant strand in the Western world is that of the human-capital school, mostly supported by neo-liberal ideology; the alternative humanistic school is concerned with a democratic, holistic approach to education and training.

Gumede, Larsson, Gustavsson and Korsgaard all argue from the latter perspective. Gumede speaks as a practitioner located in a rural part of South Africa, while the others develop their arguments theoretically, within a Scandinavian context. The history of the ideas underpinning the development of the concept of life-long learning is outlined by Gustavsson, and he points to the two different and important theoretical and ideological strands. Larsson tackles one of the most fundamental questions in educational discourse, the relationship between everyday learning and education (organized learning), in the context of life-long learning. He states that adult education must be understood as something that can change the results or the character of everyday learning. The changing relationships between the body and the mind, the hand and the head, in education are the subjects of Korsgaard's chapter. He points to the deeply embedded division between manual and mental work within Western philosophical traditions. Highlighting interesting recent trends in Europe in response to changing labour processes, he argues that the historical development of the relationship between the body and the mind in education is linked to the forms of work in which people engage at different times.

23

On the Periphery:
The Needs of Rural Women

Ellen Gumede

Marginalization means being on the periphery or margins of society. It refers to a situation where people are not at the heart of decision-making in society, and it is thus a disempowering process. This disempowerment manifests in a number of different ways: marginalized people do not enjoy sufficient opportunities to take control of their lives or to influence society as much as they would if they had decision-making powers. Marginalized groups are furthermore robbed of privileges and rights enjoyed by those in society's mainstream. In South Africa, some of the marginalized groups include women, illiterate people, youth and the disabled.

Who or what marginalizes people? Marginalization can either be a function of discriminatory legislation such as South Africa's apartheid laws, or it can be a result of societal norms, traditions, beliefs, attitudes or stereotypes. These factors, in turn, create concomitant problems where further powerful marginalizing forces such as racism and sexism emerge.

This chapter focuses on the marginalization of adult learners, in particular women in rural areas. It is true that women suffer discrimination by being women. While this is so, women in rural areas suffer discrimination by being women as well as by being mostly illiterate. Yet these women constitute a strong fibre in their families, in their communities and in their societies. They have a wide range of experiences and talents, most of which have been sharpened through observation and informal learning.

South African rural women possess a rich cultural heritage, which they cannot necessarily transfer to their school-going children because schools are Western-centred and do not relate to women's wealth of experience and knowledge. In addition, these women seldom have the support of their men because the latter are either at work in urban areas or face their own frustrations, being either unemployed or in poorly-paid jobs. African tradition has it that women have the responsibility to cook and care for the men and children. Thus, rural adult women face not only a generation and a knowledge gap vis-à-vis their children, but a challenging set of expectations from their partners or husbands as well.

Adult women and education

Many rural African women are keen to change their lives and enhance themselves; they believe that formal education will provide them with knowledge and skills to liberate themselves from poverty and their lot generally. But the adult education classes that they attend are conducted mostly in the evenings, an added obstacle in itself. Some of the further challenges that rural women in adult education face are:

The gap between formal education and their own informal education

The general adult education curriculum is not based on the experiences of rural adults, which makes it difficult for them to be inspired by it or to identify with it. Furthermore, a curriculum which does not link up with the experiences of the learner is not likely to enhance her self-esteem based on what she believes she already knows. It rejects and peripheralizes all her existing knowledge, all that she believes in and all that she has found useful in her life. This type of education perpetuates low self-esteem and disempowerment because it does not recognize that these rural learners have as much to offer as any other person. It is questionable how such a curriculum which disregards the people that it is supposed to cater for can contribute to their personal development or development in general.

No immediate employment

An additional obstacle that affects adult learners is the fact that their acquired education rarely gives them sufficient skills to be marketable in a world increasingly dominated by technology. Thus it does not serve as a mechanism for social mobility and is not as inspiring as education which gives job-related skills.

No certification

South Africa is a certificate-oriented country. While a primary prerequisite for people interviewed for prospective jobs is a qualification certificate, very few rural adult education centres provide a credible certificate. This further disempowers rural adult women and reduces their chances of finding employment.

Timing of lessons

In many rural areas adult education centres operate in the evening, an inconvenient time for most people. These centres are not usually accessible to people because of travelling distances in the vast rural areas and the lack of transport. In addition the class times are inappropriate because many people, especially women, are fatigued in the evenings. They have spent the day doing domestic chores which often includes fetching firewood by walking far from their homes. Most of the people who participate in adult education programmes suffer from real, physical exhaustion.

For women there is an added problem: women in traditional African culture are seen as subordinate to men. This compounds and expands the problems that they face. For instance, when women go anywhere they are expected to get the permission of the men, which may not come easily. Men, often unable to take care of their own lives, may manipulate women in different ways to stay home: by withholding permission to be away, or by being aggressive or abusive to women when they want to go somewhere, including attending adult education programmes.

Skills which are not transferable

A few women who are employed report that even if they are exposed to some education, the skills they learn are not transferable to other situations. This is a problem of limiting women to one place which has few benefits.

Can South Africa ignore adult education for women and rural areas?

The problem of adult education should be as much of a concern for South Africans as any level of education. Adult learners are an important social and economic resource. Neglecting them means inhibiting reconstruction and development of the densely populated rural areas. Overlooking adults with their experiences and rich cultural heritage equals the failure to capture and share in their wealth. This impoverishes the whole of society.

Recommendations

It is essential that adult education programmes are designed to be appropriate to the needs and backgrounds of the learners for which they are meant. It is equally important that research be done on the problems of adult learners in rural areas, and specifically women adult learners, in order to eradicate the myriad obstacles that are synonymous with poverty, illiteracy and patriarchy. Unless positive steps are taken, marginalization of adult learners and women will continue and, indeed, worsen.

Employed adult learners and employers should enter into negotiations to find a way in which adult education can be integrated with the experiences and cultural heritage of the learners. Finally, in-house education and training programmes should be as multifaceted as possible, so that adult learners involved in these programmes emerge as multiskilled and increasingly empowered people.

24

Life-long Learning Reconsidered

Berndt Gustavsson

The fact that human beings learn throughout life, from the cradle to the grave, is indisputable. We develop our abilities and adapt to the environment into which we are born. Most of what we learn takes place in our everyday life, whether it is in the home, in the street or in the workplace.

In a traditional society built upon handicraft and agriculture, experiences, knowledge and traditions are transmitted directly from one generation to another. When the society is modernized and industrialized, and when democratic parliamentary and other institutions are developed, the learning processes increasingly take place in schools. From the age of six, children are prepared during the next ten years for their professions and to take responsibility as adults.

It is common knowledge that school systems internationally are steeped in problems. They create inequality, often become a world of their own, dysfunctional in relation to the reality outside, and they do not prepare children adequately and appropriately for adult life. As a consequence, phenomena such as popular education and adult education appear in some societies as alternatives to the traditional schools. These are new institutions built up with the task of educating adults.

One of the main ideas behind the different forms of adult education is to build learning and knowledge upon existing personal experiences. This means that learning from one's earlier everyday life needs to be integrated with learning in an institution. The problem is that this idea does not often take place in practice in the field of adult education, because both participants and teachers tend to adopt the schooling type of learning and look upon knowledge as something isolated, existing mainly in the textbooks or in the head of the teacher.

In order to legitimize the need for adult education in society, certain concepts and ideologies appear, such as recurrent education and life-long education. Recurrent education was introduced in the debate by the

Organization for Economic Co-operation and Development in 1960 and life-long education by Unesco at the beginning of 1970. While both still exist in the learning debate all over the world, the concepts have changed content and meaning.

The point of departure in this essay is that both these concepts suffer from different weaknesses. Recurrent education tends to be reductive because it looks upon a human being as nothing else but an economic creature. As a consequence, knowledge is seen as nothing but hard currency to be put in the bank, and education as nothing else but investment in human capital.

Life-long education tends to be idealistic because it is seen to be applicable for any purpose, making it an empty concept filled with a content that is no longer able to face the problems in adult education. The concept has to be charged by a new content that corresponds to the transformation of the world since 1970.

Another confusion is that in European countries, the words 'life-long education' are currently being used in a context that does not correspond to the philosophy it had in the 1970s, but to the thoughts originally behind 'recurrent education'.

Following are the main currents in the discussion of education in a much broader sense than is usual. The first trend is the difference in origins and philosophy behind the concepts *life-long* and *recurrent* education. The second point of departure is from a humanistic perspective. Examples from different parts of the world as well as the difficulties with the humanistic tradition today will be discussed. The third point of departure is a sociological perspective on learning and education that could help explain the main contradiction in the current education discussion, between an interpretation of humanism and the theory of education as an investment in human capital. Finally, what follows is an alternative perspective of the learning process as well as possible problems of learning and education in a modern society.

Human capital and humanism

It is important to explore what the two concepts, recurrent education and life-long learning, mean and what the traditions behind them are.

Recurrent education arose, from the beginning, from the perspective of the labour market. Reintroduced in the 1980s, it considered human beings as calculating their own advantages and often referred to the individual as 'Economic Man'.[1] This picture is currently presented in neoliberal ideology and used when education is discussed in terms of market and investment in human capital. In this sense it reduces education because it concentrates on human resources as capital and economic qualities as the primary investment. The human being is more than an economic creature. This type of reductionism exists in many sciences and in this case it is the economists who make education into nothing more than economy.

If we look upon more classical motivations for education in a society, they are mainly humanistic and democratic, and they also consider education from a perspective that education of the personality and the citizen are additional dimensions of the same concept. The main mistake made by the human-capital approach is that it has neither anything to say about how people really learn nor does it elaborate on what knowledge actually is.

Life-long learning has, from the beginning, related to a humanistic tradition, where all human beings are considered capable of learning and developing their potential abilities. Life-long learning is an integrative concept in many aspects. 'Life-long' means that learning and education are possible at any age, from the cradle to the grave. It is in this sense integrative because it concerns the continuum of age. Different generations are related to each other in learning; thus one way of reaching the goal of equality in education is to educate the parents, since what children get from their homes is important in how they manage learning in school.

This leads to another form of integration: between learning in school and learning in everyday life, be it in the home, in the workplace or profession, in a social movement, or in the local society. The concept life-long learning implies, in this regard, a broad approach to knowledge and has a more holistic view of education, in which formal and informal types of learning can be integrated with one another and considered in one context.

The concept is thus described integratively in two dimensions, namely horizontally between home, local community, economic environment and the mass media; and vertically, between different stages of learning.[2]

But if the main problem with the human-capital theory is its reductionism, the problem with life-long learning is that it is used as a vision but is rather empty of content. It therefore tends to be idealistic because it does not say how it can be transformed into practice, for instance in the organization of an educational system. In addition, problems exist with the humanistic tradition in a multicultural society.

In advanced capitalist societies both recurrent education and life-long education are currently reintroduced as theories and ideologies in the discussion of how to organize education. This is also prevalent in many developing countries, albeit with different motivations and approaches. What seems to be the overall dominating trend in the Western world today in the theories of education is the human-capital school, mostly supported by neo-liberal ideology. In a context like this, even the concept 'life-long education' can be used in a rhetorical manner, without making clear the distinction between two different world-views, including the view of the human being and how learning processes and education are realized in accordance with such a view. The theory of human capital can express a view concerning the economic reasons for education in a society, but it has nothing to say about how a learning process works, or how to develop the optimal resources in a human being.

This makes the distinction necessary between what is discussed at research and policy levels, and what is practically used in education. The policy produced at central level and the practice in everyday life are often two completely different things. Some research approaches ask whether there are any connections at all between central-level policies and the local community practicalities. While there are always some connections, the relations between central and local are reciprocal.

If we look around us, the approaches to education can be analysed in terms of a deep and overall dominating contradiction between, on the one hand, education as an instrument which is utilitarian and pragmatic and where every kind of knowledge and education is intended to be transformable into practice, and the humanistic and democratic approach, with its broader and holistic ambitions on the other. This contradiction exists and it is possible to observe it at any level in the educational system, from the pupil in the classroom to ministerial level.

At the ideological level this very deep and structured tension can be observed in the discourse of education. But it has to be analysed in sociological terms and, as a consequence, the concept of life-long learning has to be reconsidered in the light of subsequent theories. If we look at the documents produced by Unesco on the subject, they are light on theory, or adapted to a world that no longer exists.

The humanistic tradition in a multicultural society

With the contradiction between unity and differences in mind, the main mistake made by the defenders of identity politics is not to realize that each minority group is also part of a greater whole. It is a very important step for different groups to identify their own culture in order to liberate themselves from cultural dominance. But when they have located themselves, there is no other possibility than to relate the culture of their own group to others. Both from a learning perspective and an ethical point of view it is necessary to have a universal outlook on education in the modern world.

The main mistake made by the defenders of the classical cultural heritage and eternal humanistic values is that they fail to realize that the Western and classical cultural heritage is one stream among many others in the world. To put just the Western tradition in a superior position in relation to others is to be imperialistic and oppressive in the classical sense.

The humanistic tradition contains many different angles, and is historically used in both an elitist and oppressive manner. It does, however, have the potential to give perspectives on the road to a democratic society built upon equality and justice. One of the cornerstones in progressive forms of humanism is that the individual educates him or herself, and develops when she or he relates to what is universally human. In this view the most humanistic saying, 'Nothing human is foreign to me', gives us the insight that every human experience and interpretation of reality is important, where and whenever it is made or expressed.[3]

This ideal is easier to discuss than to realize because the forces in societal development must be given a sociological analysis, in order for us to know about the possibilities and constraints in realizing this ideal.

Interpretation and learning

The following overview of a much more complicated theory leads to the question of what consequences it has for the process of learning and education in a life-long perspective.

If one considers education as 'nothing else' than an investment in human capital, we express a one-dimensional perspective in the system world: state power, economic muscle and expert knowledge driven by an instrumental kind of rationale. The problem is that this reductionist view of education is contradictory to what the learning process is all about.

The learning process is about your own interpretation of the world, and that interpretation starts in our everyday life. If we look upon knowledge interpreted as 'schooling', then there is a deep rift between the interpretations in everyday life and the knowledge produced in schools. This is one of the main reasons why crises can be identified in the school systems in the Western world. This is also one of the reasons why the concept life-long learning has been introduced, one of the intentions being to integrate learning in everyday life as well as school learning.

My learning process starts with my own interpretation of the world, and the new knowledge appropriated must in one way or another be integrated with my pre-understanding.[4] This means that I must have the possibility to relate my everyday understanding to the knowledge produced and transmitted in formal education. Very often this is not the case. My own experience is that knowledge in everyday life and the knowledge acquired in school differ. The consequence is that people are alienated and the possibilities to learn decrease because their rich personal experiences are not taken into account in the learning process.

The view that learning starts in everyday life is just one important first step in the process. An appropriate learning process cannot stop at the self-evident and the familiar. Therefore, the next step is to distance ourselves from our self-evident interpretations made in everyday life. This means breaking away from what we are accustomed to or have familiarity with, and becoming prepared to meet what is totally foreign and new.[5]

In turn, this leads to a new and qualitative step in the learning process which, in the best case scenario, transforms it into a more substantial level. This approach to learning and pedagogy implies the transformation and development in the progressivist tradition of Rousseau, Dewey and Freire.

It is important that individuals in a multicultural society become involved in the modernization process as well as in the rapid transformation and integration of society. The consequence of this transitional phase in society is that a new concept of what learning means needs to be constructed.

This third approach in the process can be labelled a dialectical approach to learning, which is contrary to both the progressivist and the traditional approaches. In this approach learning is viewed as a pendulum between the known, self-evident and familiar on the one side, and the unknown, distant and foreign on the other. Support for such a view can be found in modern hermeneutics (interpretational) and in a broad humanistic tradition.[6]

Social movements and learning

One of the main problems when we talk of ideals in learning and pedagogy is that educational institutions are colonized by rules and curricula, traditions and behaviour, most often summarized as the 'grammar of schooling', features that diminish people's possibilities and ambitions to learn and develop as human beings. Here one finds a conflict between learning and the institutions built up in order to increase the process of learning and education in society. It seems to be commonly accepted that strong and deep traditions are impregnated in institutional walls. This creates problems for politicians and administrators who want to transform schooling in any direction. This problem raises the question whether radicalized learning processes are possible to realize within the existing school system.

One of the main features of popular education is that learning takes place in social movements, amongst people in action. These movements and their role in the production of knowledge and learning processes are often crucial to the discussion of life-long learning. Many people have their central insights and starting-points from studies and experiences rooted in social movements.

Considered in a modern context, and in recent research, social movements are recognized as carriers of historical projects of importance to all people. They concern universal problems, such as the relation between man and woman (women's liberation movement), humankind and nature (the environmental movement), master and slave (labour movements and movements for human rights). In their praxis they themselves produce culture and new knowledge.

This view of a social movement brings us to the conclusion that a movement is identified by its concepts, ideas and intellectually motivated actions; that is, it is a producer of new knowledge and creates culture and world pictures. A social movement can be characterized by its cognitive praxis.[7]

This view tells us that it is not possible to consider scientific institutions and schools as the only producers and transmitters of knowledge. Many people learn, act and create knowledge in social movements. The question is what role this kind of knowledge plays in the normalization of learning as a necessary and continuing process taking place in the modernization of society.

Codes of learning

According to a recently formulated theory about learning, 'situated learning' or 'situated cognition', the ideal situation for learning is craft apprenticeship. Compared to learning by schooling this is more than a form of 'learning by doing', it is a different educational form of the organization of learning and teaching activity. This approach, 'learning in practice' opens up new possibilities for discussions on the relation between theory and practice, or between training and education.[8] Situated cognition is formulated as a theory of learning as opposed to what is called 'the culture of acquisition', hence the alternative is 'understanding in practice'.

The traditional school approach understands learning and teaching in terms of 'cultural transmission', which implies a stock of knowledge to be transmitted; there is no learning without teaching. The situated cognition approach assumes that the processes of learning and understanding are socially and culturally constituted in practice, in situations whose specific characteristics are part of practice as it unfolds. This division between the two different codes of learning could be based on different subjects of learning: it is one thing to learn history and how society is constructed, it is another to learn how to build a boat or repair a car.

According to the conception of a learning process described above, this is another way to formulate what can be called the first step in a learning process. That is, to start with yourself, where you are, your own familiar context. But what are the consequences if we consider all knowledge and learning as bound to the context where it exists, or to the practice where it is situated? The main question is whether the human being is capable of distancing him or herself from his or her own situation and context? If not, humankind is in trouble.

We could reformulate the problem pointed out by the situated cognition school, and say that they are right in that a first step in the learning process is that learning is dependent on situation and context. But in a modern society this is not enough. What has to be emphasized is that it is necessary in a learning process to break the everyday patterns, to turn everyday knowledge and self-evident interpretations into questions, and problematize them. One of the main challenges for the development of a modern learning process is to open up possibilities for distancing and a critical approach to knowledge, including one's own self-evident interpretation of reality, or the situation and practice in which one is involved.

One of the conclusions from the representatives of situated cognition has been deschooling. But institutions are needed in a modern society, because a critical approach to knowledge and a distancing of our own interpretations are necessary in a multicultural and modernized society.

Theory and practice

If we consider the life-long learning process from an integrative perspective it is a problem to divide 'learning in practice' and 'learning in theory'. This is the main difficulty the ANC and Cosatu have to face in South Africa, where the ambition is to break the division between training and education.[9]

The division of theory and practice is a deep tradition in the Western world, rooted in the division of labour. In Plato's time there was one class predestined to work with their bodies, the slaves, and another to govern, think and produce culture and education, the masters. This tradition follows us to the latter-day industrial society and Taylor in the twentieth century who distinguished between labour by hand and planning of the labour by brain, or the labour on the floor and at the planning office.

Even this system and organization of labour is collapsing. It shows that motivation for work and flexibility are necessary conditions for a modern working class. This means that the whole production system needs another kind of competence than just being able to repeat one movement in one and the same job, day after day. This is also one of the reasons, from the perspective of the labour market, why concepts such as life-long learning and recurrent education are being reintroduced internationally.

Human resources are in increasing demand in the competitive world markets. A developed, creative and flexible personality, able to take responsibility and co-operate, seems to be the main characteristic of the labour force of the future.[10]

This could give the impression that the humanistic tradition and the world economy walk hand in hand. They can sometimes. However, if we look more carefully at policy documents from organizations such as Unesco or the OECD, there are different views on the meaning of knowledge, learning and human beings. The interpretive meanings of different words and concepts such as 'life-long learning' and 'recurrent education' need to be clarified. It is not enough to use the right words or to be rhetorical.

The world-view behind assumptions about the nature of the human being, knowledge and learning processes must be clear and elaborated. The main mistake in this division between human-capital and humanistic approaches is that neither the schooling kind of knowledge, nor the specialist, so-called 'expert knowledge' is optimal even from a production point of view.

Some studies show a relation between high productivity and a broad general approach to education. This seems to be one of the explanations why both Japan and the USA have the highest productivity levels in the world. But if this was enough, we could live in the best of all possible worlds. However, we do not, and this is the reason why further questions are not raised about what optimal education and learning could be in the existing world, not just from a market and state perspective, but from the perspective of the human being and for the improvement of a just society.

Context and distance

The organization of a democratic educational system with equal opportunities for all has to be built upon a conscious view of the human being and how learning processes can work most effectively. This includes a conscious view of the importance of traditions and the cultural heritage of which we are also part. Although we all work and learn in our everyday lives, socially and traditionally we are not always aware of it.

Schooling considered as an institution carries its own traditions of what knowledge, teaching and learning are. To be aware of these traditions is a precondition for changing them. Considered from a learning and interpretational perspective we are all and always impregnated by the pre-understanding we carry from our everyday lives. The language and the traditions are preconditions for our understanding.

The first step to take in every learning process is to discuss our own interpretations, what is in our own heads, not only 'experiences'. If we hold on to our suppositions and take them for granted, we risk being 'home-blind', which at worst makes us frightened of the unknown.[11]

This is only one side of living in a modern and multicultural society. Different cultural groups make their own interpretations of the world. To remove oneself from the self-evident and try to see things from a distant view is one important side in a fruitful and creative learning process. The usual mistake made in schools is not to take notice of the views which the participants bring to the classroom. The precondition is to break with and distance ourselves and then to start with the known.

To take notice of and understand the different views of the world's different people in multicultural societies is a crucial first step in the creation of a modern society. If we stay with the familiar and self-evident interpretations without considering different points of view, nothing new can happen. A new quality in the learning process is to go to the foreign and unfamiliar and thereby challenge our self-evident interpretations in our everyday lives.

According to a hermeneutic, that is, understanding, approach to adult education and life-long learning, there are different methods to develop a holistic view of learning. A learning process can be considered as a circle, where the learner tries to understand that which is to be learned guided by a preconception that provides a context to which he or she can relate the unfamiliar. The learning circle can be described as the dialectical interchange of transcendence and appropriation.[12]

A learning process or educational experience is always constrained by tradition. Traditions operate at every level, in the disciplines which structure the subjects, the educational situation in itself, and the situation the student finds him or herself in. Whether we are conscious or unconscious of them, we are caught in the traditions, and they are an important part of our pre-understanding.

There are disagreements between different schools on the question of whether we are capable of distancing ourselves from traditions and studying them critically. On the one hand we have the possibility to change and transform our appropriation of the cultural heritage. But its authority over the individual's mind is not to be questioned. On the other hand there are different kinds of critical perspectives.

One step towards a critical approach is to consider the interpretations of traditions as a way of opening up 'new possible worlds', that is, to be critical in the classical sense, to be able to consider the circumstances as totally different from what they appear here and now. The name for this kind of approach is usually 'hermeneutics of suspiciousness', or 'deep hermeneutics'.[13]

This means the possibility of being suspicious of the overt or the surface of reality. It needs to be explored beyond the superficial interpretations by taking into account a variety of discourses. There are for instance three thinkers in the Western tradition who have done this in totally different fields: Freud in the field of psychology, Marx in the field of social science, and Nietzsche in questioning the basis for the whole of Western culture. This departure point takes into account that modern people are multi-faceted, communicative creatures, and have to search for truth and human right through communication with others. The focus is no longer only on the individual consciousness, but it is language and communication that turns the wheel.[14]

The next question is whether every field in the society can be a part of interpretational knowledge and understanding. If interpretation is a linguistic question, as it is considered in the dominating hermeneutic field, a critical approach could in the next step assume that there are extra-linguistic factors distorting the ideal communication and interpretation. If we think of material and hegemonic factors, such as economic status and social class – that is, power, domination and labour – are they also to be interpreted as linguistic factors?

A critical approach

If the concept life-long learning carries the potential and possibilities to create an equal and democratic educational system, a critical approach is able to tell us not just about the possibility, but also about the constraints and difficulties.

One task is to create an ideal and have a vision. There are elaborated and well-established theories within the fields of philosophy and sociology, mentioned here on the surface only, which could be deepened and used for this purpose. For instance there are open doors to transcend the rift between training and education, and how a learning-process works ideally.

Another task is to investigate the sociological barriers and historical conditions for such an ambition. There are deep traditions involved in every educational system, which have to be understood if they are to be capable of transformation. But in the process of modernization there are other obstacles, which it is quite possible to analyse, such as the specialization of expert knowledge, the knowledge of humankind and the importance of money and power.

Life-long learning realized

The life-long learning process is a free process in the humanistic sense, whereby every human being self-reliantly seeks her or his own truth of the reality in which she or he is involved. But at the same time we have to realize that a human in the modern society is only partly an autonomous and free personality.

We are bound to the traditions of which we are a part, the systems in which we are involved, and the hidden structures of which we are not totally aware. To become aware of these constraints is also part of a modern learning process. And in order to do this it is important to open up communicative possibilities, in search of the truth and human rights. One should be aware that communication and language are never free from vested power influences, in order to face them and manipulate them. Also, communication does not necessarily mean harmony and consensus because the free movement of words and messages involves contradictions, different interpretations, tensions and struggle. This is surmountable and need not be resolved through violence. As Ricoeur points out recurrently in his philosophy, the role of intellectuals is to

point out contradictions, bring them into conflict and through communication between them bring out something creatively new. This is also
our task as adult educators, whether teachers, practitioners or researchers.

Notes

1. Gesser 1985.
2. Dave 1972.
3. In my dissertation, *The Road to Education* (1991), I have analysed the humanistic tradition as an eternal contradiction between equality and elitism, free process
and goal.
4. This approach to a learning process is inspired by the hermeneutic tradition. For its relation to education, see Gallagher 1992.
5. This is inspired by Paul Ricoeur's concept, the Hermeneutics of Suspicion,
where a moment of distanciation is the second in an interpretation process (Ricoeur
1985).
6. The connection between the dialectic tradition and the hermeneutic is shown
in Weinsheimer 1985: 63 ff.
7. Eyerman and Jamison 1991.
8. Lave and Wenger 1991.
9. The first proposal for this came from Cosatu.
10. Armstrong 1992.
11. This refers to the critical ability in the classical sense that we have to imagine other possibilities than just what we have in front of our eyes here and now.
The concept distanciation is in my view closely related to this. One clear picture
of this is Ricoeur 1991.
12. Gallagher 1992: 55 ff.
13. Gallagher does not make a distinction between Gadamer's reconciliating
kind of interpretation and Riceour's deep hermeneutics. See Valdés 1991.
14. This focus upon language and communication is common to many modern
philosophical approaches from which there can be different conclusions. Here I
follow Habermas (1987) and Ricoeur (1985; 1991), who see real communication
as an existing possibility in the modern society.

References

Armstrong, M. (1992) *Human Resource Management Strategy and Action*, Kogan Page,
London.
Dave, R.H. (1972) *Foundations of Life-long Education*, Pergamon Press, New York.
Eyerman, R. and Jamison, A. (1991) *Social Movements: A Cognitive Approach*, Polity
Press, Cambridge.
Gallagher, S. (1992) *Hermeneutics and Education*, State University of New York Press,
New York.
Gesser, B. (1985) *Utbildning, jämlikhet, arbetsdelning*, Arkiv, Lund.
Gustavsson, B. (1991) *The Road to Education*, Wahlström & Widstrand, Stockholm.
Habermas, J. (1987) *The Theory of Communicative Action*, Polity Press, Cambridge.
Hirsch E.D. (1988) *Cultural Literacy: What Every American Needs to Know*, New York.
Lave, J. & Wenger, E. (1991) *Situated Learning: Legitimate Peripheral Participation*,
Cambridge University Press, Cambridge.

Ricoeur, P. (1985) *Time and Narrative, III*, University of Chicago Press, Chicago.

Ricoeur, P. (1991) 'The Conflicts of Interpretations: Debate with Hans-Georg Gadamer', in Valdés, M.J., *A Ricoeur Reader: Reflection and Imagination*, Harvester Wheatsheaf, Toronto.

Valdés, M.J. (1991) *A Ricoeur Reader: Reflection and Imagination*, Harvester Wheatsheaf, Toronto.

Weinsheimer, J. (1985) *Gadamer's Hermeneutics, A Reading of Truth and Method*, Yale University Press, New Haven, CT.

25

The Meaning of Life-long Learning

Staffan Larsson

We come into the world out of a vast nothingness. We look around, discover different rooms, reach out, touch, taste, smell. We strain body and mind to their limits. It is a full-time job, for the world is wider than our reach. 'And suddenly it is late.'

Göran Tunström[1]

The relationship between everyday learning and adult education

The relationship between everyday learning and adult education is one of the most fundamental questions in educational discourse. Far from being an issue that does not seem very exciting, this is, in fact, explosive. Questions can be raised around this issue such as: What is the meaning of education? How is it possible to legitimize the existence of education? How can teaching, study circles or training be arranged so as to result in genuine learning? Normative questions such as these cannot be answered without considering the role of everyday learning.

The relationship is one between two perspectives in educational discourse. First, there is the perspective of learning focusing on the learner, often through some learning theory. Second, the perspective of *homo docens*, or the teaching perspective, focuses on the arrangements that some agency makes in order to produce learning. The *homo docens* attitude is a perspective on the world; the attitude taken by teachers, parents or the organizers of study circles.

The arguments presented here are formed according to this *homo docens* attitude: everyday learning is analysed and addresses those who are thinking of arranging some acts with the purpose that someone should learn something.[2] In this chapter the term education is used in a broad sense, to embrace not only formal education but also study circles, training and other activities that are created through a *homo docens* attitude.

The question of everyday learning and education is not a new one. In the progressive movement at the beginning of this century, experience was regarded as the kernel of learning.[3] At the centre of this movement was a critique of schools' isolation from society. To a great extent we can recognize this perspective in contemporary discourses on knowledge and learning. The notion of 'life-long education' was introduced in this progressive context.[4]

Currently, life-long learning is a concept with many meanings used by a variety of actors. It is used as the key concept by the new government in liberated South Africa as well as by the previous conservative government in Sweden. This variety of meanings can be looked upon as a problem: life-long learning risks losing its richness and precision as a concept. It becomes too useful for too many purposes. The meaning of the term is often either obscure or meagre.

One question thus becomes urgent: What is the meaning of life-long learning? In this chapter the concept links the most fundamental aspects of learning to specific life-contexts. The concept is given a richer meaning by forming a dialogue with relevant theory and philosophy. Finally, the explicated meaning is the basis for some normative conclusions about education and training.

Everyday learning

Have you considered the phenomenon that we cannot stop thinking? All our waking moments are filled with all kinds of impressions. If we are not taking them in through our senses we are using our imagination or dwelling in memories. Our consciousness is not only filled by impressions but also by concepts and reasoning that are more or less abstract.[5] Try to imagine consciousness without content. In practice it would mean that we are not awake! Thus, every day, every week from birth until the end of our lives, our minds are constantly active. One may say that a person is doomed to think; it is beyond what we can choose to do.

It is a fundamental fact that our consciousness is nothing else than its content. We cannot imagine consciousness without a content. A closer reflection will show that this content is the world around us. Consciousness is houses, scents of flowers, texts and music or the memories of them. With the exception of activity, we are in contact with the world around us through consciousness. The world around us is known to us via consciousness. This is fundamental for our reflection on everyday learning.

Not only do we fill our consciousness with impressions and memories, they are ordered through interpretation. We construct an ordered pattern: some impressions become the background and others are in focus. Stories are constructed and thus our memory becomes ordered. We constantly interpret other people in terms of their purposes and the meaning they are expressing. The interpretations are often executed automatically – we 'see' a car and not something that we can reflect on in order to become convinced that it is a car.

Interpretation is thus not something we do at certain moments. Instead, it is done constantly. The interpretations we make constitute our personal knowledge.[6] The interpretations order the world around every person, regardless of whether others consider them to be true. We are not only doomed to think; we are doomed to interpret. This is a fundamental fact of life.[7] It is also fundamental for the meaning of the notion 'learning'.

In everyday use we think of interpretation as something reflected upon. In my use of the notion 'interpretation' this is not the case. Interpretation can be thematized, that is, reflected upon as well as taken for granted. Our consciousness functions on different levels: we focus on something, something else is in the periphery and other things are beyond our awareness. When we talk with a woman, we focus on what she is saying and let the rest of her concrete appearance remain in the background, though still in our awareness. In our way of speaking and acting towards her, we take for granted many presuppositions about her. However, we can be aware of them through our interaction with her and perhaps we may be forced to revise our presuppositions. Learning can in fact be so defined: as a change in our interpretation of something.[8]

An important aspect of this perspective is the assumption that we always have some kind of 'pre-understanding' when we approach a situation, a text or a person. We are no *tabula rasa*. Our history of experiences has formed us and this is what we carry with us in our encounters with the world. Our interpretations are thus formed by the social interactions, cultures and places we have experienced. There is no neutral point of view from where we can understand the world. Even language affects our way of understanding the things we encounter. Language is beyond the individual and exists before we enter the world as individuals. Thus, we are not only doomed to think and interpret; we find ourselves caught in an already-existing system for interpreting the world. This is shaped by social interaction and we are formed by our interaction with others in everyday contexts.[9] In contemporary societies, however, we often meet several systems of interpretation; in this way we often leave the dense closed culture with a consistent world view. On this basis we form our individual interpretations of the world around us.[10]

Our individual experiences also form us, and in principle everyone is on different ground. Our interpretations are thus formed by the place in which we are and have been both geographically and socially.[11] We interpret the world differently according to the place where we are and the person we have become. Where we are in space and time is fundamental for our experiences and interpretations, and thus for our learning.

We are also active, not always but often. The activity can be very elaborate and reflected upon, but can also be completely outside aware-ness.[12] Reflection is often considered as a 'higher stage'. This is a prob-lematic view. In one philosophical tradition, pragmatism, the relation between thought and action, is quite different. Here functional activity is not governed by reflection. Reflection is rather the consequence of a break in the smooth routine activity; the actor becomes puzzled and starts an inquiry to solve the problem. The solution then becomes routinely performed. Behind this way of thinking there is the idea of an adaptation of actions to the environment in terms of effective action.[13] This was only meant to illustrate the complicated relation between thought and action.

Knowledge that becomes routinely performed action often 'disappears' from awareness. Learning to drive a car can be taken as an example. The beginner concentrates on the gear-stick and the clutch and the brake-pedal, and how to move hands and feet. Once we are more skilled we focus more on the traffic outside the car and eventually we are not really aware of the way in which we move our feet. This illustrates the develop-ment of a sequence that starts with reflection and ends with skilled au-tomatic activity.

Thus it is clear that development of action is an important part of learning. It is also obvious from the examples that there is often a relation-ship between thought and action. However, this relationship has many facets and should not be conceived of in a simplistic way.

Through our activity we can affect the world around us. If the content of consciousness is our interpretation of the world, then the activity is the way we can change something outside our body. Our interpretations can be important and thus there is an interplay between interpretations and skill in action. But we can also take a passive attitude: there is much interpretation going on that does not result in activity.

Consciousness and action between body and world

Through consciousness and action we stand in a relation to the world around us. It has been said that we are living in a 'life-world', a world that has its centre in our body but is extended to our surroundings, that is the content of our consciousness and the object of our actions. Consciousness and actions are *between* our body and the surroundings. This is the place where learning occurs, thus learning changes the rela-tions between ourselves and our surroundings. We cannot imagine either thought or action without presupposing both the individual and the sur-rounding world. This life-world is formed by its existence in space and time, simply because its content is a world that is situated in space and time. Thus we are formed by the situation in which we live, since it is the content of our lives.

The consequence of this perspective becomes a definition of learning. Learning is a change in the interpretations of the world around us or the change of action in terms of an enhanced skill. Besides pure reflexes this is our individual knowledge. While learning is a natural process that takes place in everyday life, we do not often think about it as learning. It is possible that we learn when we read the newspaper, or work or talk with someone. We can learn by simply participating in action.[14] It can also be a question of noticing, and developing our awareness about different aspects, for example a carpenter's awareness about the structure of wood.[15] Finally, learning can also be something that we think of as learning, such as our struggle to understand how to play bridge, or when someone participates in a course to learn to read and calculate.

When we talk about knowledge, it is important to be aware that knowledge is not necessarily an individual phenomenon. For example, knowledge has been materialized in all kinds of machinery, tools and other kinds of technology in a way that makes it possible for individuals to have access to the fruits of knowledge without knowing a lot themselves. We can use the knowledge that there is in the whole of television technology with very limited personal knowledge. We can use cars and computers in a similar way without any knowledge about their construction. In this way we can 'extend' our knowledge by, for instance, buying technology. Another important collective side of knowledge is the fact that knowledge often resides in an organization of individuals' specialized knowledge. This is often the case in workplaces.[16]

Some fundamental assumptions about the nature of everyday learning have been put forward. The following section looks at the relation between everyday learning and education. This is followed by a discussion dealing with the consequences of the fact that persons have different life-worlds.

Everyday life is always somewhere

In everyday life we are constantly interpreting. However, different people live in different contexts. Concretely this means that we are geographically situated in different places. It also means that we live in different social circumstances. Furthermore, we are placed in different cultures and in a specific historical situation. This is fundamental for the kind of interpretations we make. These circumstances are also fundamental in terms of learning, in terms of the challenges that will provoke a change in interpretation of something. Therefore we have to reflect on the character of everyday life in different places and the possibilities for learning. Two aspects of everyday life are prominent because they occupy a large proportion of the time that forms our lives, namely working life and the use of mass media.

The empirical facts show a correlation between working life and use of mass media. Those who have little to learn from working life often use the mass media in a way that produces little knowledge: interpretations that are seldom challenged. A Swedish investigation of mass-media use has found that the modernization processes in our time have meant fewer differences between men and women.[17] However, class differences have sharpened. In the case of television, this has to do with an increasing differentiation in viewing practices. News as a genre is not as common as a shared practice; rather it is becoming a 'highbrow' practice.

Everyday life produces an accelerating knowledge gap

Everyday life produces a constantly growing gap between those on the one hand who are forced or provoked or seek to learn, and those on the other who are in a somewhat different position, where learning is seldom experienced. The differences in terms of knowledge are not only a question of differences in formal education. Differences in formal education segregate people in terms of what kind of everyday life they will have. Then everyday life operates as differentiating contexts. Since everyday life forms the whole of life, it will have a strong impact in the long run.

On the meaning of adult education

A discussion of adult education must be based on learning in life generally. Adult education as well as education generally must be understood as something that can change the results of everyday learning or the character of everyday learning. The arguments in this chapter are normative, they do not describe how adult education or training actually works, but how it should work. When people start studying they arrive with their interpretations of all kinds of phenomena they will meet as content in a course. These interpretations will be changed if the learning is meaningful. The contribution of adult education has to be judged in relation to how it changes everyday learning and everyday life.

The meaning of adult education has to do with changing the patterns in which adults are caught. What does this mean? Adult education has often legitimized its existence by referring to its role in bringing about increasing equality. The arguments so far have shown that learning in everyday contexts operates towards an increasing inequality. A realization of an increasing equality must effect the differences that the educational system has produced, as well as those that are produced in everyday life. However, the empirical results in terms of participation show an unequal distribution in adult education too; if adult education is going to contribute to equality, its practice has to be changed, and geared towards those who have least knowledge.[18]

Adult education is an opportunity also for those with limited formal education. If everyday learning is not prominent among those with a limited education, one should consider the possibility that adult education can contribute and thus open a way to learning that would otherwise be closed. The conclusion is that contemporary adult education contributes more to equality in opportunities than in results.[19]

A third more pragmatic perspective could be complementary to the one mentioned above. The focus here is on the situations in which adults are placed and the learning needs they have in order to enhance this situation. In this perspective the value of knowledge is relative to the situations where it can be of use.[20] Thus, there can be no common core. In terms of equality, adult education is contributing as long as it is instrumental in relation to equality in other aspects of life: economic, legal or power relations of all kinds. The main point in this context is that adult education should be evaluated against the norm that it promotes equality in these kinds of aspects.

Interpretations and skills must be challenged

When the student intends to participate in a course, her consciousness is filled with many thoughts, interpretations, memories and perhaps experiences of action that are relevant for the content in the course. According to our earlier definition, learning will take place when the existing interpretations and skills are changed. If this change is going to be possible, existing interpretations and skills must be challenged.

One problem in this context is a lack of ambition: where the interpretations that can be developed are the same as the ones the student already has. The distance between different interpretations can reside in a group where members have different views. From a number of empirical studies where one can follow the change of interpretations in a pre-test/post-test-design, one can conclude that some students have rather advanced interpretations from the very start and that not much is accomplished by participating in terms of learning.[21] Another problem arises when there is too large a gap between message and pre-understanding. In this case there will be no contact, because the student cannot see the link between the message and her own understanding of a relevant phenomenon.

One reason for lack of challenges is the attitude among some teachers who think of students as empty bottles that can be filled with knowledge. Often this is reinforced by the thought that good results in tests are the consequences of teaching, without considering other sources.

The conception behind the demand for a challenge can be traced to the enlightenment movement. In this school of thought, the aim was to challenge superstition and myths. The aim was to spread 'light', that is, rational knowledge emanating from a scientific discourse. It is possible to analyse this as a struggle between interpretations. The enlightenment perspective has inspired educators during the last centuries in struggles against racism and myths about women. However, the perspective has been criticized from many angles, often for its claim to have a privileged position in terms of truth.[22] Another side is its elitism.[23] However, a rational attitude can be defended, if it is reformulated. One can look upon learning as a process, where new conceptions or interpretations are added to old ones. In this way individuals and collectives can reflect on the relative value of different interpretations. In this perspective learning need not necessarily be a question of forcing someone to accept a certain version.[24]

Learning context must promote authentic learning

The next criterion for adult learning is based on the assumption that learning can be deep or superficial. Everyone is familiar with the phenomenon of memorizing. This kind of approach to learning is intimately linked to institutionalized learning. It is difficult to imagine someone who tries to memorize an article in a newspaper. Memorizing is a rare technique in everyday life. It is a study technique that is used when students have to report their reading in tests or similar situations, where someone else defines the requirements and the reader tries to foresee them. The impact is often meagre.[25] From the perspective of life-long learning the problem with memorizing is the lack of influence on everyday life and learning. Learning becomes an activity that is only linked to the educational institution; relevant everyday interpretations are not affected. The only effect on everyday learning is the indirect consequence of educational merits, that is, that someone will have a working life that is productive for learning.

Unfortunately, schools have traits in common that promote what can be called alienated learning. It is part of what Tyack and Tobin called the 'grammar of schooling', a rather uniform structure that has dominated for more than a hundred years.[26] Students adapt to this grammar and its often artificial way of handling knowledge: dividing it into small pieces that can be handled during a specific period of time under the condition that all students must perform the same activity at the same time. Those who participate will often abandon their own engagement in understanding something for the sake of an instrumental attitude: to learn only what is demanded. This attitude is learned in school contexts by the constant repetition of the same structures day after day, week after week and year in year out. Adults, too, are marked by this.

Authenticity in learning is thus a delicate thing. One aspect is what has been called genuine interest[27] – that can be a starting-point for learning or the effect of being confronted by something. Another dimension has to do with the contact between everyday interpretations and what is learned in organized learning settings. If there is no contact, the effects in terms of making everyday life more productive as a learning context will be limited.

The Dane Grundtwig, who inspired the creation of folk high schools, used the metaphor of life and death when he talked about learning. Knowledge can be thought of as dead or alive. Grundtwig's analysis of his contemporary schools at the beginning of the nineteenth century is still useful. A more recent intellectual, Habermas, also refers to a concept that is close to the meaning of 'authenticity' in his work about 'communicative action'. In his work this is one basis for differentiating between the rationality that resides in communicative action and linked to life-worlds and the one that is instrumental and strategic and linked to systems.[28] However, in a postmodernist discourse the idea of authenticity is a myth or redundant, since it presupposes a subject with some kind of identity, which is denied within that school of thought.

Content must be relevant

Knowledge is often functionally related to contexts. To read and write are arts that are meaningful in the perspective of communication in certain (literate) societies. Mathematics can be useful in practical situations as when working out taxes or the comparison of prices of cans of different sizes in a shop. These situations often do not exist in more formal arrangements of education. There is a gap between the situations where something is learned and used. Furthermore, schools are often anachronistic in the choice of content. Latin was an important subject in Swedish secondary schools until the end of the 1960s. At that time the chances of using that particular language in everyday life had been limited for more than a hundred years. Democratic attitudes have been introduced in Sweden at least since the end of the nineteenth century. In ordinary schools, however, authoritarian forms still often dominate,[29] in spite of objectives that favour democratic forms. However, if one looks at adult education in Sweden and compares it with ordinary schools, one is struck by the flexibility for change among the popular education institutions to become relevant for participants.[30]

Relevance means a great deal in terms of how difficult something is to understand. The critique of Piaget in the 1970s involved the difficulties demonstrated in isolating cognitive structures from content. If a certain logical problem was given concrete expression that related to everyday contexts, almost everyone could solve it. If the same logical problem was presented in a more abstract version hardly anyone could solve it.[31] The effects of relevance are twofold. First, it is important to provide opportunities for participants to learn at all. Second, it is important in relation to the opportunities that learning will have any impact on everyday learning.

The ability to judge

Many messages we are confronted with in everyday life attempt to persuade us. Power is not only executed by economic and political means, it is also a question of having the upper hand with regard to the content of consciousness. Foucault uses the expression 'discourse' for the span within which we talk about the world, which also indicates what is excluded. Thus we are objects for all kinds of efforts where different organizations, companies, churches and political parties try to impose their definition of truth on us. They want to have power over the discourse. In the masses of messages to which we are exposed everyone needs to be able to judge. The main problem in our time is not lack of information – it is lack of means to choose something for yourself. Women and men must be able to evaluate the messages, arguments and propositions in a critical way. They must judge. This kind of 'talent' is in a way superior to other kinds of knowledge, since it is not a question of learning, but the evaluation of what has been learnt. It is the basis for a well-founded commitment to a certain standpoint. In order to reach a standpoint, you have to consider conflicting arguments, be aware of the weak spots in arguments, recognize the interests behind the messages and think critically about the empirical plausibility in propositions about the real world. The judgements could be enhanced by use of social interaction, where arguments can be criticized.[32] Contemporary developments in theories of democracy stress this kind of judgement as central to the notion of democracy – a deliberative democracy.[33]

The judgements of our time are perhaps not based on a complete picture of the world. This idea has been eroded by the problems faced by all-embracing systems of thought. The ancient idea of 'phronesis' – good judgement in a specific case – is thus needed.

A good adult education must not only have the qualities of challenging everyday interpretations, be relevant and have a genuine meaning for the students – it must also be aware that all those interpretations that are communicated in educational discourse must be subordinated to the judgement of specific cases in everyday life.

Notes

1. Tunström 1993: 20.
2. Barnett 1973.
3. Dewey 1966; Dewey 1963; Dewey 1975.
4. Borgström 1988.
5. Husén and Postlethwaite 1994.
6. Idhe 1977; Gallagher 1992.
7. Bengtsson 1988.
8. Marton *et al.* 1977; Gallagher 1992.

9. Mead 1976; Wittgenstein 1978; Idhe 1986.
10. Berger and Luckmann 1967.
11. Lave and Wenger 1991; Chaiklin and Lave 1993.
12. Chaiklin and Lave) 1993.
13. Wennerberg 1966.
14. Chaiklin and Lave 1993.
15. Molander 1993.
16. Hutchins 1993.
17. Reimer 1994.
18. SCB 1991.
19. Härnqvist 1989.
20. Gumede, Chapter 23 in this book.
21. Alexandersson 1985; Marton *et al.* 1984; Ramsden 1988.
22. Habermas 1972; Von Wright 1987.
23. Gustavsson 1991.
24. Habermas 1991.
25. Svensson 1976.
26. Tyack and Tobin 1994.
27. Dewey 1975.
28. Habermas 1991.
29. Larsson 1993.
30. Larsson 1995.
31. Donaldson 1980; Johnsson-Laird *et al.* 1972.
32. Habermas 1991.
33. Res Publica 1994.

References

Alexandersson, C. (1985) *Stabilitet och förändring, En empirisk studie av förhållandet mellan skolkunsdap och vardagsvetande*, Acta Unitersitatis Gothoburgensis, Göteborg.
Barnett, S.A. (1973) 'Homo Docens', *Journal for Biosocial Science*, No. 5.
Bengtsson, J. (1988) *Sammanflätningar. Fenomemologi från Husserl till Merleau-Ponty*, Daidalos, Göteborg.
Berger, P.L. and Luckmann, T. (1967) *The Social Construction of Reality*, Penguin, Harmondsworth.
Borgström, L. (1988) *Vuxnas kunskapssökande – en studie I självstyrt lärande*, Brevskolan, Stockholm.
Chaiklin, S. and Lave, J. (eds) (1993) *Understanding Practice, Perspectives on Activity and Context*, Cambridge University Press, Cambridge.
Dewey, J. (1963) *Experience and Education*, Collier Books, New York.
Dewey, J (1966) *Democracy and Education*, The Free Press, New York.
Dewey, J. (1975) *Interest and Effort in Education*, Southern Illinois University Press, Cambridge.
Donaldson, M. (1980) *Hur barn tänker*, Liber, Lund.
Gallagher, S. (1992) *Hermeneutics and Education*, State University of New York Press, Albany, NY.
Greene, M. (1994) 'Chapter 10: Epistemology and Education Research: The Influence of Recent Approaches to Knowledge', *Review of Research in Education*, Vol. 20, AERA, Washington DC.
Gustavsson, B. (1991) *Bildningens våg: tre bildningsideal I svensk arbetarrörelse 1880–*

1930, Wahlström and Widstrand, Stockholm.

Habermas, J. (1972) *Knowledge and Human Interest*, London.

Habermas, J. (1991) *The Theory of Communicative Action, Volume 1, Reason and the Rationalization of Society, Volume 2, Lifeworld and System: A Critique of Functionalist Reason*, Polity Press, Cambridge.

Härnqvist, K (1989) 'Comprehensiveness and Social Equality', in Ball, S.J. and Larsson, S. (eds), *The Struggle for Democratic Education, Equality and Participation in Sweden*, The Falmer Press, New York.

Husén, T. and Postlethwaite, T.N. (eds) (1994) 'Phenomenography', *The International Encyclopedia of Education*.

Hutchins, E. (1993) 'Learning to Navigate', in Chaiklin, S. and Lave, J., *Understanding Practice, Perspectives on Activity and Context*, Cambridge University Press, Cambridge.

Idhe, D. (1977) *Experimental Phenomenology, An Introduction*, G.P. Putnam's Sons, New York.

Idhe, D. (1986) 'On Non-foundational Phenomenology', *Publikantioner från institutionen förpedagogik*, Göteborg University, June.

Johnsson-Laird, P.N., Legrenzi, P.C. and Sonino-Legrenzi, M. (1972) 'Reasoning in a Sense of Reality', *British Journal of Psychology*, Vol. 63.

Larsson, S. (1993) 'Initial Encounters in Formal Adult Education', *Qualitative Studies of Education*, Vol. 16, No. 1, pp. 45–65.

Larsson, S. (1995) 'Folfbildningen och vuxenpedagogiken', in Bergstedt, B. and Larsson, S. (eds.), *Om folkbildningens innebörder*, MIMER, Linköping, pp. 35–57.

Lave, J. and Wenger, E. (1991) *Situated Learning*, Cambridge Unversity Press, Cambridge.

Marton, F. *et al.* (1977) *Inlärning och omvärldsuppfattning*, Almqvist & Wiksell, Stockholm.

Marton, F., Hounsell, D. and Entwistle, N. (eds) (1984) *The Experience of Learning*, Scottish Academic Press, Edinburgh.

Mead, G.H. (1976) *Medvetandet, jaget och samhället. Från en socialbehavioristisk synpunkt*, Argos, Kalmar.

Molander, B. (1993) *Kunskap I handling*, Daidalos, Göteborg.

Ramsden, P. (ed.) (1988) *Improving Learning: New Perspectives*, Kogan Page, London.

Reimer (1994) *The Most Common of Practices: On Massmedia Use in Late Modernity*, Almqvist & Wiksell International, Stockholm.

Res Publica (1994) *Tema liberalism och kommunitarism*, No. 27.

SCB (1991) *Levnadsförhållanden, Rapport 67*, Vuxmas stidoede; tagamde 1975–1989, Örebo.

Svensson, L. (1976) *Study Skill and Learning*, Acta Universitatis Gothoburgensis, Göteborg.

Tunström, G. (1993) *Under tiden*, Albert Bonniers Förlag, Stockholm.

Tyack, D. and Tobin, W. (1994) 'The "Grammar" of Schooling: Why Has It Been So Hard to Change?', *American Educational Research Journal*, Vol. 31, No. 3.

Von Wright, G.H. (1987) *Vetenskapen och förnuftet, Ett försök till orientering*, Bonniers, Borgå.

Wennerberg, H. (1966) *Pragmatismen*, Rabén and Sjögren, Stockholm.

Wittgenstein, L. (1978) *Filosofiiska undersökningar*, Bonniers, Stockholm.

26

The Worlds of the Hand and of the Mind

Ove Korsgaard

Today's conception of education is to a large extent connected to the school as an institution. It is difficult to imagine a society without schools where education is still possible. Educational history is practically always written as a history of schools. That, however, does not give a complete picture of the educational structure of a society, as the overwhelming part of education in most societies has been connected with the workshop, not with the school.[1]

In pre-industrial society the workshop was the 'ideal-typical' place for education, building on concrete relations between master and apprentice. The master–apprentice education constituted a rich social structure in which a decisive element in the learning process was the observation of masters, skilled workers and other apprentices in their work. The master was the foreman and the role model. The apprentices participated in mutual learning activities with a minimal education compared to the present concept. Through actual participation in production they gradually learned to carry out more complicated parts of the finished product. With occasional education the apprentices moved towards becoming masters in their trade. The decisive learning process was participation in technical production; trade skills were developed through imitation over a period of time. Education took place in the association between master and apprentice and was based on the mimetic principle as a pedagogical method – learning took place by observing, doing and imitating.

To obtain the skills necessary to be a farmer or craftsman, until a few centuries ago, was something which was not interfered with by the state or the church. Those in each generation followed in the footsteps of their fathers and mothers and learned from an early age what was necessary for participating in the work on the farm or in the workshop. Schools, for many, were out of the question and emerging generations learned what was necessary from their elders and masters.

In ancient European society there seemed to be a division of responsibility between the workshop and the church. The workshop took care of skills training while the church took care of general education. Educating craftsmen and farmers for their job was not the concern of the authorities but educating them as citizens had a high priority. In this process, however, the Reformation accentuated a new phase. To learn the principles of Christianity came – with the Reformation – to be regarded as absolutely necessary. The church became the great educator and the parson became the religious teacher. The church set the goal for public education and, consequently, the teachings of the church became the framework for the adult's public life in civil society.

The principles of the teaching can be read in the catechism of Martin Luther. In a society where the Bible was the foundation for societal education, writing and arithmetic were less important than reading. These two subjects, therefore, became voluntary in school. Parents had to pay extra for arithmetic and writing tuition.

In a society where Christianity was the ideological foundation of the state, it was absolutely necessary to know the principles. It was more important than it is today to know – or confess to – the fundamental rules of democracy. The bringing up of children on the teaching of the catechism became the foundation of the education of citizens.

Industrialization and academization

In pre-industrial society the facilitation of knowledge took place in a direct meeting between older and younger generations within the farming environment, the kitchen or as part of the guild-apprentice schemes.

Historically, the decisive change in the dissemination of knowledge took place when the classroom begins to replace the workshop as the main place for learning. This change from workshop to classroom developed in a process which is as long as the history of enlightenment.[2]

Gradually, the school took over still more of the learning tasks from the workshop and educational tasks from the church. A still greater part of the teaching was moved from the workshop to the classroom: from the 'world of the hand' to the 'world of the mind'. Thereby, more and more teaching processes became academized. The popular way of learning was replaced by an academic approach where the pattern of knowledge is systematized and separated from the individual way of living. The same development was seen regarding the passing on of knowledge, as it became attached to a pedagogy which was based on the classroom and not on the workshop.

The development from practical knowledge to theoretical knowledge, from the workshop to the classroom, constitutes a qualitative change in the historical process. In the pre-industrial farmer and craftsman society adults and children had access to much practical knowledge. With the development of industrial society, theoretical knowledge became increasingly important for the structuring of qualifications. To learn something became to a large extent a question of filling 'Mind' into the body's reservoir. In this tradition the 'Mind' was regarded as ennobling of mankind, comprising the human intellect, the language and related phenomena.

There is a qualitative difference between workshop learning and the academic learning tradition. One of the differences is that authentic or primary experiences, such as experiences we have through palpable contact with our surroundings, were replaced with authoritative or secondary experiences, for instance experiences of others which are explained especially through textbooks. There is a great difference between becoming a blacksmith by 'seeing and trying' and becoming a machine-technician by 'reading and understanding'. But the strength of the school was that it could offer some authoritative experiences which were not available in the workshop.

From the beginning of industrialization there were, however, philosophers and pedagogues who would continue using the workshop as the place for learning and education. John Locke was one of the first to stress the importance of primary experiences in the learning process; he advocated combining physical work with teaching. Jean Jacques Rousseau also promoted the idea. His revolutionary book *Émile* (1762) is based on the presumption that primary experiences should be the foundation for teaching. Émile should be taught the carpentry trade, not so that he can become a carpenter, but to have an education as a human being. Also, there was the Danish educator, philosopher and historian Grundtvig, who had the vision that the workshop should be the basis for the schooling of boys. In a school publication from 1836 he wrote: 'The only good school for citizen life of which I have any perception is in the houses of clever and striving citizens.'[3] Grundtvig also acted as he preached. When his sons, Johan and Svend, became candidates for confirmation they were placed as bookbinding and carpentry apprentices – presumably against their mother's wishes.[4]

Neither Rousseau's Émile nor Grundtvig's Johan and Svend were to be educated for life as craftsmen but they were to learn to use their hands and bodies in the workshop in order to acquire a proper general education. Later, the idea of using the workshop-model in education was put forward by pedagogues such as John Dewey, Celestin Freinet and Georg Kerschensteiner. These pedagogues agreed to organize the school in such a way that theory was tested in practice. Their pedagogical model had its foundation in people's practical achievements; working life should be the obvious focal point in the life of the school. The school should be a picture of what happened in society at large.

It has, however, proved very difficult to combine work with education. Even though Rousseau's *Émile* is regarded as a key text in the history of pedagogy, his thoughts about primary experiences and working with the hands did not show the way for the school and pedagogy in industrial society. Neither were Grundtvig's thoughts about workshop training being favoured over classroom education accepted. On the contrary, the development went from authentic to authoritative experiences, from the workshop to the classroom, from the 'world of the hand' to the 'world of the mind'.

To include manual work in education seems to be in conflict with fundamental structures in the development of industrial society. The most important division of labour in industrial society has been between intellectual and manual work. Correspondingly, the most important divisions within the educational system have been between the intellectual and the manual subjects, between general knowledge and practical knowledge, between the activity of the mind and the activity of the hand. (These concepts should be understood in the 'ideal-typical' way where the activity of the hand also implies brain-activity.)

The difference between hand and mind, between the practical and the theoretical, has been a fundamental obstacle which a number of pedagogues have tried, in vain, to overcome. Why this idea had no effectiveness was described in the following way by the American Von Borstel:

> Intellectuals do not like it because it asks them to put down their books for a while and pick up a tool. Middle class parents do not like it because it expects all children to engage in manual activities commonly associated with the lower classes. Poor parents do not like it because, to them, education is a means for the children to join the ranks of the government-maintained paper-pushers.[5]

Although there have been other points of view, there has been a general agreement that the change from the 'world of the hand' to the 'world of the mind', from authentic to authoritative experiences is most important in the qualification of the labour force. It has also been met with approval that the textbook was the starting-point for general education. When the school became the key institution of society a close connection between knowledge and education was established. The cognitive dimension became dominant in educational efforts. By and large, knowledge and education became two sides of the same coin: an educated person was a knowledgeable person.

The post-industrial society

That the advanced industrial societies find themselves in a new structural change was already mentioned by Daniel Bell in 1973 in his book *The Coming of Post-Industrial Society*.[6] In this book he describes the development from pre-industrial societies to post-industrial societies, a development which 20 years ago was only at its beginning but which has since become quite detectable. One of Bell's main points was that we shall live in a society based on research and know-how, where a great part of the population will be working with information and symbols. And this point of view seems too true. There has been a dramatic change from blue-collar to white-collar work. The forecast says that in the year 2000 about 75 per cent of all wage-earners in Denmark will be doing white-collar work. More than half of this number are expected to have an advanced education. In this kind of production more people make less use of their bodies.

During the last 25 years a new system for creating prosperity has developed. This system is totally dependent on communication and the exchange of data. In an advanced economic system the work is no longer connected to things but to symbols. Hard manual work has been exchanged for knowledge and information. Prosperity is no longer based on muscle power but on brain power.

What does it mean for the school that the body is on its way out of production? Does it imply a further change in education: from the workshop to the classroom? From authentic to authoritative experiences? From the 'world of the hand' to the 'world of the mind'? Or does it mean a break with the logic which has caused this change? We do not know. No society has previously been through a development towards a post-industrial society, as Bell calls it.

My hypothesis is that the educational structure of a society changes qualitatively when the society converts from 'hand work' to 'mind work'. This does not mean that authoritative knowledge will be of less importance in the future. If society is to be still more scientific and if production increasingly is based on experiences made in the laboratory or at the desk, as seems to be the case, theoretical knowledge will continue to play a fundamental role in the education systems of the future.

In spite of this, development will not just show a continuation of what has happened during the whole industrialization process – that is, a further shift of education from the workshop to the classroom. There are several reasons why a break will occur in this development logic. Although we shall not reach 'the schoolless society' which Ivan Illich speaks of as an ideal, in future there will be a greater difference between education and schooling than we have known in the industrial society where the two concepts have a tendency to melt into each other.

I shall mention three reasons for this development.[7] First, the need for knowledge in a society based on research and knowledge will reach a level where the school can no longer keep a monopoly on supplying the educational requirements of society. It will surely be both too expensive and inadequate to achieve 'life-long learning' using the school and the classroom as a point of departure.

Second, the new information technology will radically open up new possibilities for the dissemination of knowledge and know-how. In the future, education will not, as is the case today, be based on pedagogy in a school-like fashion. This shift is formulated in the new keyword: from educating to learning, which is now extensively heard.[8] Information technology gives the individual far greater possibilities for scheduling a learning process which is based on a co-ordination between different dissemination systems. Earlier, one was dependent on teachers, textbooks, classrooms and libraries, but more and more it will be possible to become educated via a number of electronically distributed common programs. The learning process will become more like the master–apprentice principle than the schoolroom education principle.

Third, and in this connection decisively, it seems that the change in society from hand work to mind work weakens the connection between general education and knowledge. There are many indications that knowledge is about to lose its function as the foundation of education. Undoubtedly, information technology will change the status that bookish knowledge has had. Know-how and information will no longer be a resource relatively difficult to obtain and to which only a part of the population has access. The new information technology will make know-how and information a mass product, easily accessible and cheap. It is, therefore, conceivable that in the future there will not be the same prestige attached to know-how and information as when the book culture was at its peak.

Once again we shall see a difference between knowledge and general education. In the post-industrial society the educational process will include features which will resemble the way in which the learning process for the majority was organized in the pre-industrial, almost schoolless society.

While acquisition of knowledge increasingly starts from symbols and a monitor's pictures, it seems that general education is more oriented towards those symbolic and articulate forms of expression which are connected to the hand and the body. The body is to a lesser degree marked by hard muscular work. It is no longer shaped as a 'peasant-body' or 'labourer-body'. The body now is increasingly part of the identity-shaping and self-promotion of the individual. With the body being freed from material production, it seems that it more and more becomes part of cultural production.

In many societies there are members of an upper class who have not done any physical work, but for whom sports and other kinds of bodily expressions have played a great role in the education process. For instance, important ingredients of the practical–aesthetic activities of the Japanese Samurai were flower binding, tea ceremonies, calligraphy, bowmanship and dancing. There is, however, a big difference between having a nominal upper class without physical work and a society where only a minority will have done physical work in the classical sense.

In the post-industrial society one will not only study but also practice in order to obtain a proper education. This implies a shift in the educational process: from explicit knowledge to expressive abilities.

Features within the master–apprentice way of learning will thus be rehabilitated in the post-industrial society. As a factor in the changing of society from the 'world of the hand' to the 'world of the mind' it seems that the relation between the mute base and the articulate superstructure will be radically changed once again.

Notes

1. That the history of education has been seen through the eyes of the history of schools is, for example, shown in an article by headmaster Morten Bredsdorff about the Danish school system from 1942. He refers to the British diplomat Moleworth, who in 1692 painted a rather negative picture of life in Denmark. He stressed, however, one thing, namely the level of enlightenment. The Danish commoners had good reading and writing abilities. But that could not be the case, writes Bredsdorff. A survey from 1735 shows that at the most there were schools in every second parish. Bredsdorff here equates reading ability and school attendance. It does not occur to him that the two institutions, the church and the home, could pass on these abilities. Dansk Folkeoplysning 1942: 11 (Korsgaard 1996).
2. Jensen 1987.
3. Grundtvig 1836.
4. Korsgaard 1986.
5. Nabudere 1995.
6. Bell 1973.
7. Korsgaard 1996.
8. Cf. for example the introduction from Unesco to the fifth international conference on Adult Learning to be held in Hamburg, Germany, in July 1997. Here the earlier use of the phrase 'adult education' has been subsequently changed to 'adult learning'.

References

Bell, D. (1973) *The Coming of Post-Industrial Society: A Venture in Social Forecasting*, New York.
Grundtvig, N.F.S. (1836) 'Det Danske fiir-kløver partisk betragtet', in *Grundtvigs skoleverden*, Vol. II, 1968.
Jensen, F. (1987) *Det tredie, Den postmoderne udfordring*, Amadeus, Denmark.
Korsgaard, O. (1986) *Kredsgang, Grundtvig som bokser*, Gyldendal, Denmark.
Korsgaard, O. (1996) *Kampen om lyset: Dansk voksenoplysning gennem 500 år*, Gyldendal, Denmark.
Nabudere, D.W. (1995) 'Education with Production and the Philosophy of World Education', in *Reflections on the Concept of World Education*, issued by the Association for World Education.

About the Contributors

Maurice Amutabi is a lecturer in the Department of Development Studies in the Institute for Human Resource Development at Moi University in Kenya. He is active in a number of community development and literacy projects, both as an academic and as an activist.

Mignonne Breier is a researcher at the University of the Western Cape (UWC). She co-ordinated the UWC team of the Social Uses of Literacy Research Project, a joint project involving the Centre for Adult and Continuing Education (CACE) and the Department of Adult Education at the University of Cape Town. She is currently a senior researcher at the Education Policy Unit, UWC.

Michael F. Christie is currently a senior lecturer in the Education Faculty of the Northern Territory University, Australia. He lectures in the area of adult and vocational education and has over twenty years' experience of visiting remote Aboriginal communities in order to supervise trainee teachers. His doctorate was on race relations between Aborigines and colonists in early Victoria, Australia.

Norman Fry is currently the director of the Northern Land Council, but prior to that he spent many years as the Assistant Director of the Faculty of Aboriginal and Torres Strait Islander Studies. He has been an Aboriginal activist all his life and is active in land claims by the Larrakia people in the Darwin area of Australia.

Jeanne Gamble is a research coordinator for the National Training Board's investigation into education, training and development practices in South Africa. She is based at the Department of Adult Education, University of Cape Town. She has worked as an industrial trainer and lecturer of workplace trainers.

Ellen Gumede obtained her teacher's certificate at Adams College, Natal, South Africa. She taught at eight government schools before being promoted to principal of St Christopher junior school. She retired from school teaching in 1990, and embarked on adult education in 1991.

Berndt Gustavsson is a researcher in the field of popular and adult education in the Department of Education and Psychology, University of Linköping, Sweden. His doctorate was in philosophy and the history of ideas.

Chan Lean Heng earns her living as a lecturer in feminist social work and is completing her PhD on educational work with factory women in Malaysia. However she prefers the identity of a feminist popular educator. She is a founder member of the Workers' Education Centre, the first women workers' centre in Malaysia.

Lillian Holt is the principal of an independent school, Tauondi, which is largely self-funded and provides a bridge for young Aboriginal adults into tertiary education. She is an active member of a number of Aboriginal organizations in Australia, as well as a contributor to the work of international adult education bodies such as the Asia South Pacific Bureau of Adult Education and the International Council of Adult Education.

Charlene Houston works as a volunteer in her local community and works full-time for an NGO, the Development Action Group, on housing projects in Cape Town. She recently represented DAG at a conference in Holland on support for housing delivery in South Africa.

Keith Jackson is the principal of Fircroft College in England. He has been involved in and has written extensively on adult education and community development in the United Kingdom over the last thirty years.

Ove Korsgaard has for several years been the principal at a Danish folk high school. He is now a researcher a the Royal Danish Institute for Educational Studies and an associate professor at the University of Odense. He is President of the Association for World Education, a NGO with consultative status with the United Nations. He has published several books about the history of body culture and the history of adult education, including *Kampen om Lystet. Dansk voksenoplysning gennem 500 ar* (The Fight about the Light: Danish Adult Education through 500 Years, 1997).

Staffan Larsson is a professor of adult education at Linköping University, Sweden. His research is concerned with different aspects of adult education in Sweden, and includes *Paradoxes of Teaching* (Instructional Science, 1983), *Initial Encounters in Formal Adult Education* (Qualitative Studies in Education, 1993) and in translation from Swedish, *The Study Circle Society* (1996). Larsson was a visiting scholar at Stanford University in 1987/8. He is a part of the Adult Education Research Group at Linköping University, which comprises more than 25 researchers investigating adult education from different perspectives.

Rosemary Lugg is a researcher with a special interest in Adult Basic Education and Training. One of the high points of her working life has been to set up a small, independent research agency called Adult Learning Opportunities (ALO), of which she is a co-director. This has given her the freedom to work on some exciting and innovative projects in South Africa, including the National Union of Mineworkers ABET research project.

Linzi Manicom left South Africa as a political exile in 1976. She lived and worked as a researcher and community worker in Tanzania and Mozambique before moving to Toronto, Canada, in 1984. She works as a freelance writer and editor in the field of women's organizing and gender issues in global economic restructuring. She is a PhD candidate at the Ontario Institute for Studies in Education, working on a dissertation on gendered state formation in South Africa. She has recently co-edited a book with Shirley Walters: *Gender in Popular Education: Methods for Empowerment* (Zed Books, 1996).

Judith Marshall is a popular educator and writer who has worked for many years in the areas of adult literacy and training, international development and solidarity. She spent eight years in southern Africa, mainly focusing on work-place literacy in Mozambique. Her book recounting these experiences, *Literacy, Power and Democracy in Mozambique*, explores the meanings women and men attached to literacy and schooling during the tumultuous social changes of the mid-1980s. For the past five years she has worked with the Steelworkers Humanity Fund, one of Canada's new, labour-based development funds. She co-ordinates the education and linkage activities of the Fund, and is project officer for its southern Africa programme.

Mizana Matiwana is the provincial co-ordinator of the National Progressive Primary Health Care Network in the Western Cape Province, South Africa. She has been working to facilitate community involvement in health care for the past four years. The work includes the training of communities so that they can participate effectively in the process of transforming the health system of the country.

Elana Michelson is an Associate Professor of Cultural Studies at Empire State College, State University of New York and has worked extensively as a trainer and consultant on experiential learning and adult education in the USA and internationally. Dr Michelson is co-author of *Portfolio Development and Adult Learning: Purposes and Strategies* and author of numerous articles on the social, epistemological and political ramifications of the theory and practice of experiential learning. Her most recent work, on the recognition of prior learning in South Africa, has focused on the potential role of trade-union and anti-racist struggles in the development of policy.

Mildred Minty first began teaching as a volunteer high-school science teacher in west Malaysia. After working as an adult educator in the community college system of the Canadian province of Newfoundland and Labrador for several years, she became involved in regional economic development activity with the former Economic Recovery Commission. She currently works for the Department of Development and Rural Renewal in the Policy and Strategic Planning Division. One of her responsibilities is to work with the economic zones to help them integrate education, training and human resource development into their strategic economic plans.

Daniel Moshenberg is a member of the Women's Leadership Group/Grupo de liderazgo de mujeres, of the Tenants and Workers Support Committee/Comite de apoyo de inquilinos y trabajdores, of Alexandria, Virginia. He is also an Associate Professor of English at the George Washington University, where he directs the Expository Writing Program. In 1995, he worked as a Fulbright Distinguished Lecturer at CACE at the University of the Western Cape, in women's literacy promotion and development. He teaches, writes and wonders about literacy and literacy cultural practices.

Pauline Murphy is a senior lecturer and director of the Womens' Opportunities Unit, School of Social and Community Sciences, University of Ulster, Jordanstown Campus, Northern Ireland. She also chairs the NI Training for Women Network and the NI Community Education Association. She has pioneered a distinctive holistic approach to education and training for women which she prefers to describe as personal, professional and political development for women. She was inspired by achievements in South Africa to re-double her efforts in her professional and voluntary work in Northern Ireland to help shape a just, peaceful and empowering society for future generations there – including for her own four children.

Ali Osman is a PhD student at Linköping University, Sweden. His current interest is multicultural education, and he is working on a thesis on the social construction of educational identity in multicultural Sweden. The focus of this study is the adult education system, specifically the municipal adult education system and the folk high schools.

Teresa Quiroz Martin is co-ordinator of the Masters Project in Social Policy and Local Development at the Arcis University in Santiago, Chile. During her years of exile from Chile, among other posts she was director of the Latin American Centre of Social Work in Peru. She is also a former director of the School of Social Work at the Catholic University of Chile. She has published on women and development, local development and participatory research.

Joe Samuels is the chair of the Adult Educators and Trainers Association of South Africa (AETASA), which has pioneered the running of a national Adult Learners Week. He is a lecturer and co-ordinator of the Continuing Education programmes at CACE, University of the Western Cape. He is actively involved in a number of policy-oriented adult education and training structures locally and nationally.

Tony Sardien has been working as an adult educator in the area of anti-racism and gender at CACE, University of the Western Cape, since 1995. Before joining CACE he worked at SACHED, an NGO in Cape Town, as a co-ordinator of the Basic Course for Adult Educators. This was a national programme working with civic, trade-union, development and other activists. He is interested in the processes of globalization as these affect gender, class and 'race' relations.

Tammy Shefer has a long commitment to women's struggles in South Africa and has been involved in gender training within a range of areas, including leadership skills training with unionized women workers and education against woman abuse. More recently, beginning with a project at CACE, she has been involved with developing and implementing an integrated approach to challenging the multifaceted and interconnected forms of oppression and inequality existing in the South African context. She is currently a lecturer in the Psychology Department at the University of the Western Cape.

Minnie Venter-Hildebrand is an independent researcher and editor, and director of the Research and Management Agency, Cape Town. She has worked extensively in the higher education and adult education fields, as researcher, documentalist and editor. She is the editor of *Prospects for Progress: Critical Choices for Southern Africa* (Maskew Miller Longman, Cape Town), which was shortlisted for the Alan Paton Literary Award in 1995. She has worked as a contract consultant for the National Commission on Higher Education (a South African presidential commission), the South African Ministry of Education, USAID projects and various South African academic institutions.

Shirley Walters is an activist, educator and academic who has been active in a wide range of cultural, educational and women's organizations in South Africa over the last twenty years. She is the founding director of CACE and Professor of Adult and Continuing Education at the University of the Western Cape. She has worked as a school teacher, industrial trainer, community educator, researcher and academic. She recently co-edited (with Linzi Manicom) *Gender in Popular Education: Methods for Empowerment* (Zed Books, 1996).

Michael Welton received his MA in Anthropology and PhD in Educational Studies from the University of British Columbia. He is currently Professor of Adult Education at Mount St Vincent University, Halifax, Nova Scotia. He has published four books, his most recent being *In Defence of the Lifeworld: Critical Perspectives on Adult Learning* (1995). His interests include the history and social theory of adult learning. Currently, he is focusing his social theoretical work on developing a conceptual and research framework to study the role of adult educators in maintaining a vital civil society.

Jonathan Winterton is a senior lecturer in Industrial Relations and co-ordinator of the Work Organisation Research Unit at the University of Bradford Management Centre. He is a consultant to the ILO, the OECD, the European Commission and the Development for Education and Employment, and has a long association with the coal industry. His major books include: *Coal, Crisis and Conflict: The 1984–85 Miners' Strike in Yorkshire* (with R. Winterton, Manchester University Press, 1989); *Public Enterprise in Transition: Industrial Relations in State and Privatised Corporations* (with A. Pendleton, Routledge); *Managing Human Resources* (with C. Molander, Routledge, 1994); and *Restructuring within a Labour Intensive Industry: The UK Clothing Industry in Transition* (with I. Taplin, Avebury, 1996).

Ruth Winterton is a lecturer in Industrial Studies in the Department of Adult Continuing Education at the University of Leeds, and tutor in Adult Education at the Northern College, Barnsley. She has undertaken extensive research on vocational training issues, and has co-authored several government reports, including; *Collective Bargaining and Consultation over Continuing Vocational Training* (Employment Department, 1993); *Implementing NVQs: Barriers to Individuals* (Employment Department, 1995); and *The Business Benefits of Competence Based Management Development* (HMSO, 1996).

Index